THE GIRL IN THE TEXT

Transnational Girlhoods

EDITORS: Claudia Mitchell, *McGill University*; Bodil Formark, *Umeå University*; Ann Smith; *McGill University*; Heather Switzer, *Arizona State University*

Girlhood Studies has emerged over the last decade as a strong area of interdisciplinary research and activism, encompassing studies of feminism, women and gender, and childhood and youth and extending into such areas as sociology, anthropology, development studies, children's literature, and cultural studies. As the first book series to focus specifically on this exciting field, *Transnational Girlhoods* will help to advance the research and activism agenda by publishing full-length monographs and edited collections that reflect a robust interdisciplinary and global perspective. International in scope, the series will draw on a vibrant network of girlhood scholars already active across North America, Europe, Russia, Oceania, and Africa, while forging connections with new activist and scholarly communities.

Volume 1
The Girl in the Text
Edited by Ann Smith

Forthcoming:

Ethical Practice in Participatory Visual Research with Girls and Young Women
Edited by April Mandrona, Relebohile Moletsane, Astrid Treffrey-Goatley, Lisa Wiebesiek

Living Like a Girl
Edited by Maria Vogel and Linda Arnell

For a full volume listing, please see the series page on our website:
www.berghahnbooks.com/series/transnational-girlhoods.

THE GIRL IN THE TEXT

Edited by
Ann Smith

berghahn
NEW YORK • OXFORD
www.berghahnbooks.com

First published in 2019 by
Berghahn Books
www.berghahnbooks.com

© 2019 Berghahn Books

All rights reserved. Except for the quotation of short passages
for the purposes of criticism and review, no part of this book
may be reproduced in any form or by any means, electronic or
mechanical, including photocopying, recording, or any information
storage and retrieval system now known or to be invented,
without written permission of the publisher.

Library of Congress Cataloging-in-Publication Data
Names: Smith, Ann. | Smith, Ann, PhD in Feminist Literary Theory editor.
Title: The girl in the text / edited by Ann Smith.
Description: First Edition. | New York : Berghahn Books, [2019] | Series:
  Transnational girlhoods ; 1 | Includes bibliographical references and
  index.
Identifiers: LCCN 2019001628 (print) | LCCN 2019017333 (ebook) | ISBN
  9781789203257 (ebook) | ISBN 9781789203233 (hbk : alk. paper) | ISBN
  9781789203240 (pbk : alk. paper)
Subjects: LCSH: Girls. | Girls in literature.
Classification: LCC HQ798 (ebook) | LCC HQ798 .S567 2019 (print) | DDC
  305.23082--dc23
LC record available at https://lccn.loc.gov/2019001628

British Library Cataloguing in Publication Data
A catalogue record for this book is available from the British Library

ISBN 978-1-78920-323-3 hardback
ISBN 978-1-78920-324-0 paperback
ISBN 978-1-78920-325-7 ebook

Contents

List of Illustrations — vii

Introduction
The Girl in the Text: Representations, Positions, and Perspectives
Ann Smith — 1

Chapter 1
Naughtiest Girls, Go Girls, and Glitterbombs: Exploding Schoolgirl Fictions
Lucinda McKnight — 13

Chapter 2
"This Is My Story": The Reclaiming of Girls' Education Discourses in Malala Yousafzai's Autobiography
Rosie Walters — 29

Chapter 3
The Girl: Dead
Fiona Nelson — 45

Chapter 4
Girl Constructed in Two Nonfiction Texts: Sexual Subject? Desired Object?
Mary Ann Harlan — 60

Chapter 5
Perfect Love in a Better World: Same-Sex Attraction between Girls
Wendy L. Rouse — 77

Chapter 6
Narrating Muslim Girlhood in the Pakistani Cityscape of Graphic Narratives
Tehmina Pirzada — 94

Chapter 7
Confronting Girl-bullying and Gaining Voice in Two Novels by Nicholasa Mohr
Barbara Roche Rico — 111

Chapter 8

"Like Alice, I was Brave": The Girl in the Text in Olemaun's Residential School Narratives
Roxanne Harde 127

Chapter 9

Girl, Interrupted and Continued: Rethinking the Influence of Elena Fortún's Celia
Ana Puchau de Lecea 143

Chapter 10

Lolita Speaks: Disrupting Nabokov's "Aesthetic Bliss"
Michele Meek 158

Chapter 11

Hope Chest: Demythologizing Girlhood in Kate Bernheimer's Trilogy
Catriona McAra 174

Chapter 12

The Girl in the GIF: Reading the Self into Girlfriendship
Akane Kanai 190

Chapter 13

Girls' Perspectives on (Mis)Representations of Girlhood in Hegemonic Media Texts
Paula MacDowell 207

Chapter 14

Using Fiction, Autoethnography, and Girls' Lived Experience in Preparation for Playwriting
Genna Gardini 223

Index 239

Illustrations

Illustration 6.1
Jiya and *Burka Avenger* in a Burka Avenger Poster (2012).   98

Illustration 6.2
Gogi in the village from the *Going Gogi* book (2009).   102

Illustration 7.1
Mural featuring Nicholasa Mohr by El Mac and Cero.   112

Illustration 11.1
Joseph Cornell, Untitled (Pink Palace), ca. 1950.   175

Illustration 11.2
Kate Bernheimer, A Lovely Naked Girl, 2001.   186

Illustration 12.1
Ex-boyfriend problems.   200

Illustration 12.2
Struggling to act cool.   194

for Claudia Mitchell, the woman in my text

INTRODUCTION
The Transnational Girl in the Text
Transnationalism Redefined?

Ann Smith

If transnationalism, in the literal sense, has to do with the ways in which borders between nation-states are becoming less rigid and more porous rather than impermeable, I want to begin by suggesting that the term can function, too, as a way of describing a weakening of cultural and other ethnic imperatives. Tsitsi Dangarembga's *Nervous Conditions: A Novel* (1988) seems to me to have illustrated this kind of transnationalism three decades ago, long before this notion became a topic of general interest. This work of fiction, set in what was then Rhodesia before the war of liberation, is about a young girl, Tambudzai, known as Tambu, who is given the opportunity to go to school, at the age of thirteen, only because her brother, Nhamo, has died. African girls were then (and many still are) caught up in a kind of nationalism that is fostered by, and demonstrated in, the historically and culturally held belief that African girls, particularly rural ones, are not to be educated; only boys are. It is worth quoting from the opening paragraphs at some length because here we see, at once, that Tambu, writing as a young woman years later, rejected this aspect of African nationalism even as a girl.

> I was not sorry when my brother died. Nor am I apologising for my callousness, as you may define it, my lack of feeling ... Therefore I shall not apologise but

begin by recalling the facts as I remember them ... that put me in a position to write this account. For though the event of my brother's passing and the events of my story cannot be separated, my story is not after all about death, but about my escape ... about my mother's ... entrapment; and about Nyasha's rebellion – Nyasha, far-minded and isolated, my uncle's daughter, whose rebellion may not in the end have been successful. (Dangarembga 1988: 1)

Nyasha, Tambu's cousin and friend, serves as foil to the protagonist. Strictly speaking, as mentioned above, transnationalism suggests that borders between nation-states have become (or are becoming) less stringent, uncompromising, and, even, weakened. We can see this in the ways in which temporary migration puts pressure on migrants to adopt and display the values of the host nation and become assimilated into it so, when Nyasha's father, Babamakuru, the headmaster of the mission school, sent by the missionaries to study in England for five years to earn a degree, took Nyasha and her brother, Chido, with him, Nyasha did this so well that she was unable to cope with the requirements of her return to rural Africa. Unlike those who emigrate and form or join ethnic transnational communities in which their own values are espoused along with some of those of the host nation, Nyasha succumbed to what Tambu's mother, Mainini Ma'Shingayi, calls "the Englishness" (202) evident even at the mission, a far-flung outpost of England itself. In a sense Nyasha becomes an English national in her eschewing of all things African. But, because the borders, as it were, between Rhodesia and England are not in any way porous for her, when she returns to rural Africa she cannot assimilate back into her family and community. She reads *Lady Chatterley's Lover* despite her mother's objection that "books like that ... are no good for you" (75) until her father confiscates it, contravenes African custom by eating before her father has finished his meal and talking back to him, and smokes cigarettes. However, Tambu copes with the border-crossing between her rural African village and the relatively sophisticated milieu of the English mission school and back again for school holidays although not, it is true, without some difficulty. At the mission she discover[s] that using a knife and fork was not as easy as it looked" and realises with great embarrassment that her "place [at the table] looked as though a small and angry child had been fed there" (82). Back at home for Christmas, she eats the breakfast "hunks of bread cut thick, spread with margarine and taken with tea poured out of a huge enamel kettle ... in which the milk and water were boiled up together ... [although] she would have preferred egg and bacon" (134), the quintessential English breakfast. She cannot clean the latrine that has fallen into a state of unhealthy filth well enough so she "[goes] back into the bushes as [she] had done before the latrine was built" (123). For Tambu these borders between what is acceptable in England and Africa and what is unacceptable are permeable; she accommodates the differences.

Given that the "nervous conditions" of Dangarembga's title refer to Jean-Paul Sartre's recognition, in his Preface to Franz Fanon's *The Wretched of the Earth*, that "the status of the native is a nervous condition introduced and maintained by the settler among colonized people with their consent" (1963: 20), we watch Nyasha's loss of the freedom she experienced in England manifest itself as an eating disorder representative of such a nervous condition. For Dangarembga, this eating disorder of the adolescent Nyasha is not related to her compliance to normative standards of female beauty and attractiveness but serves as a metaphor for the inappropriateness of her response to such nationalist oppression in its unstrategic excessiveness. "Exerting control over what one eats is not the answer to the patriarchal control of [girls'] access to learning and education in Southern Africa; to fade away is to give up" (Smith 2000: 252) and it is this recognition that empowers Tambu to pursue her education. Nyasha, the (English) nationalist becomes seriously undernourished and fades from the text as Tambu, the African transnationalist, chooses to return to school instead of staying behind in the village to help look after her.

In this novel, Tambu's adolescence itself "becomes metonymic of a developing political and feminist consciousness" (Smith and Mitchell 2001: 291). She struggles to deal with the appeal of the elite privilege of education, endorsed by patriarchy, yet recognizes that this is the only way out of poverty available to her; this benevolent patriarchy both empowers and oppresses her. For Tambu, the transnationalist, education is the impermeable border between poverty and achievement. For Nyasha, the nationalist who relished this privilege, education is her undoing.

We see Tambu dealing with the overwhelming sense of her own worthlessness as a poor black girl, but, as Roberta Trites reminds us, if we are to read fiction we need an "understanding of the subjunctive ... [the] ability to understand possibility and potential" (2016: viii), so we are not surprised by the concluding sentences.

> Quietly, unobtrusively and extremely fearfully, something in my mind began to assert itself, to question things and refuse to be brainwashed, bringing me to this time when I can set down this story. In was a long and painful process for me, that process of expansion. (1988: 203)

Introducing the Chapters in this Volume

There are many different ways of introducing authors and their chapters to the readers of a book. Since these chapters first appeared as articles in *Girlhood Studies: An Interdisciplinary Journal* 10(3) in 2017 (with the exception of "Using Fiction, Autoethnography, and Girls' Lived Experience in Preparation for Playwriting" by Genna Gardini because we could not finalize it in time), I have chosen to use the abstracts that were published in the journal to introduce the work of these writers. I have also used the abstract that was part of Gardini's original submission but have no way of referencing this use except by mentioning it here.

In her chapter, "Naughtiest Girls, Go Girls, and Glitterbombs: Exploding Schoolgirl Fictions," Linda McKnight considers "the struggles, denials, and ambivalences that produce and are produced by reading the schoolgirl. In her creative article with its glitterbomb "incendiary fragments of memory and media" detonating, as it were, on the pages she discusses the "postfeminist entanglement in the ongoing re-configuration of the schoolgirl, with [its] implications for policy and practice in education and for cultural and girlhood studies" (McKnight 2017: 7).

In "'This Is My Story': The Reclaiming of Girls' Education Discourses in Malala Yousafzai's Autobiography," Rosie Walters discusses the implications of how "young women's and girls' education activists represent themselves" in relation to "the way in which Yousafzai negotiates and challenges discourses around young women, Pakistan, and Islam." Walters concludes that "a truly emancipatory understanding of girls' rights would look not to the words and policies of powerful organizations but, rather, to young women themselves" (Walters 2017: 23).

Fiona Nelson, in "The Girl: Dead," expresses her concern with what she calls the "dead girl genre of Young Adult (YA) literature"—books that she describes as being "artifacts of a culture that allows little to no sexual agency or subjectivity for (living) teenaged girls and young women." She observes "that *dead* has come to be promoted as a viable sexual subject position for young women" and worries that these novels "might actually nurture a culture of bullying and suicide" (Nelson 2017: 39).

In her chapter, "Girl Constructed in Two Nonfiction Texts: Sexual Subject? Desired Object?" Mary Ann Harlan investigates the ways in which two popular nonfiction texts, *American Girls: Social Media and the Secret Lives of Teenagers* (2016) by Nancy Jo Sales and Peggy Orenstein's *Girls and Sex: Navigating the Complicated New Landscape* (2016) construct girls "as sexual subjects and desired objects." She points to the dissonance between what these two authors say about girls and what girls themselves have to say about how they "navigate society's expectations and constructions of them as sexual subjects" (Harlan 2017: 54).

Wendy L. Rouse, in "Perfect Love in a Better World: Same-Sex Attraction between Girls," explores the "impact of shifting cultural norms" on the lives of lesbian girls in the late nineteenth and early twentieth century. Given the "growing anxiety about the potential sexual undertones of female friendships" as sexologists began to focus on homosexuality as pathology, the literature being produced and consumed by adults led to "tragic consequences for [girls] who resisted efforts to conform to heteronormative expectations regarding their future" (Rouse 2017: 71).

Tehmina Pirzada, in "Narrating Muslim Girlhood in the Pakistani Cityscape of Graphic Narratives" focuses on two graphic novels, *Gogi* (1970–the present) by Nigar Nazar and *Burka Avenger* (2013–the present) by Haroon Rashid, to examine "the empowering portrayal of Muslim girlhood that these works offer in addition to advocating for the rights of Muslim girls." She is interested in how they rework the "western superhero trope to foreground [the] everyday heroism of these protagonists" (Pirzada 2017: 88).

In "Confronting Girl-bullying and Gaining Voice in Two Novels by Nicholasa Mohr," whom she describes as "an important but critically overlooked author of the Puerto Rican Diaspora," Barbara Roche Rico examines the representation of bullying in two novels by Mohr. She explores "the emergence of the female subject from behind her self-definition as a victim of girl-bullying" and shows how the protagonist's "involvement with art enables her to move from the role of object to that of subject" and how this "brings [her] to a deeper understanding of her culture and herself" (Roche Rico 2017: 105).

Roxanne Harde's chapter, "'Like Alice, I was Brave': The Girl in the Text in Olemaun's Residential School Narratives" traces the journey of the eponymous Indigenous girl who wanted to become a student in a residential school so that she could acquire the literacy that would enable her to read *Alice in Wonderland*. Through her "determination, courage, and resilience … [she] draws on … her culture" and [on this] British novel [in order to find] her own methods of resisting colonial oppressions and asserting Indigenous agency" (Harde 2017: 121).

Ana Puchau de Lecea's focus in "Girl, Interrupted and Continued: Rethinking the Influence of Elena Fortún's *Celia*" is on "the ways in which Fortún, through her shifting characterization of Celia as increasingly subversive presented herself as a female author offering alternative models of femininity to her readers through the character Celia and the social context of the series." She is interested in how "Fortún's ideological influence on female writers" (Puchau de Lecea 2017: 137) helped ensure the narrative continuity of Spanish literature after the Civil War.

Michele Meek's point of departure in "Lolita Speaks: Disrupting Nabokov's 'Aesthetic Bliss'" is that "a contemporary analytical shift from valuing the aesthetics to a consideration of the ethics of [*Lolita*] has led to restricted critical readings" of this novel. Her concern is with Lolita's victimization that, for her, disrupts Nabokov's "aesthetic bliss." Meek looks at three revisionary texts, all written by female authors, that "give voice to the girl in the text" in acknowledgement of [her] "sexual desire and agency" (Meek 2017:152).

In "Hope Chest: Demythologizing Girlhood in Kate Bernheimer's Trilogy," Catriona McAra, "invoking and explaining the relevance of literary theories related to caskets," uses the metaphor of the hope chest "as both a toy and a cultural repository" that she locates "at the heart of a trilogy of fairy tale novels." She uses the hope chest to discuss the social transition in these novels of the "child-woman—a hinge-like cultural figure whom Bernheimer represents metaphorically through boxes of accoutrements containing memories and prophecies" (McAra 2017: 168).

Akane Kanai, in "The Girl in the GIF: Reading the Self into Girlfriendship," explores "the practice of reading as a form of social participation in girlhood in digital spaces." For her, "readers' aesthetic and social participation" in the circulation of blogs that "use GIFs (looping, animated images) and captions to articulate feelings and reactions relating to everyday situations … is key to the formation of digital publics in which readers come to recognize themselves as girls through calls to common feeling" (Kanai 2017: 184).

In "Girls' Perspectives on (Mis)Representations of Girlhood in Hegemonic Media Texts," Paula MacDowell notes that "media texts are constantly projecting … conflicting and influential messages" about and at girls. She discusses her analysis with "10 girl co-researchers (aged between 10 and 13)" of these "taken-for-granted meanings that need to be understood, questioned, interrupted, and transformed." She reports on the production by these girls of a "Public Service Announcement (PSA) to represent how girls and girlhood are (mis)represented in well-established and hegemonic media discourses" (MacDowell 2017: 201).

Genna Gardini explores Sheila Kohler's *Cracks* (1999) in "Using Fiction, Autoethnography, and Girls' Lived Experience in Preparation for Playwriting" to unpack her "personal experience of being educated in a heteronormative, anglicized South African boarding school." Gardini "tracks [her] attempts to use and problematize some of Kohler's ideas in an autoethnographic research process with a group of young women to explore the genesis of [her] play, *Handsome Devil*." She explores "the use of discussion and journaling as a way of integrating and documenting [the] findings [of the group]."

Chapters Speaking to Chapters

The contributors to this inaugural volume of our new series, Transnational Girlhoods, present us with a range of perspectives on girlhood as evoked by their understanding of how the girl in the text works not only in terms of geographic location but also in relation to their positionality. The girl is presented as central to liberating pedagogical practice and educational activism in British Australian Lucinda McKnight's taking on of neoliberalism in curricula that affect girls in Australia and this chapter speaks to Rosie Walters's work on Malala Yousafzai's autobiography in which she (Yousafzai) reclaims the discourses about education and girls and young women in Pakistan and Islam. The girl is implicated in adult-created forms of (often very dangerous) determinism as Fiona Nelson, Wendy L. Rouse, and Mary Ann Harlan point out. Nelson's interest is in the genre of contemporary Young Adult literature in the US that focuses on dead girls and might well encourage suicide, and this is in conversation across time with Wendy L. Rouse's chapter on how the writings of early twentieth-century British, Austrian, and German-Austrian sexologists blighted the lives of lesbian girls and young women in the US so severely that some saw suicide as the only way out. Harlan's description of how two non-fiction US texts construct girls as both sexual subjects and objects (as does the dead girl genre and the writings of the sexologists) and her point about how the authors do not listen to what girls have to say about themselves underly, theoretically if not chronologically, what concerns both Nelson and Rouse.

Girls in texts are presented as fictional heroes who empower themselves and others with lasting effect in Pakistan in Tehmina Pirzada's chapter, in Barbara Roche Rico's in Puerto Rico, in a Canadian Residential School in Roxanne Harde's chapter, and in Spain for Ana Pucheau de Lecea. All four authors, in being concerned about the ways in which the reconstruction of the girl relies on her own initiative and on her assuming agency have much to say to each other and to the authors mentioned above.

Representations of the child-woman evoke discussions of the relationship between desire and ethics for Michele Meek and a consideration of how the child moves into womanhood in a trilogy of US fairy tales for Catriona MacAra. Meek's exploration of the notion of sexual consent in *Lolita* (1955) by Russian-born American Swiss Nabokov (1955) as well as her concern with the act of giving voice to girls addresses Harlan's use in her chapter of the words spoken by girls themselves along with MacDowell's insistence on privileging the words of her girl coresearchers. MacAra's investigation of Kate Bernheimer's (2001, 2006, 2011) use of her own transition from child into woman during the late 1960s and early 1970s in the US in her fairy tales resonates with Roxanne Harde's description of how Margaret (Olemaun) Pokiak-Fenton and her daughter-in-law Christy Jordan-Fenton narrated Pokiak-Fenton's own experiences in the 1940s as a student in a Residential School in Canada. Both these chapters are in conversation with Barbara Roche Rico's examination of the ways in which author Nicholasa Mohr's own experience is evident in that of her girl protagonist, Felita, and with Genna Gardini's autoethnographic approach in working with a group of young women whose collective written and spoken responses to their own experience of girlhood influenced her writing of the play, *Handsome Devil*, about what it might mean to be a girl in a South African school. In turn, this chapter can be seen to be in conversation with many other chapters whose emphasis is on the voices of girls.

The participation of the girl in digital and media texts is explored in relation to different publics. For Akane Kanai, writing from Australia, reading can be an act of social participation in digital spaces when bloggers and their readers, whom they call girlfriends, share similar experiences of particular feelings. These girlfriends would find much in common with Paula McDowell's coresearchers—a different public of 10 girls from 3 elementary schools in Vancouver, Canada—who created a PSA in response to how girls are misrepresented and constructed in media texts.

Understanding a Different Kind of Transnationalism

I want, now, to suggest how my notion of the kind of analogous transnationalism and nationalism that I put forward in relation to Tambu and Nyasha in Dangarembga's *Nervous Conditions* (1988) might work in other ways in these chapters. This might prove useful as we consider the implications of transnational girlhood studies and transnational girlhoods.

Ana Puchau de Lecea's chapter on the influence of Elena Fortún's series, "Celia and Her World" on later women writers demonstrates beautifully my suggested re-defining of transnationalism to include the process of weakening borders other than those between nation-states. Thanks to Fortún as (re-defined) transnationalist, the seemingly impermeable border surrounding the depiction of girls in Spanish fiction as necessarily subservient and marginalized was ruptured and this led to the creation of what were known as weird girls in Spanish literature; the girl was reconstructed as a non-conforming independent rebel.

If McKnight's suggestion that we can refigure the schoolgirl through liberating pedagogical practice suggests that the rigid boundaries that surround her are weakening, the action of some Melbourne parents in the 1990s who withdrew their daughters, but not their sons, from private schools because they could no longer afford the fees, as McKnight reminds us, might stop us in our tracks. Seeing this feminist re-figuration as analogous to transnationalism in the face of the nationalism of such conservative parental discrimination would allow us to see the schoolgirl as she is and not as these parents see her. Similarly, just as Dangarembga's (1988) fictional Tambu did in Rhodesia, Malala Yousafzai, as Rosie Walters points out, worked against what we might think of as the nationalist policy of her birthplace, Pakistan, that sees girls as unworthy of being educated, even before she was shot. What could be described as Yousafzai's transnationalist insistence on troubling these borders imposed by authoritarian discourses of control over girls allows them to speak for themselves.

Three of the contributors whose chapters deal with fictional texts, Fiona Nelson, Tehmina Pirzada, and Barbara Roche Rico, offer other interesting ways in which this re-defined transnationalism can be seen to operate in relation to girlhood studies. I would like to suggest that Fiona Nelson points to the construction by Young Adult literature authors and publishers of an alarming border that separates the desirable dead from the less desirable living. If we agree that nationalism is about preserving borders Nelson's worries that these novels might lead to bullying and suicide are indeed well-founded. If girlhood studies sees itself as transnationalist in the sense that I am proposing, this border needs not to be weakened so much as smashed to bits. That there are no books about dead boys—and I am not suggesting that there should be—makes this imperative even more urgent because popularity is associated with being dead if you are a girl. In relation to Tehmina Pirzada's chapter my suggested analogy appears to hold up: these cartoons that we could describe as transnationalist serve to create great gaps in the border between nationalist traditional and stereotypical portrayals of Muslim girls and their representation in these novels as super-heroic. Barbara Roche Rico considers the fictional representation of a Puerto Rican girl, Felita, who self-defines as an object—a victim of bullying—until her story-telling grandmother helps her to move away from hatred and the desire for revenge. Felita learns to exercise agency as an artist and finds her own subjectivity. This, in turn, leads to her coming to understand herself and appreciate her culture. There are echoes here of Tambu's ability to make permeable that seemingly impermeable border between seeing herself as object unworthy of being educated and as agentic subject in search of an education. Both girls exercise a kind of transnationalism.

Roxane Harde offers us an account of a cultural border-crossing that calls Dangarembga's (1988) novel to mind. Olemaun, an Indigenous Canadian girl, returns home from her Residential School after an absence of two years. She struggles to re-assimilate into her Inuvialuit culture because, in part, she cannot speak her own language and she cannot eat the food she grew up on. Countering the kinds of colonial benevolent patriarchy that led to the predicament shared by Nyasha and Olemaun requires a kind of transnationalist border-crossing with which both girls struggle and that neither of them appears able to manage.

Michele Meek's examination of the ways in which revisionary texts reposition Nabokov's Lolita as an incest victim and also as a girl with sexual desire makes it clear that the border between sexual consent and non-consent is extremely shaky. The issue of consent as a non-negotiable border between all girls and women and their potential sexual partners must be taken up by transnational girlhood studies.

Catriona MacAra's consideration of how the hope chest, as symbol for Bernheimer, in being both conservative and transgressive, challenges the conventional societal expectation of girls and girlhood. Perhaps this could serve to make less impermeable that border between so-called good or conservative girlhood and so-called bad or transgressive girlhood?

Reading Wendy L. Rouse's chapter might show how easy (and how convenient for my argument) it is to imagine an uncrossable border between the experiences of lesbian girls and what the sexologists were saying at the turn of the nineteenth century and early into the next one. If we replace those sexologists with contemporary homophobes the border is no different and the need for a transnational sundering of it is obvious.

For Genna Gardini the border between idealized girlhood and the experience of real lived girlhood needs to be broken down if girls are to be believed, taken seriously, and have their voices heard and respected. This also involves breaching the border between fictional romantic idealized notions of girls' boarding schools and the reality of these institutions.

As we read Akane Kanai's chapter and Paula McDowell's we are reminded of the rigid border (known as the digital divide) between those girls who have access to computers and other devices that link them to the internet and those who do not. Kanai reminds us of another border—that between the active participation of girls and their need (as perceived by themselves and others) to be girlishly non-threatening. While the weakening of the digital divide border may be beyond the ability of transnational girlhood studies to remedy, the second must be attended to. MacDowell's chapter responds to this in her attempt to breach the border between how girls are misrepresented in the media and how they see themselves by having her co-researchers—10- to 13-year-olds drawn from a larger group of 30 Caucasian, Chinese, East Indian, Greek, Japanese, Jewish, Romanian, Spanish, Thai, and Turkish girls—create a media text that narrates their own stories and do just this in presenting themselves as they wish to be seen.

If we agree with my extending the definition of transnationalism to include the breaking of conceptual ethnic and cultural borders or, at least, making them permeable, we can open up possibilities for transnational girlhood studies to make a huge difference in the lives of girls around the world and even more so if this includes the actualization of the notion of transnational girlhood that would involve girls interacting with each other, perhaps as activists or perhaps as colleagues and friends, across borders—geographical, cultural, ethnic, economic—to form virtual neighborhoods.

Acknowledgements

I am most grateful to the authors and the reviewers, to Vivian Berghahn, Camille LeBlanc, and Amanda Horn of Berghahn Books, to Pamela Lamb for creating the excellent index, and to Claudia Mitchell for coming up with the title.

ANN SMITH has been the managing editor of *Girlhood Studies: An Interdisciplinary Journal* since its inception. Formerly a lecturer in the Department of English, University of the Witwatersrand, South Africa, where she specialized in literary theory with a particular focus on feminism and queer theory, she is now an adjunct professor in the Department of Integrated Studies in Education at McGill University, Montreal.

References

Dangarembga, Tsitsi. 1988. *Nervous Conditions. A Novel.* London: The Women's Press.
Sartre, Jean-Paul. 1963. "Preface." In *The Wretched of the Earth*, Franz Fanon, Trans. Constance Farrington, 7–31. New York: Grove.
Smith, Ann. 2000. "Girl Power in Nervous Conditions: Fictional Practice as a Research Site." *McGill Journal of Education* 35 (3): 245–260.
Smith, Ann, and Claudia Mitchell. 2001. "Reading Adolescence in Some Southern African Fiction." In *Spaces and Crossings*, ed. Rita Wilson and Carlotta von Maltzan, 289–300. Frankfurt am Main: Peter Lang.
Trites, Roberta. 2016. "Foreword." In *One Child Reading. My Auto-Bibliography*, Margaret Mackey, vii–ix. Edmonton, AB: The University of Alberta Press.

CHAPTER 1

Naughtiest Girls, Go Girls, and Glitterbombs
Exploding Schoolgirl Fictions

Lucinda McKnight

Schoolgirl and Title Girl

Schoolgirl, as a term, is an oxymoron. The negative charge between metaphoric tenor and vehicle provides the frisson that sustains this trope. The word schoolboy is redundant, rarely used; school and boy go together so naturally that the adjective is unnecessary. Schoolgirl retains an element of surprise, and reminds the reader subliminally that girls did/do not always go to school. The word girl in any title offers this same frisson: a whole book about a girl? Really? A journal called *Girlhood Studies*? This contradiction in terms, that girl is important, salient on the cover in the title font, and yet culturally understood as something much less, is readily demonstrated when the reader makes the switch and substitutes boy in a popular title, like that of the *Go Girl* series.

We do not need to say, "Go boy!"; boys inherently go, they move, they travel, they can appear and disappear at will—sons running out to play unsupervised in the park after school, or husbands racing out the door to

---

Notes for this section can be found on page 26.

work. "Go boy," used as verbal incitement to action or attitude is a metaphor with no energy for human males; titles excite when they provide the reader with that contradiction in terms, that mental hook of intrigue and unexplored im/possibility. *Embroider Boy* might be such a title, but may have limited appeal for publishers in markets with fiercely heteronormative pedagogies.

This chapter responds to the call to consider how girls are represented in works with girl in their titles and takes as a starting point this heteroglossic friction within the word schoolgirl and in the very notion of a protagonist being a girl. To explore this concept, I take an autoethnographic and narrative approach, drawing on the trans-generational and trans-genred collection of books found in my own house with girl in their titles: two volumes in Enid Blyton's *Naughtiest Girl in the School* (1940–1952) series; contemporary tween sensation *Go Girl: Brilliant Besties* (Badger 2013); Valerie Walkerdine's academic *Schoolgirl Fictions* (1990), and my recently completed and bound thesis, *The Glitterbomb: Designing Curriculum and Identity with Girls' Popular Culture* (2014). These books in my bookshelves as a white, Anglo middle-class Australian are about schoolgirls and I draw on my lived experience as girl, mother, stepmother, and teacher to both perform and move beyond a comparison of the girls' fiction titles found there.

In the process, I am in dialogue with Walkerdine's *Schoolgirl Fictions* (1990) and complicate notions of reading the girl. Yet I would not want to stop in a girls' studies ghetto, and, as in my other work (McKnight 2015a, 2015b), seek to use concepts and insights of girls' studies for broader impact; I intend this chapter to be a discussion of reading that is also in dialogue with theory around reading and teaching texts, such as key literary works by Stanley Fish (1980) and Louise Rosenblatt (1968) on notions of pinning down and releasing meaning.

Key Concepts, Inspiration, and Research Design

By using the word heteroglossic in relation to metaphor, I refer to Mikhail Bakhtin's (1981) guiding philosophical trope of heteroglossia, a continual life struggle between centrifugal forces spinning meaning apart and centripetal forces that cohere. The compound noun schoolgirl comes together on the line, the intimate kerning between letters pulling them together. Yet schoolgirl simultaneously breaks apart, with a crack like the gunshot that wounded Malala Yousafzai. School is not necessarily a place where girls belong. My work has demonstrated that this is also conceivable in my own cultural and geographical contexts (McKnight 2014, 2015a, 2015b).

In the recession of the 1990s, parents at the school in suburban Melbourne where I was teaching began withdrawing their girls, claiming that they could afford private education for their sons but not for their daughters. The schoolgirl is a modern and tenuous phenomenon, a novelty. The schoolgirl must still be described and defined by the adjective school, a word associated but not assumed, so that agentive school and vulnerable girl are only contingently linked. Borrowing from Walkerdine (1990), we might perceive that the girl makes a phallic claim to learning, or indeed to the power of being in a title, yet has no phallus.

Through this chapter I contemplate the girl represented and addressed by the texts discussed, and the struggles, denials, and ambivalences that produce and are produced by reading the protagonist schoolgirl of these titles as an ongoing material and discursive reconfiguration simultaneously invested with capacity and girled into helplessness. In doing this work, I am indebted to a number of feminist thinkers and writers, including Walkerdine (1990), Frigga Haug and Others (1987), Frigga Haug (2000), Madeleine Grumet (1976), Claudia Mitchell (2016), Claudia Mitchell and Sandra Weber (1999), Dorothy Smith (1987), Judith Butler (1997), Angela McRobbie (2009), Patricia Williams (1991), and Susanne Gannon and Bronwyn Davies (2006). I seek first to describe their influence through explaining and then enacting the creative research design developed during my doctoral work to explore representations of schoolgirls.

My study involved working with a group of female teachers to design curriculum around girls' popular culture, with a focus on the stories we, as co-researchers, tell during our collaboration, rather than on a curricular end product. This is an approach advocated by curriculum theorist Grumet (1976), who encourages us to think about how teachers experience themselves in their work, rather than the teaching plans they produce.

A progressive concept when proposed, this idea is experienced today as even more radical in a neoliberal educational imaginary obsessed with outcomes (Reid 2010); eschewing outcomes also fits with Dorothy Smith's (1987) feminist advice to find standpoints outside of dominant discourse for sociological research. The study contemplates how curriculum design occurs in the context of broader media culture and involves the performance of gendered identities—coercively gendered yet with this very coercion providing opportunities for speaking back, as Judith Butler (1997) suggests—as researchers conjure past, present, and future simultaneously as we professional adult women continue to negotiate our identities as schoolgirls, as always already girlwomen, in another oxymoronic formulation. We are all grown up, but like the girl in the title of the book we read and the film we watch, we are always girled. We are always becoming girls, even as we are always becoming teachers (Mitchell and Weber 1999) through an ideological maelstrom of cohering and disintegrating discourse (Bakhtin 1981).

I also wrote narrative vignettes linking my own and my young daughter's consumption of popular media texts to our design work and shared these with teacher co-researchers, who wrote back with their own stories. Through this collegial memory work (Haug and Others 1987; Haug 2000; Gannon and Davies 2006) we enmesh professional dialogue and personal anecdote with fiction and with the political social commentary of the news media with which we engage, and forge ways of imagining our girlselves and girlstudents outside of dominant linear curricular discourses (Smith 1987), as well as seeking productive ways to read girls in the texts we teach.

Models for Collecting and Writing

Walkerdine's *Schoolgirl Fictions* (1990) provided invaluable inspiration for this work. She uses an eclectic collection of chapters both critical and creative to explore alternative and multiple constructions of schoolgirl identities. Using poststructuralist and psychoanalytic theory, she desires to "blow apart the fictions through which we have come to understand ourselves" (1990: xiv); this informed my own guiding metaphor of the glitterbomb, the girly intervention both effete and powerful, with fragments of stories, meeting transcripts, illustrations, photographs, screen captures, and theory detonating traditional thesis chapter (and book chapter) structure in a heteroglossic orgy of delight and dismay.

As with Walkerdine's montages, Walter Benjamin's strategy for writing vignettes is, according to John Hughes, "to dip in and take a quotation out of context, mount it into a dialectical image and see what sparks fly" (1992: n.p.), further heteroglossic work of synthesis and release that proved generative for my study. Patricia Williams (1991) also achieves an alchemical forging of anecdote, story, and legal discourse in her work, bringing together professional legal debate and personal fury at injustice.

Troubling Neoliberal Curriculum and Reading as Comprehension

So, as naughtiest girl researcher I sought to undermine neoliberal certainties of curriculum, and as go girl mother of young children, to obtain a doctorate and return to the workforce by using concepts from a marginalized field to do mainstream critique. In doing this, I also drew on the work of Rosenblatt (1968) and Fish (1980) to trouble the very notion of finding and studying a girl in any text. There is a particular urgency in returning to these theorists in a contemporary context. In Australia, conservative forces behind a new national curriculum have re-framed the senior study of literature into what teachers involved in my study described as a tickbox meeting of requirements (McKnight 2015a, 2015b). New Victorian interpretations of this curriculum insist that students draw on literary theorists in their exam responses, raising fears of an ever more prescribed regurgitation of taught responses.

Rosenblatt, while reading now as profoundly and problematically humanist, not to mention dismissive of popular culture, reminds teachers that "the literary work exists in the live circuit set up between reader and text" (1968: 25), not in the text reified by new criticism, or even solely in the reader's mind. Fish (1980) goes so far as to suggest that a text is made anew by every reader in the context of membership of interpretive communities. These perspectives serve to destabilize the study of literature as comprehension, or teacher-licensed explication of theoretical positions, yet they still fall short. A circuit is too neat. Interpretive communities are based on flawed assumptions of sameness (Eagleton 1983).

If we borrow the electricity of Rosenblatt's circuit, and the creativity of Fish's invention of the text, and bring these along with awareness of Bakhtin's combustible competing forces of heteroglossia to reading or making the girl in the text, we can get started. Add in Benjamin's synthesis of past, present, and future into fragmented flash (described in Hughes 1992), Butler's (1997) performative and iterative identity, and McRobbie's (2009) heteroglossic compression of post-feminism into hyperfeminized top girl, isolated, diminished, and simultaneously enabled, and we have the theoretical components of a glitterbomb, an intervention into conventional understandings of how we frame and interpret a given girl text, or any text, in fact. The contradictory components of the glitterbomb exemplify the concept of post-feminist discursive complexity (Gill 2007) and trouble easy renderings of representation.

I turn now to the popular texts that participate in shaping the schoolgirl, providing background to their contexts that may resonate with readers' own memories and imaginings.

The Girls in and on the Texts

While I was writing my thesis on creating curriculum around girls' popular culture and reading Walkerdine (1990), I was also reading girls' fiction, as a pre-service Literacy teacher educator and as a mother of a girl who was four when I began and seven by the time I had finished writing my thesis. I have these books on our shelves, yet when the editor of this special issue asked me for the publication details of the particular works I would be citing I found these difficult to provide. I had re-read two of prolific post-war British author Enid Blyton's *Naughtiest Girl* books: *The Naughtiest Girl is a Monitor* ([1945]1997), in an Enid Blyton centenary edition from a second-hand shop, and *The Naughtiest Girl Again* ([1942]1987), a yellow-paged edition handed down from Amy's[1] much older step-sister. I had read the compilation edition *Go Girl: Brilliant Besties* (2013).

Yet the writing I would do around these texts, about the girls conjured up by them would not be confined by these editions; I am working also with remembered and storied editions and girls. It is impossible to read *The Naughtiest Girl* in 2016 without experiencing my own childhood readings and re-readings over many years. As I read, I am also aware of my mother's love of these books and my visceral memories of other Enid Blytons with pen and ink illustrations coloured by her own careful schoolgirl hand, and of our conversations about the books and shared thrill at the naughtiest girl's exploits. If this sounds as though I am waxing nostalgic, the reader may be reassured by Mitchell and Weber's assertion that nostalgia can be used purposefully to claim a history, or territory (1999). Fiction books with girl in the title were rare in my experience and there was enormous delight in this protagonist who was like a girl from a girls' annual story luxuriously developed as a proper, novel-length character. Then, of course, there was the frisson, for us as good girls, of the naughtiest girl, the girl who makes trouble.

The covers of my lost childhood editions are easily found online. Looking at the cover art highlights the nature of these works as both written and graphic. The naughtiest girl of the 1970s is wild, dirty, and fun, rendered in brilliant primary colours, with her ratty hair and slouchy socks. The naughtiest girl of the 1980s in my step-daughter's edition is more androgynous and muted. The naughtiest girl of the centenary edition is retro, in a plaid dressing gown and beside a fancy gold centenary medallion. The 1980s edition contains apparently original illustrations of 1940s schoolgirls contrasting incongruously with the cover. The 1990s edition has retro-style drawings that cannot quite replicate the perfect marcel waves of 1940s school girl hair, the hair of my grandmother's 1941 wedding photo.

My grandmother married a man she did not love since her father would not let her break off her engagement. He would not allow her to make trouble. This stylized, sinuous marcel line invites me to segue into story, into embodied forms of knowledge (Weber 2008) and into the crafting of my glitterbomb, the securing of meaning even as it exceeds my intentions.

First, I will introduce briefly the *Go Girl* series. *Go Girl* is published in Australia but is a global phenomenon, and has so-called headquarters online; a mock embroidered logo has tabs for games and glitter. The series of over 40 books can be purchased as individual books, or as chunky sets, such as our *Brilliant Besties* (2013),which contains five short novels as chapters: *Sleepover* (McAuley 2013a); *Birthday Girl* (Badger 2013); *Secret's Out* (Perry 2013a); *Music Mad* (McAuley 2013b), and *Flower Girl* (Perry 2013b).

I read these books as teacher/researcher/mother/girl and as I read I am simultaneously feeling the hundreds of button and loop fastenings on my silk bodice closing me into my 1985 bridesmaid's dress; wondering what my daughter will make of the cool girl who lies; estimating a reading level for the book; and noticing that every single one of the 83 illustrations shows the go girl on her own and often miserable, unlike the more social and happy illustrations in the *Naughtiest Girl* books. The schoolgirl in the text, the naughtiest girl, go girl, Walkerdine girl, thesis-writing girl is always in the making, always juxtaposed, always shot through with other words (Bakhtin 1981) and images, intertextually linked by visual line and printed word, coming into focus and blurring even more.

In the following section, I seek to create a glitterbomb around the notion of the girls in these texts, a playful collection of fragments packed tightly that simultaneously explodes meaning, with identities pulled this way and that via competing heteroglossic addresses; this is not always comfortable for the reader who experiences these contradictory forces by re-making these images in further fragmented formulations. The white space here is vital to allow room for this discomfiture and resonance.

What forms, for readers identifying as women, from the following prompts? What memories flash up, superimposed, in the instant, with imaginings of our present young daughters, nieces, friends, and students, and the hopes or fears we have for their futures? In reading we perform suppression, projection, identification, and resistance, with bedtime story and political debate enmeshed.

The Glitterbomb

'Hallo, Kath! What are you so busy about? Let's see.'
She bent over Kathleen's work. 'My goodness!" she said. "What tiny stitches – and how nicely you've worked the roses! I wish I could sew like that. I want a handkerchief case.' (Blyton [1942]1987: 127)

> The next morning before school, Casey spent ages on the computer making pretty invitations. She put daisies all around the border, just like the daisies that decorated Tamsin's peg at school. (Perry 2013: 236)

1984: English Literature was my favourite school subject. We met Keats etcetera, but one of our set texts was *Women and Fiction*, a collection of short stories by and about women. Was this actually the first time I had read something at school written by a woman? I remember Tolkien, Hardy, Hartley, Shakespeare, Steinbeck, Barstow, Bradbury, Brecht… wait, there was Harper Lee. But I thought she was a man anyway. I do think Jane Austen was there in Year 11 but I have only a fleeting memory of empire line bodices on a fuzzy old television adaptation, probably of *Pride and Prejudice.* Just writing those male authors' names tows me back to the twentieth century, all tweed and pipes, and even further, to coal fires and gas lamps lit by maids. (Personal thesis vignette, "The Winding Sheet" (2012), remembering *1984*)

A judge who was verbally abused by a defendant reciprocated at a court hearing where he was being sentenced for breaching an antisocial behaviour order. John Hennigan, 50, who had breached the order by using racist language towards a black woman and her two children told Chelmsford crown court judge Patricia Lynch QC that she was 'a bit of a cunt.' And Judge Lynch replied: 'You are a bit of a cunt yourself.' (*The Guardian*, 11 August 2016)

> 'No quarrels with anyone – no bad tempers – no silly flare-ups!' said Elizabeth to herself. She knew her own faults very well. (Blyton [1997]1945: 3)

The children are making constructions from Lego; we are concerned here with the actions of three children: a three-year-old girl, Annie, and two four-year-old boys, Sean and Terry. The teacher's name is Miss Baxter. The sequence begins when Annie takes a piece of Lego to add on to a construction she is building. Terry tries to take it away from her to use himself, and he resists…
Terry: You're a stupid cunt, Annie. (Walkerdine 1990: 4)

> 'Our girls are demure,' said the principal smugly, with a tight smile. (Diary note 2015 from tour of a prospective school for my daughter)

The moment Iris stepped out from behind the curtain and into the light her nerves vanished. (McAuley 2013b: 359)

This will be my first job interview in ten years or so since I had my children. The role is Head of Senior School, with some English teaching, and they want someone with a deep understanding of curriculum theory. My grandmother taught at this school. On the website, leaves fall softly from an ancient tree, history realised in a dreamy animation carpeting a private girls' grammar school world. Motto: Educating Tomorrow's Woman. The girls in the photographs are in smart knee length plaid, with clean skeletal traceries of white bordering their navy blazers. In Years 7 to 9 they all pursue the SHINE Award. (Personal thesis vignette, "Shine" 2013)

> There was another outburst of cheering and clapping. 'Good old Elizabeth!' shouted somebody. 'Trust her to ask something for the school, and not for herself.' (Blyton [1942]1987: 213)

She will shine. (Extract from print advertisement for private girls' school, 2012)

In the 1940s, starting secondary school and her period, my mother had to wear an elastic belt around her waist, with dangling straps front and rear, to which she secured a chafing wedge of sanitary napkin. Above that she wore a suspender belt to hold up her twisty stockings, then enormous bloomers, and then an itchy woollen tunic with further belt. Under her tunic she wore a shirt with a starchy collar that cut a raw line in her skin, and a tie. My mother still cannot wear any garment that touches her neck. She is still that girl, wrestling with the trappings of schoolgirlhood. (Diary notes, 2016)

> Girls are victims of cruelty, but they rise above their circumstances by servicing and being sensitive to *others*—selflessness. (Walkerdine 1990: 98)

>> [Reflecting on lesson re girls' magazines that do not take a feminist stance.] I try to imagine the gap between my private world and my teacher persona that might facilitate this silence in my pedagogy. What is in that gap? What feelings? What desires? What fears? The words that come to me—I test them out and write them here—are these: *I do not want to make trouble.* (Personal thesis vignette, "Lesson Plan" 2012)

> Naughtiness in young children, for example, is to be expected, validated and associated with masculinity. (Walkerdine 1990: 49)

[On giving a talk at a school.] Students flood in and seize the chairs; many have to sit on the floor around the edges of the room, where they cannot even see the screen. A beautiful girl sits right at my feet, and raises her hand keenly at every question, despite the restless tide behind her, the boys ignoring the rhythmic *shhhing* of Jess and Rachel [teachers], who hover at the back. The girl's hand is often the only one, and I work hard to elicit more from the others, but she shines through, her golden corkscrew curls bobbing—a tween Shirley Temple. (Personal thesis vignette, "What They Did to Her" 2013)

> The staffroom is full of women eating cottage cheese or grapefruit.
> Each of them knows about diet and eating and sexuality. They are willing to talk about these, caught inside what they are: the unique combination of worker and woman, dependent and independent, free and trapped. (Walkerdine 1990: 29)

> Sign across driveway of co-educational school: Tradesmen's Entrance. Two girls out of twenty in woodworking class. (Diary note from tour of prospective school 2015)

'Let's visit the Party Princess website. She might be able to help.' Seconds later a girl appeared on the screen wearing a tiara and holding a present. 'That's the Party Princess,' explained Sophie. 'She knows everything there is to know about parties.' Sophie clicked on the WHAT'S HOT section.

> Party Princess
>
> WHAT'S HOT RIGHT NOW? MOCKTAIL PARTIES!
> - Wear your best clothes
> - Serve brightly coloured soft drinks and juices in tall glasses
> - Offer unusual snacks on silver trays
> - Play croquet
>
> Annabelle grinned. 'That's it!' she said. 'I'll have a mocktail party!' (Badger 2013: 101)

Melbourne mother angry girl can't wear pants as part of school uniform. (Woods 2016) (Diary note of newspaper headline)

> [On attending a symposium] At the end of the long day, a very senior academic in our faculty says of a couple of his doctoral colleague co-presenters, 'Well, the girls have kept us on track.'… I know that whatever else I might wish to be, I do not wish to be a girl. (Personal thesis vignette, "The Girls" 2012)

> Being a girl isn't what it used to be. IT'S BETTER. (Barbie *I Can Be* Facebook app. Mattel 2012)

Back to the job interview. First question. 'Where did you go to school?' asks the Principal. It's not something that, at 46, I put on my CV. I answer, naming an academic private girls' school. The Principal and Vice Principal, both women slightly older than me, look at each other and smile. 'Yes. You look like a Presbyterian Ladies' College girl.' My face falls into dismay, they misunderstand, and attempt to reassure me. 'Don't worry, it's a compliment.' Next question. I am wasting their time, with my shades of grey, in a navy and white world. (Personal thesis vignette, "Shine" 2013)

> I'm in control
> I broke the mould
> The girl you see
> Is up to me. ("Here I Am" song lyrics from *Barbie the Princess and the Popstar* (2011))

'That girl will drive me mad,' thought Mam'zelle to herself, 'with her spots and her greasy hair and her pale face. How she whines!' (Blyton [1987]1942: 44)

> Rachel (teacher co-researcher, from meeting transcript, 2012):
> There's one of mine, and I wouldn't be surprised if she was still sitting there playing with her little dolls. She's gorgeous, absolutely gorgeous … but she's very young.

Lucinda is poised to write an excellent thesis. She has completed a full draft which has been read by [her] supervisors. We are all in agreement that the thesis has the potential to address the issues with which Lucinda is concerned in a startlingly fresh and original way. It breaks the mould of theses as they are traditionally done in Education. (Supervisor's response, Higher Degree by Research Annual Review, 2014)

> 'Oh, I do feel so happy, Julian.'
> 'You've a right to,' said Julian. 'Funny person, aren't you? Naughtiest Girl in the School—and Best Girl in the School!' (Blyton [1945]1997: 214)

>> The increased prominence of the colour pink and other 'girly girl' characteristics will likely be a key influencer of Millennial women's consumer behaviour throughout their lifespan. (Young and Hinesly 2012: 7)

I enter the classroom. GOOD MORNING GOBLINS AND PRINCESSES announces the whiteboard in a chunky font. CLICK AND DRAG YOUR ICON TO MARK THE ROLL. On one side of the screen, an army of boy goblins waits, while princesses preen on the other, separated by a large castle. Battle lines are drawn. Maybe they will fight it out over the chores when they get inside the castle, like the rest of us. Even the teacher has an identical princess icon with her name on it. (Personal thesis vignette, "Goblins and Princesses" 2013 written after taking my daughter to school)

> Rachel (teacher co-researcher):
> Some of the Year 9 girls who went up to City Band, they wore suits. Half of them going up dressed like they were going to a disco, then a couple of them— there was just this sort of 'I'm not going to participate in this'—wore suits. So I think you'd have quite a few who think that this is something they don't relate to.

On the school tour we follow the familiar pattern of various lectures in a hall followed by a walk around led by some photogenic and charming senior students. It all goes smoothly until we reach the gym. Here we pause in a dark breezeway; we cannot see the gym because dark paper has been stuck all over the windows. We ask why. The students tell us: 'We had to do this because the girls didn't feel comfortable using the gym without it. The boys were looking through the windows and hassling them. So we're trying to get more girls in.' (Diary notes from school tour 2012)

> 'Such a nasty woman.' US presidential candidate Donald Trump on his opponent, Hillary Clinton, in their third and final televised debate. (NBC News, 19 October 2016)

Complaints have been made against a judge who verbally abused a defendant in a retaliatory exchange after he launched a foul-mouthed tirade at her from the dock, the Judicial Conduct Investigations Office (JCIO) has said. Judge Patricia Lynch QC was sentencing John Hennigan at Chelmsford crown court for his ninth breach of an antisocial behaviour order in 11 years when the exchange took place. Lynch's withering comments came when Hennigan, 50, told her she was 'a bit of a cunt,' to which she retorted: 'You are a bit of a cunt yourself. Being offensive to me does not help.' After Hennigan shouted back 'Go fuck yourself,' she replied: 'You too.' (Davies 2016)

> The complaints to the School Meeting were so serious that the two judges and the Jury took a long time to discuss them. In the meantime, the rest of the

> children also discussed the matter among themselves. Not many of them were for Robert, for he was not liked, but on the other hand most of the boys and girls felt that Elizabeth had no right to lose her temper so fiercely.
> 'And after all,' whispered one child to another, 'she was the naughtiest girl in the school last term, you know.' (Blyton [1942]1987: 30)

What if a girl wanted to be a goblin? What if a boy wanted to be a princess? Heaven forbid. I am dying to ask if Amy could have been a goblin, but I don't want to be the troublesome teacher mum doing a PhD in education who spoils all the lovely fun everyone is having. Must be a nice supportive mummy princess too, and slide my icon back home to my ivory tower… The other mothers are probably thrilled about the new roll call. Many of them have long blonde hair. They don't need a grey-brown goblin mother with her grimaces upsetting all the loveliness. This PhD is turning me into a goblin, though: I am grumpy all the time. (Personal thesis vignette, "Goblins and Princesses" 2013)

> Lola let her eyes wander back up to her mum's face. Her cheeks were brushed lightly with rouge, and her eyelashes looked longer and darker than normal. With her hair up and wispy, she looked …
> 'Mum…' Lola breathed, 'You look, you look …'
> 'Like a princess. A big princess!' Tess finished for her. (Perry 2013b: 436)

Fragments of Glitter

The girl in the text, the girl made by any arrangement of drawn lines and letter signifiers, is a flimsy typographic stencil layered into a much more elaborate collage, always in formation. The elements of this collage are always calling each other into being, always relational, struggling to assert diachronic depth and linearity, and flatter synchronic juxtaposition so that we can make meaning even as multiplicity spins meaning away.

Conclusion

This chapter complicates, rather than complies with, the notion of the girl in the text as an entity that readers can identify, study, and compare. My daughter is addicted to Blyton's cliff-hangers and experiences the static, conversation-focused, individualized go girls as unbearably dull. Blyton's covers suggest camaraderie, rebellion, and adventure while the go girls stand stiffly on their own, in glossy pink gear, on a glossy pink background of shiny pink hearts. Blyton's girls see boys as friends. The go girls see them as boyfriends. There are myriad points for textual comparison that lead us only to historical determinism and conclusions such as *girls were different back then* or *girls are hyperfeminized today*.

Instead I put these titles to work differently to demonstrate how, for readers identifying as girls or women, reading about any girl is to participate in the ongoing negotiation of our own schoolgirl fictions in the moment. I propose that this negotiation takes the form of competing discourses and materially realised memories of both restraint and loss of control, of flyaway hair, and shame at the spreading flower of blood on the skirt of our school uniform; of being a good girl, and yet having the capacity to call a man a cunt.

Walkerdine quotes Catherine Clement, whose emancipatory story echoes her own:

> "As I found my own voice in analysis, droning on day after day, it gradually took the place occupied for so long by the schools. One day it was inevitable that I should cease to be a schoolgirl" (1990: xi).

In contrast, informed by my writing and arranging to inquire, I propose that women readers never cease to be schoolgirls. We are always the girl in our own title, the protagonist in our own story who must act inside the oxymoron of claiming agency despite broader contexts that deny it. We are yesterday's, today's and tomorrow's woman (girl) all at once. We can never detach ourselves from how she is represented; we are still becoming her, making her as we think, write, and speak. In relation to education and the study of literature, we can never deliver her as the answer to a comprehension question, or as a dispassionate reading that does not recognize this ongoing and difficult coalescence.

If negotiation is understood also as tension, then we can connect with the rage Walkerdine (1990) finds in the gap between socialization and capacity, a heteroglossic space. Between what pulls in and what spins out, friction creates an incendiary spark. My daughter suddenly tells me she can no longer play on the playground equipment at school because boys are looking up her uniform skirt. I buy her five pairs of short leggings to wear under it. Within a week a notice comes home from school telling us leggings under uniforms are banned. I imagine Amy, with her leg hooked over the playground bar, spinning and spinning as she loves to do, a Catherine Wheel spinning off a spark that could burn down the school.

I hope this writing and the constellation of theory invoked here might spark other scholars to incorporate these ideas into their own formulations, work with them in further artful collecting and collaging to think about the process of figuring the girl. By taking up any of these rhetorical prompts into their own assemblages, other writers can expand the parameters of my own lived experience as a white, cis-gendered, middle-class girl and bring other heteroglossic, or oxymoronic tensions to bear.

Where, decades after Walkerdine's *Schoolgirl Fictions* (1990), are the other flashes of anger at always being girled, always tied to what is most designated as most abject in culture (Weber and Mitchell 1995)? Where are the other girls simultaneously empowered by a title, by the monitor's badge, the doctoral trencher, the judge's gavel, or even leadership of the so-called free world? These schoolgirl stories continue to detonate, for example in the work of Melissa Wolfe (2016), whose filmed accounts of school uniform shame resonate with my own descriptions. It would be exciting to collect and juxtapose more contradictory stories and fragments, to explore how the girl in the text is also and always figured by the girl in the world.

LUCINDA MCKNIGHT is a British Australian senior lecturer in pedagogy and curriculum at Deakin University, Melbourne. Her background is in English Literature, Fine Arts, and Women's Studies and she works in pre-service teacher education. She has written on girls and education for a range of journals and is a published fiction writer and poet. She is particularly interested in metaphor and has studied its role in girls' popular media texts and research methodologies. As a feminist teacher and researcher, she is keen to trouble gender binaries through the enactment of research designs involving creative approaches.

Note

1. I have used pseudonyms for my daughter and coresearcher teachers.

References

Badger, Meredith. 2013. "Birthday Girl." In *Go Girl: Brilliant Besties*, 89–179. Richmond, Australia: Hardie Grant Egmont.

Bakhtin, Mikhail. 1981. *The Dialogic Imagination: Four Essays*, ed. Michael Holquist. Austin: University of Texas Press.

Blyton, Enid. [1942] 1987. *The Naughtiest Girl Again*. London: Fontana Paperbacks.

Blyton, Enid. [1945] 1997. *The Naughtiest Girl Is a Monitor*. London: Hodder Children's Books.
Butler, Judith. 1997. *Excitable Speech*. New York: Routledge.
Davies, Carolyn. 2016. "Complaints Made after Judge Trades Insults with Defendant in Court." *The Guardian*, 11 August.
Eagleton, Terry. 1983. *Literary Theory: An Introduction*. Oxford: Basil Blackwell.
Fish, Stanley. 1980. *Is There a Text in This Class? The Authority of Interpretive Communities*. Cambridge: Harvard University Press.
Gannon, Susan, and Bronwyn Davies. 2006. *Doing Collective Biography*. New York: Open University Press.
Gill, Rosalind. 2007. "Postfeminist Media Culture: Elements of a Sensibility." *European Journal of Cultural Studies* 10 (2): 147–166.
Grumet, Madeline. R. 1976. "Toward a Poor Curriculum." In *Toward a Poor Curriculum*, ed. William F Pinar and Madeleine R Grumet, 67–87. Dubuque, IA: Kendall/Hunt Publishing Company.
Haug, Frigga. 2000. "Memory Work: The Key to Women's Anxiety." In *Memory and Methodology*, ed. Susannah Radston, 155–178. New York: Berg.
Haug, Frigga, and Others. 1987. *Female Sexualisation: A Collective Work of Memory*. Trans. Erica Carter. London: Verso.
McAuley, Rowan 2013a. "Sleepover." In *Go Girl: Brilliant Besties*, 1–85. Richmond, Australia: Hardie Grant Egmont.
McAuley, Rowan. 2013b. "Music Mad." In *Go Girl: Brilliant Besties*, 275–365. Richmond, Australia: Hardie Grant Egmont.
McKnight, Lucinda. 2014. "The Glitterbomb: Designing Curriculum and Identity with Girls' Popular Culture." PhD diss., Deakin University.
McKnight, Lucinda. 2015a. "Is the Frame Broken? Seeking New Metaphors for Textual Study in English." *English in Australia* 50 (2): 7–14.
McKnight, Lucinda. 2015b. "Still in the Lego (Legos) Room: Female Teachers Designing Curriculum around Girls' Popular Culture for the Coeducational Classroom in Australia." *Gender and Education* 27 (7): 907–927. doi:10.1080/09540253.2015.1096920.
McRobbie, Angela. 2009. *The Aftermath of Feminism: Gender, Culture and Social Change*. London: SAGE.
Mitchell, Claudia, and Sandra Weber. 1999. *Reinventing Ourselves as Teachers: Beyond Nostalgia*. Taylor and Francis elibrary. http://site.ebrary.com.ezproxy-m.deakin.edu.au/lib/deakin/docDetail.action?docID=10054861 (accessed 24 February 2017).
Perry, Chrissie. 2013a. "Secret's Out." In *Go Girl: Brilliant Besties*, 183–274. Richmond, Australia: Hardie Grant Egmont.
Perry, Chrissie. 2013b. "Flower Girl." In *Go Girl: Brilliant Besties*, 369–455. Richmond, Australia: Hardie Grant Egmont.

Quinn, Ben. 2016. Judge and defendant exchange insults in court. *The Guardian*, 11 August. https://www.theguardian.com/uk-news/2016/aug/10/judge-defendant-john-hennigan-exchange-insults-chelmsford-court (accessed 24 February 2017).

Reid, Alan. 2010. "Accountability and the Public Purposes of Education." Australian Education Union. http://www.aeufederal.org.au/Publications/2010/NS/AReid.pdf (accessed 26 May 2014).

Rosenblatt, Louise. 1968. *Literature as Exploration*. London: Heinemann.

Smith, Dorothy. 1987. *The Everyday World as Problematic*. Boston: Northeastern University Press.

Walkerdine, Valerie. 1990. *Schoolgirl Fictions*. London: Verso.

Weber, Sandra. 2008. "Visual Images in Research." In *Handbook of the Arts in Qualitative Research*, ed. J. Gary Knowles and Ardra L Cole, 41–53. CA: SAGE.

Weber, Sandra, and Claudia Mitchell. 1995. *That's Funny You Don't Look Like a Teacher: Interrogating Images, Identity and Popular Culture*. London: Routledge.

Williams, Patricia J. 1991. *The Alchemy of Race and Rights: Diary of a Law Professor*. Cambridge: Harvard University Press.

Wolfe, Melissa. 2016. "Refracting Schoolgirls: Pedagogical Intra-Actions Producing Shame." *Discourse: Studies in the Cultural Politics of Education* 38 (5): 727–739. doi: 10.1080/01596306.2016.1143451.

Woods, Emily. 2016. "Melbourne Mother Angry Girl Can't Wear Pants as Part of Uniform." *The Age*, 16 May.

Young, Amy M., and Mary D Hinesly. 2012. "Identifying Millenials' Key Influencers from Early Childhood: Insights into Current Consumer Preferences." *Journal of Consumer Marketing* 29 (2): 1–15.

Filmography

Hughes, John. 1992. *One Way Street Fragments for Walter Benjamin*. Canberra: Ronin Films. Videorecording.

NBC News. 2016 "The Third Presidential Debate: Hillary Clinton and Donald Trump (Full Debate)." https://www.youtube.com/watch?v=smkyorC5qwc

Norton, Zeke. 2012. "The Princess and the Popstar." UK.

CHAPTER 2

"This Is My Story"
The Reclaiming of Girls' Education Discourses in Malala Yousafzai's Autobiography

Rosie Walters

In 2014, the year she turned 17, Malala Yousafzai released a second version of her autobiography, rewritten for her own generation, detailing her fight for girls' education. In it, she reflects on her childhood in the Swat Valley in Pakistan, her campaign against the Pakistani Taliban, or Tehrik-i-Taliban Pakistan (TTP), their attack on her in October 2012, and her move to the United Kingdom. Having blogged, lobbied politicians, and spoken publicly since a young age, Yousafzai was propelled into international fame after surviving an attack by two TTP gunmen while sitting on the bus home from school. Since then, she has given speeches at the United Nations, made a film, and told her story through countless interviews and in the two versions of her autobiography. Her story resonated in the West in a post-9/11 context of "save the Muslim girl" stories (Sensoy and Marshall 2010: 309; see also Yaqin 2013). Leigh Gilmore and Elizabeth Marshall write, "The 'veiled' brown girl in need of saving figures as the static vulnerable girl in the rescue discourse Laura Bush used to rally support for the U.S. military invasion [of Afghanistan]" (2010: 680). Yousafzai's story also resonates with powerful campaigns at the highest levels of international politics that advocate investment in girls' education in developing countries as the solution to global poverty. With programs such as the Nike Foundation's Girl Effect, the UN Foundation's Girl Up, and Plan International's Because I Am a Girl, international development policy has embraced a narrative in recent years that sees girls in developing countries as untapped resources whose untold potential to boost economies is restrained by outdated cultural norms. These narratives reproduce tropes that see former colonies as being in a childlike phase of development, unable to protect their own (especially female) citizens; they have been used to justify a range of Western interventions. For some, Malala Yousafzai's story has been adopted into such discourses by the West (see Olesen 2016). Indeed, in a recent study of UK newspaper coverage of her story, I analyzed how it was underpinned with gendered and orientalist understandings that ultimately positioned the UK as Yousafzai's protector and savior (Walters 2016). However, one aspect that has been undertheorized in the literature is how Yousafzai herself negotiates such discourses. She is patronized by the very same Western institutions that would claim to be rescuing her while simultaneously rejected by many in her home country who see her as complicit in a Western political project that is anti-Islam and anti-Pakistan. Much has been written about the newly emergent discourses that see powerful actors mobilizing in the name of girls in developing countries (see Khoja-Moolji 2015a; Koffman and Gill 2013; Moeller 2014), yet little has been done to understand how girls negotiate these discourses. In this chapter I analyze how Yousafzai, addressing her own age group, subverts these discourses by contextualizing her story, challenging assumptions that readers might make about her childhood, and turning the gaze back onto the West. In doing so, I argue that girl studies scholars have a duty to pay heed to the everyday acts and representations with which girls resist powerful discourses.

Feminist scholars in literary studies have documented the historical absence of women's writing from critical discussions of autobiography. This is intrinsically linked to the very nature of the genre that "functions as the closest textual version of the political ideology of individualism," and therefore, "is gendered as 'male'" (Gilmore 1994: 1). The autobiographical "I" is tied closely to an Enlightenment understanding of the self: "[A]ll 'I's are rational, agentive, unitary. Thus the 'I' becomes 'Man,' putatively a marker of the universal human subject" (Watson and Smith 1992: xvii). The 'I' in autobiography adopts an objective, individual, and rational position in a journey of discovery. Recent work by feminist scholars, however, has shown how women authors have challenged this model of the self through "a more dialogical conception of Selfhood as something which is essentially social and relational" (Moore-Gilbert 2009: xvii). Furthermore, Lee Quinby (1992) argues that as a genre, autobiography and its assumptions about subjectivity are inherently tied to the post-Enlightenment West. Nevertheless, some postcolonial writers have used it as a means to subvert Western human rights and development discourses by positioning, "Western readers as those in need of schooling" (Gilmore and Marshall 2010: 682–683).

I adopt a feminist, postcolonial, and poststructuralist framework. As Ofra Koffman and Rosalind Gill write, it is an approach that "recognizes that global inequalities that are gendered and racialized remain entrenched" (2013: 85). A poststructuralist analysis of autobiography rejects the notion that there is a single, unified subject to be represented truthfully or otherwise by the author (Smith 1990). It seeks to analyze the ways in which the subject enters into dialogue with discourses about identity and truth (Gilmore 1994). While dominant discourses come to shape society's understandings, individuals can and do have agency to negotiate or even reject them. My approach, therefore, is to "read against the grain," with the purpose of seeking out "that which [evades] the dominant discourse" (Khoja-Moolji 2016: 9). My intent was to find the instances in which Yousafzai negotiates, or subverts, the dominant discourses surrounding girls' education. The themes of the findings were thus dictated largely by the literature on those discourses, including my own previous findings on representations of Yousafzai in UK newspapers. These included the portrayal of "Third World"—especially Muslim—girls as passive victims in need of rescue by the West, the assumption that Western societies have achieved gender equality and are thus best placed to help other societies do the same, and the fixation on investment in individual girls rather than collective action as a solution to gender inequalities. After many close readings of the autobiography, I selected over 7,500 words of relevant passages and coded them according to these themes. The examples given in this chapter then, are just a few of the many that I could have cited. Without denying that Yousafzai's story, and at times her representation of it, resonate deeply with problematic Western constructions of Muslim societies (Khoja-Moolji 2015a), in this chapter I analyze the many occasions on which she reclaims her story from those discourses. In highlighting this, I hope to act as an "ally" to girl activists in making the world "a more respectful place for female youth" (Kearney 2009: 22). If, as Gilmore and Marshall state, "How women of color use autobiography to talk back to the construction of the permanently vulnerable girl is an important and yet undertheorized area of feminist resistance" (2010: 668), then how girls of color do the same is theorized to an even lesser extent. My previous study analyzed 223 UK newspaper articles and found that in over 424 quotations, Yousafzai herself was cited only 47 times. In other words, despite journalists embracing Yousafzai's cause of girls' education, "nearly nine times out of ten they still rely on someone else to explain how this theme is significant" (Walters, 2016: 664). Read in this context, the concluding statement to the prologue of her autobiography "I am Malala and this is *my* story" (Yousafzai 2015: 7, emphasis added) signals that this retelling represents both Yousafzai's resistance to Western depictions that would silence her, and her response to her attackers who climbed onto her school bus and demanded to know, "Who is Malala?" (2015: 7).

In the following section, I summarize the extensive literature on girls' education discourses in international development and the many ways in which these discourses resonate with neoliberal, individualistic visions of empowerment that posit girls in developing countries as being in need of rescue by the West. In the following three sections, I analyze instances in which Malala Yousafzai counters these discourses in her self-representation before discussing the implications of these findings for the study of girlhood.

The "Girl Powering" of International Development

In what Koffman and Gill refer to as the "girl powering" (2013: 86) of international development, nongovernmental organizations, national governments, global governance institutions, and transnational corporations have converged in recent years around a hegemonic discourse that sees girls' education as the solution to many development problems. Starting with the Nike Foundation's launch of the Girl Effect in 2008, a vast array of actors have embraced discourses that see girls as having the potential to lift entire communities out of poverty if only they are given formal schooling (Switzer 2013). These discourses unproblematically link the rights and interests of young women in developing countries with the achievement of international development goals by arguing that when investment is given to an adolescent girl she will reinvest the benefits in her own community. This logic sees young women as deserving of an education, not because they have an equal right with young men to such opportunities, but because they are a winning investment opportunity. It is important, of course, to clarify that some girls' organizations are setting out their own alternative vision of girls' empowerment. For example, the Malala Fund provides a platform for Yousafzai herself. Her blog entries on the site are often deeply political, including statements about girls' rights and a recent post criticising President Trump's travel bans, thus making space for girls themselves to challenge powerful people and institutions. However, such organizations also need to speak to, and at times adopt, dominant discourses in order to be heard in international fora.

While calls for investment in educational opportunities for young women would be welcome for many, the girl powering of international development is problematic in many ways. First, as a representational regime it masks the extractive nature of the relationship between some of the very same organizations funding these initiatives and the communities they purport to be helping. Following the Girl Effect logic, interventions by powerful actors in developing countries are benevolent and efficient solutions to inequalities resulting from outdated cultural norms in those countries. Heather Switzer (2013) points out that this serves to discourage critique of the structural relationships that cause inequalities, and to discourage collective organizing by women to address the many forms of discrimination that they face. Second, as Switzer goes on to say, many of the campaigns promote a simplistic model of young women's empowerment that ignores the diverse injustices faced by young women and focuses almost entirely on providing them with primary education as a means to gain workplace skills. Third, underpinning the Girl Effect's claims to be raising awareness of adolescent young women's unique potential and abilities is an essentialist and individualistic narrative that places the responsibility for solving some of the world's most pressing issues, which the international community has so far failed to do, firmly on the shoulders of children. As Kathryn Moeller, reflecting on her experience of ethnographic fieldwork in a project in Brazil funded by Girl Effect, argues, "The Girl Effect is not what one would ask of her or his own child ... It asks them to be responsible for the lives, well-being, and futures of those far beyond themselves, including their families, communities, their nations, and the world" (2014: 599). It is an extension of neoliberal discourses in the West, in which young women are seen as either can-do girls or girls-at-risk, with untold potential, as long as they do not make the wrong choices (Harris 2004). This discourse plays out in the lives and on the bodies of young women in developing contexts who are offered educational opportunities if they, in turn, accept individual responsibility should the supposedly wrong choices mean that they ultimately fail. As one recent blog post by the Girl Effect in Rwanda put it, girls should "commit to live an exemplary life" (Girl Effect 2015: n.p.). Fourth, as part of a discursive regime that Özlem Sensoy and Elizabeth Marshall label "missionary girl power" (2010: 296), initiatives such as the UN Foundation's Girl Up, which encourages girls in the West to set up clubs and fundraise for UN girls' education projects, place young women in the West in the role of the "sisters, saviors, and 'BFFs'" (Koffman et al.: 161) of their counterparts in developing countries. They appeal to patronizing narratives that see girls in postcolonial states as being in need of rescue while remaining silent about the many enduring inequalities that Western young women may face in their own communities. Finally, in what Projansky calls the "spectacularization" of girlhood, we are invited to gaze at spectacular girls like Yousafzai, to marvel at their abilities, and achievements, but also to watch in horror if weakness, the wrong choices, or the inability to cope with the pressure of society's expectations might lead them into a "spectacular descent into at-risk status" (2014: 4). Girls are spectacular and they are a spectacle; they are not, however, to be supported in this particular discursive regime which has little or nothing to say about the many girls who, for whatever reason, do not measure up to this individualistic vision of success.

It is in this context that Malala Yousafzai's story emerged, "more or less pre-packaged" by discourses that see Western-style education as the only way to counter the perceived "backwardness" (Olesen 2016: 315) of developing countries, and, in particular, Muslim countries (see also Thomas and Shukul 2015). Indeed, analysis of the coverage of her story in UK newspapers revealed a tendency to present the UK as a "paternalistic, caring benefactor, and champion of gender equality" (Walters 2016: 665) in providing medical treatment and safety for Yousafzai in the aftermath of the attack. The way in which powerful actors in the West have embraced Yousfazai's story is viewed with suspicion in her homeland where skepticism ranges from a sense that her story has overshadowed the stories of other victims (particularly of drone strikes), to a conspiracy theory that her attack was faked in order to undermine the Pakistani state (Olesen 2016). When her first autobiography (Yousafzai 2014) was released, some in Pakistan even started to observe an "anti-Malala day" in protest at passages in it about the author Salman Rushdie (Khoja-Moolji 2017). Yousafzai herself describes how it was "hard news" when she learnt of this response to her story. "People … said I was a bad Muslim. People … even said my father had shot me as a stunt so we could live overseas in luxury" (2015: 177). It may perhaps also have come as hard news then that her first autobiography was seen by some to "[rearticulate] the trope of victimized Muslim women" (Khoja-Moolji 2015b: 552). While the first book (2014) does not explicitly define its intended readership, it was published at a time when Yousafzai was taking her campaign to decision-makers at the highest levels of international politics. This, along with its having been coauthored by war correspondent Christina Lamb, might explain Shenila Khoja-Moolji's findings that it frequently reproduces Western discourses about Pakistan and Islam. The second book (2015), however, was written for Yousafzai's own age group, and includes discussion questions and activities for school classes. Writing for those still in school may have allowed Yousafzai to assume that her readers would have little prior knowledge about Pakistan, the Taliban, or Islam, thus enabling her to explain her story on her own terms. Furthermore, the fact that she rewrote the book a year later may have given Yousafzai time to reflect on her representation in the West and in Pakistan, and on the reception of her first book. There is a marked difference in the description of some events and impressions between the two versions. For example, while Yousafzai discusses enjoying watching the US television show *Ugly Betty* in the first version, it is only in the second that she describes reaching the conclusion while watching it that women in the US face many forms of oppression (to which I will return presently). Undoubtedly, the choice of the successful author of young adult novels, Patricia McCormick, as coauthor of the second version will have contributed to the different tone. However, without having been party to the numerous discussions, resulting in deletions and alterations, that would have constituted the editing process, it is impossible to gauge whether the different content and tone is a result of the influence of the two coauthors, or whether it is Yousafzai herself who strategically adopts different voices to reach the two different audiences. In either case, I concluded that a search for examples of Yousafzai's resistance to representations and appropriations of her story in the second version of her autobiography (2015) would yield interesting results. I chose to read this text as speaking to, and against, attempts by those in both the West and in Pakistan to appropriate Yousfazai's story. In doing so, I aim to contribute to an area that remains undertheorized in the literatures on girls' education discourses and on autobiography—girls' own interpretations and self-representations. Catherine Driscoll (2002) argues that girlhood is often portrayed in both popular culture and academic literature solely in relation to a future role as woman, and indeed, though many autobiographical accounts of girlhood exist, they are almost invariably written by adult women reflecting on a journey of becoming (Gilmore and Marshall 2010). The structural marginalization of children generally, and girls in particular, makes it almost impossible for a girl's own story to emerge in a format such as this autobiography, with such global readership. Malala Yousafzai's writing, therefore, offers a unique chance to analyze the ways in which a girl has written a "counterpedagogy of childhood" (Gilmore and Marshall 2010: 678), one that resists patronizing assumptions about postcolonial girlhood.

No Rescue Required: Girls, Resistance, and Agency

The first trope of colonial discourses that Yousafzai challenges in her writing is the attempt to "construct the colonized as childish and inferior subjects, in need of the paternalistic guidance and rule of their superiors" (Narayan 1995: 133). In the aftermath of her shooting, the UK media repeatedly reported her to be younger than she was, describing the then 15-year-old as 14, while commentators persuaded readers of the need to do "everything humanly possible" to protect "little Malala," this "vulnerable girl," and "precious jewel" (Kelly 2012). The portrayal of Yousafzai as younger makes her appear more vulnerable and in need of rescue. Yousafzai's second autobiography, however, tells another tale. When discussing her fifteenth birthday, she reflects, "This birthday felt like a turning point for me. I was already considered an adult—that happens at age fourteen in our society. But it was time for me to take stock, to think about my future. I knew for certain now that I wanted to be a political leader" (Yousafzai 2015: 125). Her assertion of adulthood exposes the ways in which the perception of Yousafzai as young or childlike is very much a Western one. Indeed, while Western news served to make her seem younger than she was, she herself describes doing the very opposite. For example, when asked by the US ambassador how old she was she "straightened [her] posture to look as tall as possible," before adding a year onto her age in the hope that he would listen more carefully to her thoughts on girls' rights as a result (2015: 104). She also describes the reaction of a friend of her father who, after hearing her speak about her cause, was shocked to discover she was then only 11. He exclaimed, "She is *pakha jenai* ... wise beyond her years" (2015: 94).

As I noted, UK newspapers also placed Yousafzai in a passive role in her own story, emphasizing her victimhood over her survival, citing (predominantly male) politicians, doctors, and even Taliban spokespersons instead of her. They persistently used passive voice constructions that reduced her to the "shot Pakistani girl" (Walters 2016: 656). In girls' education discourses girls in developing countries are portrayed as having incredible potential but this must be unleashed through Western intervention, so they are simultaneously depicted as potentially agentic but also as passive, inactive, and awaiting rescue. Again, Yousfazai's self-representation tells a different story.

She describes how, when the TTP had threatened to target girls' schools, her teachers believed that it would be too dangerous for Yousafzai and her classmates to travel to school in their uniforms. She obeyed their wishes. However, she recounts, "That day I chose my brightest pink *shalwar kamiz*" (2015: 80)—a garment that would have made her stand out clearly—as an act of defiance. She describes her anger at people's assumption that her father is the cause of her activism, "as if he forced me to speak out. As if I didn't have a mind of my own" (2015: 188), and she describes being "furious" after the attack by the Taliban, "Not that they'd shot me. That I hadn't had a chance to talk to them. Now they'd never hear what I had to say" (146). Her self-depiction is not of a vulnerable little girl but one of a courageous young woman, with an important political cause, who is furious, not only at people's underestimations of her, but also at the attackers who shot her down before she had a chance to tell them why she felt they were wrong.

Elsewhere, Yousafzai also challenges portrayals of Muslim and Pakistani women more broadly. While the challenge is less unambiguous here, particularly when she discusses visits to her female relatives outside of Mingora who are mostly illiterate, reading against the grain one sees that there is much that does not conform to representations of the "average third world woman" (Mohanty 1991: 56) or indeed the "Oriental woman" who "never spoke of herself … represented her emotions, presence, or history" (Said 2003: 6). Among the many examples she gives of girls and women who are willing to defy the orders of not only the TPP, but also their own male relatives, she also tells stories that complicate Western assumptions about passive women and controlling men. For example, when Yousfazai decides that she will not veil her face, it is her mother, portrayed as the most devout of her family, who disapproves. Yet, her mother not only respects her wishes but even defends her: "Even if my mother disagreed with my choice—and even if her friends criticized her—she stood up for me" (2015: 83). Yousafzai's portrayal of Pakistani womanhood is complex. While her description of the hardships she faced under the Taliban will no doubt resonate with Western discourses, she complicates them by showing how different geographical and class contexts can have an impact on women's lived realities, and how the women around her stand up for themselves and the women around them. It is a tale full of acts, both small and large, of resistance.

Yousafzai also resists attempts to depoliticize her story as just another example of third world girlhood. While dominant Western discourses see movements such as the Taliban as the result of supposedly traditional attitudes, or of a strict reading of the Quran, Yousafzai is keen to address the role of Western intervention in filling their ranks. She describes a conversation she had with President Obama.

> I told him I did not like his drone strikes on Pakistan, that when they kill one bad person innocent people are killed too, and terrorism spreads more. I also told him that if America spent less money on weapons and war and more on education, the world would be a better place. (2015: 194)

Similarly, she tackles the Pakistani government's failure to protect girls' schools from the Taliban head on when she meets the Prime Minister while collecting an award. She writes that she "presented him with a list of demands," including the rebuilding of girls' schools that have been destroyed (2015: 114). Yousafzai even uses her book as an opportunity to admonish the West on its failure to meet the needs of those fleeing the conflict in Syria. "People who are safe and who aren't in need should be paying for this because these refugees do not want luxury ... All they want is peace" (2015: 214). Yousafzai is not the voiceless, passive victim that "save the Muslim girl" discourses would imply. Neither does she represent herself as in need of rescue by the West, as girls' education discourses might. Rather, she is asking politicians and publics to listen to her deeply political message, to confront the consequences of Western interventions and failures in her region, and to grant those who have suffered as a result the rights that the West purports to promote worldwide.

I Am Malala as Ethnography of the West

Another form of resistance in *I Am Malala* is the way that Yousafzai resists the dominant "polarizations that place feminism on the side of the West" (Abu-Lughod 2002: 788). She does so by conducting a sort of "ethnography of the West" (Moore-Gilbert 2009: xxii-xxiii). In descriptions that mirror Orientalist travel writing, the West becomes a fantastical place, at times incomprehensible and at times comprehensible only through (often unfavorable) comparisons with home. She is surprised to find she likes New York: "Many people in Pakistan have been told that the United States is a dark and godless place, but everyone I met there was quite nice" (2015: 193). While her home, the Swat Valley, has often been described as "the Switzerland of Pakistan," Yousafzai labels New York as being "like a developed Karachi" (2015: 194). She makes no effort to disguise the ambiguity, and, at times, distaste she feels for her new home of Birmingham, and of struggling to adapt to a culture in which "we are just a few feet away from the next house, but for all we know of our neighbors, it might as well be a mile" (2015: 180).

Part of this study of the West involves analyzing gender relations and scrutinizing claims of greater equality. She describes how in Pakistan, when her father encouraged her to watch an *Ugly Betty* DVD to help improve her English, she concluded, "Although Betty and her friends had certain rights, women in the United States were still not completely equal; their images were used to sell things. In some ways, I decided, women were showpieces in American society too" (2015: 88). Upon moving to the UK, Yousafzai and her mother are fascinated by women going out in short skirts and bare legs in mid-winter and wonder whether their legs are made of metal to be able to withstand the cold, and Yousafzai is amused by the way in which her classmates roll up their skirts to make them shorter at school, but roll them back down again before going home to their parents. She chooses to wear her school uniform skirt down to her ankles, and her thankfulness that a few other Muslim girls in her class do the same suggests an interpretation that such a move might have an impact on her ability to fit in. The society she portrays is one in which girls' clothing will be scrutinized by their parents and peers alike, with very real consequences, thus challenging the idea that she would encounter restrictions or be judged on her choice of clothing only in her home country of Pakistan.

Finally, the "save the Muslim girl" discourses that emerged post-9/11 not only place feminism "on the side of the West" (Abu-Lughod 2002: 788) but also link it with secularism, negating the possibility of Muslim feminism. However, Yousafzai herself emphasizes her Muslim faith at many points during her narrative, including perhaps the most traumatic part of her story. When she wakes up in the Birmingham hospital unsure where she is and unable to communicate it is the hospital's Muslim chaplain who comforts Yousfazai, reciting the "beautiful, soothing words of the Holy Quran" (2015: 135). She also describes her campaign for girls' education as being sanctioned by her faith, writing that it was her mother's quoting from the Quran that persuaded her to continue in spite of the risks. "'Falsehood has to die,' she said. 'And the truth has to come forward'" (78). These moments disrupt the dominant discourses that see girls' education and girls' rights more broadly as inherently secular or Western.

Resisting Spectacularization

Malala Yousafzai cannot resist being a spectacle. In fact, she acknowledges and even embraces this role: "When you have such a public role and so many people counting on you, I believe you must always act in the way people expect of you" (2015: 184). She can and does, however, resist being seen as spectacular. Among other character traits, she describes her difficulty in getting out of bed in the morning, her tendency to fight with her siblings—"I may be an advocate for free speech and human rights in public; but with my brother, I admit, I can be a dictator" (2015: 186)—and her nervousness before giving an assembly at her school, despite having previously addressed the United Nations. Her self-portrayal is grounded in the everyday and the unspectacular.

Furthermore, while her story is frequently cited as an example of spectacular girlhood, in which girls "succeed because they embrace neoliberal narratives of individual choice and agency that ignore community partnerships, solidarity, and support from adults and girls alike" (Bent 2016: 107), Yousafzai constantly champions her classmates in Pakistan and credits others with her achievements. She stresses that "any one of us could have achieved what I had" (2015: 115), and she describes the collective action she and her classmates took for girls' education. She credits her best friend Moniba as the class's "public-speaking champion" (72), and, when praised for her own eloquence, she writes, "It wasn't me, Malala, speaking; my voice was the voice of so many others who wanted to speak but couldn't" (73). She refuses to speak out without the support of her mother, saying, "Because if I didn't have her support it would be like speaking with only half my heart" (78), and she credits her parents and their support for her eventual successes. Finally, she shows the many acts of bravery by others that have made her own campaigning possible including, for example, her teachers' decision to keep the school open despite the threats against them. As Emily Bent writes, spectacular discourses erase "the sociocultural and geopolitical support systems that make girls' exceptionality possible" (2016: 108). They obscure the support that girls require from fellow girls, parents, teachers, and youth workers, activists, policy makers, and communities to be able to bring about change, not because of a lack of ability but because of their position in society as children and as female. Although the book's front cover may claim to be about "one girl" who "stood up for education and changed the world," Yousafzai's writing shows how at every step of the way, she was helped and supported by others and that with the same help and support, other girls could achieve great things too.

Conclusion

The choice to read against the grain in this analysis has emphasized the moments of resistance in Malala Yousafzai's autobiography that disrupt powerful narratives. This methodological choice is a concerted attempt to fill the gaps in the literature on girls' education discourses that to date have treated such discourses largely as all-powerful. There is much to be critiqued and questioned in the recent focus by powerful Western actors on girls in developing countries, and the models of empowerment it puts forward, a project to which my previous work has contributed. However, that such discourses exist does not mean that they are automatically taken up. Depicting Yousafzai as a young woman whose story has been coopted by powerful discourses in the West is not that different from depicting her as a young woman whose voice was silenced by the Taliban. Both do not go far enough in acknowledging her agency. This chapter suggests the potential for scholars of girlhood studies to analyze the ways in which girls resist such discourses and tell their stories according to their own vision of what empowerment would mean.

Often, the study of narratives of girlhood has focused on what they can tell us about adult women's political agency. Yet the study of girlhood must also analyze girls' political agency in its own right. Malala Yousafzai's politics nearly robbed her of the chance to become an adult woman. We should not, therefore, analyze her story for what it might tell us about womanhood, but rather for what it tells us about girlhood. She portrays a girlhood that is deeply political, agentic, and that must constantly negotiate between competing and conflicting discourses that would threaten to constrain it. This matters in and of itself, and it matters for what it can tell us about the potential for girls to articulate and bring about their own vision of an empowered girlhood, with the support of activists and communities alike, and thus to open up more possible ways of being a girl.

Acknowledgments

This research is funded by the Economic and Social Research Council. I would like to thank the two anonymous reviewers and the editor for their helpful comments on this article.

ROSIE WALTERS is a postgraduate researcher at the University of Bristol. Her research focuses on girl power discourses in international politics by analyzing various prominent campaigns that posit girls' education as the solution to global poverty. She focuses particularly on juxtaposing representations of young women in the media and in policy with the ways in which they represent themselves. Rosie is also an Editor at Large of E-International Relations, the world's leading open access website for students and scholars of international politics.

References

Abu-Lughod, Lila. 2002. "Do Muslim Women Really Need Saving? Anthropological Reflections on Cultural Relativism and Its Others." *American Anthropologist* 104 (3): 783–790. doi:10.1525/aa.2002.104.3.783.

Bent, Emily. 2016. "Making It Up: Intergenerational Activism and the Ethics of Empowering Girls." *Girlhood Studies: An Interdisciplinary Journal* 9 (3): 105–121. doi:10.3167/ghs.2016.090308.

Driscoll, Catherine. 2002. *Girls: Feminine Adolescence in Popular Culture and Cultural Theory*. New York: Columbia University Press.

Gilmore, Leigh. 1994. *Autobiographics: A Feminist Theory of Women's Self-Representation*. New York: Cornell University Press.

Gilmore, Leigh, and Elizabeth Marshall. 2010. "Girls in Crisis: Rescue and Transnational Feminist Autobiographical Resistance." *Feminist Studies* 36 (3): 667–690.

Girl Effect. 2015. "12+ Programme Graduates Commit to Live an Exemplary Life." http://girleffectcountryblogs.com/2015/11/13/12-programme-graduates-commit-to-live-an-exemplary-life/ (accessed 20 October 2015).

Harris, Anita. 2004. *Future Girl: Young Women in the Twenty-First Century*. London and New York: Routledge.

Kearney, Mary Celeste. 2009. "Coalescing: The Development of Girls' Studies." *NWSA Journal* 21 (1): 1–28.

Kelly, Lorraine. 2012. "We Must Help Malala, Terror of the Taliban." *The Sun*, 12 October.

Khoja-Moolji, Shenila. 2015a. "Suturing Together Girls and Education: An Investigation into the Social (Re)Production of Girls' Education as a Hegemonic Ideology." *Diaspora, Indigenous and Minority Education* 9 (2): 87–107. doi:10.1080/15595692.2015.1010640.

Khoja-Moolji, Shenila. 2015b. "Reading Malala: (De)(Re)Territorialisation of Muslim Collectivities." *Comparative Studies of South Asia, Africa and the Middle East* 35 (3): 539–556. doi:10.1215/1089201X-3426397.

Khoja-Moolji, Shenila. 2016. "Doing the 'Work of Hearing': Girls' Voices in Transnational Educational Development Campaigns." *Compare* 46 (5): 745–763. doi:10.1080/03057925.2015.1084582.

Khoja-Moolji, Shenila. 2017. "The Making of Humans and their Others in and through Transnational Human Rights Advocacy: Exploring the Cases of Mukhtar Mai and Malala Yousafzai." *Signs* 42 (2): 377–402.

Koffman, Ofra, and Rosalind Gill. 2013. "'The Revolution Will Be Led by a 12-Year-Old Girl': Girl Power and Global Biopolitics." *Feminist Review* 105 (1): 83–102. doi:10.1057/fr.2013.16.

Koffman, Ofra, Shani Orgad, and Rosalind Gill. 2015. "Girl Power and 'Selfie Humanitarianism'." *Continuum: Journal of Media and Cultural Studies* 29 (2): 157–168. doi:10.1080/10304312.2015.1022948.

Moeller, Kathryn. 2014. "Searching for Adolescent Girls in Brazil: The Transnational Politics of Poverty in 'The Girl Effect'." *Feminist Studies* 40 (3): 575–601. doi:10.15767/feministstudies.40.3.575.

Mohanty, Chandra Talpade. 1991. "Under Western Eyes: Feminist Scholarship and Colonial Discourses." In *Third World Women and the Politics of Feminism*, ed. Chandra Talpade Mohanty, Ann Russo and Lourdes Torres, 51–80. Bloomington: Indiana University Press.

Moore-Gilbert, Bart. 2009. *Postcolonial Life-Writing: Culture, Politics and Self-Representation*. London: Routledge.

Narayan, Uma. 1995. "Colonialism and its Others: Considerations on Rights and Care Discourses." *Hypatia* 10 (2): 133–140. doi:10.1111/j.1527-2001.1995.tb01375.x.

Olesen, Thomas. 2016. "Malala and the Politics of Global Iconicity." *The British Journal of Sociology* 67 (2): 307–327. doi:10.1111/1468-4446.12195.

Projansky, Sarah. 2014. *Spectacular Girls: Media Fascination and Celebrity Culture*. New York: New York University Press.

Quinby, Lee. 1992. "The Subject of Memoirs: *The Woman Warrior's* Technology of Ideographic Selfhood." In *De/Colonizing the Subject: The Politics of Gender in Women's Autobiography*, ed. Sidonie Smith and Julia Watson, 297–320. Minneapolis: University of Minnesota Press.

Said, Edward. [1978] 2003. *Orientalism*. (5th ed.) London: Penguin.

Sensoy, Özlem, and Elizabeth Marshall. 2010. "Missionary Girl Power: Saving the 'Third World' One Girl at a Time." *Gender and Education* 22 (3): 295–311. doi:10.1080/09540250903289451.

Smith, Sidonie. 1990. "Self, Subject and Resistance: Marginalities and Twentieth-century Autobiographical Practice." *Tulsa Studies in Women's Literature* 9 (1): 11–24. doi:10.2307/464178.

Switzer, Heather. 2013. "(Post)Feminist Development Fables: The Girl Effect and the Production of Sexual Subjects." *Feminist Theory* 14 (3): 345–360. doi:10.1177/1464700113499855.

Thomas, Elsa Ashish, and Rashid Narain Shukul. 2015. "Framing of Malala Yousafzai: A Comparative Analysis of News Coverage in Western and Pakistani Mainstream English Print and Alternative Media." *Media Asia* 42 (3–4): 225–241. doi:10.1080/01296612.2016.1142248.

Walters, Rosie. 2016. "'Shot Pakistani Girl': The Limitations of Girls Education Discourses in UK Media Coverage of Malala Yousafzai." *British Journal of Politics and International Relations* 18(3): 650–670.

Watson, Julia, and Sidonie Smith. 1992. "Introduction: De/Colonization and the Politics of Discourse in Women's Autobiographical Practices." In *De/Colonizing the Subject: The Politics of Gender in Women's Autobiography*, ed. Sidonie Smith and Julia Watson, xii-xxxi. Minneapolis: University of Minnesota Press.

Yaqin, Amina. 2013. "Autobiography and Muslim Women's Lives." *Journal of Women's History* 25 (2): 171–184. doi: 10.1353/jowh.2013.0020.

Yousafzai, Malala, with Christina Lamb. [2013] 2014. *I Am Malala: The Girl Who Stood Up for Education and Was Shot by the Taliban*. London: Weidenfeld and Nicolson.

Yousafzai, Malala, with Patricia McCormick. [2014] 2015. *I Am Malala: How One Girl Stood Up for Education and Changed the World*. London: Hodder and Stoughton.

Filmography

Horta, Silvio. 2006–2010. *Ugly Betty*. USA.

Chapter 3
The Girl
Dead

Fiona Nelson

> Story is for a human as water is for a fish—
> all-encompassing and not quite palpable.
> (Gottschall 2012: xiv)

In the weeks following the Netflix release, in 2017, of its series, *Thirteen Reasons Why*, based on Jay Asher's 2007 novel of the same title, the media was full of reports of the popularity of the show with teens and its distinct unpopularity with parents, educators, and youth counsellors. While some teens argued that the show is an entertaining, educational, realistic glimpse into the harshness of high school life, some adults countered that the series romanticizes and glorifies suicide, presenting it as an effective revenge mechanism and possibly triggering vulnerable teens to consider suicide themselves. The fact that both camps were so passionate speaks to the central power of story. As Jonathan Gottschall argues, humans are the only species so thoroughly constituted in, through, and by story. Our waking lives are spent consuming and constructing stories and "even when the body goes to sleep, the mind stays up all night, telling itself stories" (Gottschall 2012: xiv).

Notes for this section can be found on page 58.

But do they matter, these stories we tell? Certainly, consumers of stories might feel affirmed, challenged, comforted, or alienated. It is difficult, however, and research has failed, largely, to find direct links between the consumption of any one popular culture item and radical changes in behavior. In other words, it is probably unlikely that watching one television series, even one so widely consumed and discussed, would lead a teenager, not otherwise inclined, to suicide. The concern, of course, is with those teens who are already vulnerable and perhaps considering suicide. My additional concern is not simply with this one story but with how this story is a constitutive element of a larger cultural discourse. This story is a piece of a bigger story and those larger stories, those cultural narratives, are the water we swim in. Bronwyn Davies famously argues that "stories are one of the primary means that adults use to make available to children the kind of rational ordering of the social world that they themselves believe in" (2003: 29). Children arrive into, and grow up in a world where the stories are pre-told, although also always evolving. Language, Davies argues, "makes social and personal being possible but it also limits the available forms of being to those that make sense within the terms provided by the language" (2003:1). According to Davies, the stories told by adults to children and youth play a foundational role in establishing the world as a particular kind of place and gender as particular ways of being in that world.

Thirteen Reasons Why (2007) is a book written by an adult, published by adults, adapted and produced for television by adults, and commercially promoted by adults. While in the broadest sense, the book is about teen suicide as is the TV series, it is more accurately about a teen girl's suicide. Certainly, teens of any (or no) gender might be able to identify with elements of the story, and parents of any child might find something to worry about in it, but this book needs to be considered in the context of an entire genre of YA fiction that is telling a particular story about girls' lives and deaths. I would argue that the Netflix adaptation of this one book represents a massive jump in the mainstreaming of this narrative about teen girls.

Two areas of research interest come together for me in this chapter. The first is an increasing concern with the sorts of gender-based bullying faced by girls and young women. In particular, I am attentive to the phenomenon of young women being sexually victimized in some way, often online and/or on video, and then being bullied about their sexuality and/or victimization to the point where they attempt to commit suicide or actually do so. The World Health Organization (2014) has reported that suicide has become the leading cause of death, globally, for girls aged 10 to 19. Massimiliano

Orri et al. found that "despite a large number of research and prevention programs, the attempted suicide rate among youth is increasing" (2014:1). We cannot know how many of these suicides are linked to bullying and sexual victimization but what is striking is that suicide has taken over as the leading cause of death among girls and young women at the same time as a genre of YA literature glorifying and romanticizing dying and death has been burgeoning. It is this genre of YA literature that is my second area of research interest.

YA literature is a rapidly expanding field, with entire bookstore aisles dedicated to it. My concern with YA books is as cultural artifacts. I am interested in the types of messages and narratives that are currently considered appropriate and timely for a certain age group (and, I would argue, gender) of people. These books constitute a vital component of the cultural/historical milieu within which girls and young women experience and make sense of their lives and sexualities.

I will focus here on a portion of the sub-genre of YA literature that I call the dead girl genre. I am concerned with books in which the death of the central teenage female character figures prominently. Often, she appears as the posthumous narrator or, if the book is told in the third person, the posthumous protagonist. For the purpose of this analysis, I will further distinguish two subtypes of this genre—the definitely dying and the indisputably dead.[1] I do not include the many books in which the central female character is undead—a vampire or a zombie, for example, because these, I would argue, belong to a different genre. This distinction gets fuzzy when the central character in a dead girl book is referred to as a ghost, or when she has the ability to inhabit the body of a living person. Nonetheless, her status as dead, rather than in some way undead, is never disputed within the book itself.

There is not a parallel genre of dead boy books. Although a small number of recent books have featured teen boys who grapple with mental illness and suicidal ideation, we do not see analogous examples of dead boys posthumously telling their stories. One of my central areas of questioning thus has to do with the narrative and imaginative purposes served by dead girls that could not be served by live ones. What are the messages circulating in our culture, in this case via YA novels, about girls' lives and deaths, and about what they should be doing with those lives, and during those deaths?

Because the stories are my data, I will begin by describing a sample of books in each of the two sub-genres and then I will go on to examine some of the themes and trends evident across these books.

Definitely Dying

In these books, the central character's death is inevitable and imminent. In John Green's *The Fault in our Stars* (2012), 16-year-old Hazel is dying of metastasized thyroid cancer. In a support group for teens with cancer, she meets Gus, who has bone cancer. They become good friends, Gus using his sick kids' wish to take Hazel to Amsterdam to track down her favorite author. In Amsterdam they find the author, although not with the results Hazel had hoped for. Hazel's interest in the author stems from her concern about her own mother and what will happen to her after Hazel has died. In the course of the book, Hazel is reassured that her mother will be alright, that her mother will in fact continue to exist after Hazel has died. This conflation of her own death with the death of one or more family members is not uncommon across this genre, as I will discuss shortly.

In Amsterdam, Hazel and Gus also become lovers. There is a sense that the usual rules governing teenage sex and its consequences do not apply to them. Fate will perhaps make an exception for two teens dealt such tragic hands. This relationship is presented as the pinnacle of Hazel's life and it is thus heartrending when Gus dies. The sadness of Hazel's own death is perhaps mitigated by the possibility that she might be reunited with Gus.

In Jenny Downham's *Before I Die* (2007), 16-year-old Tessa is dying of leukemia. She writes a list of things that she wants to do before she dies, the first of which is to feel the weight of a boy on top of her; she wants to experience sex. On learning of this, Zoey, her best friend, dresses Tessa up and takes her to a club where they pick up two young men and return to their apartment for sex. Tessa's experience of sex is unremarkable and she moves on to other items on her list, including saying yes to everything for a day, trying drugs, and breaking the law. She assumes she will not have time to fall in love but it is on her list anyway. Sure enough, she meets Adam, the new teenage boy next door, and they fall in love. They become lovers and this is the sex that is meaningful and beautiful. When she tells her father that she wants Adam to move in and stay with her every night, her father consents. Again, there is a sense that the usual rules do not apply. In fact, this is made explicit throughout the book, starting with Zoey's telling her, the first night they head out to have sex with strangers, that "there are no consequences for someone like you!" (10).

This would appear to be true. Although Tessa uses a condom the first time she has sex with the stranger, no form of contraception is ever mentioned again in relation to Adam. She is also let off a shoplifting charge and forgiven for stealing her father's car and driving without a license. For Zoey, however, who is not imminently dying, there are serious consequences. She (who was the provider of the condoms on that first fateful night) begins a relationship with the young man she picked up in the bar but, when she discovers she is pregnant, she is abandoned by both him and her family. She decides to keep the baby and accept state assistance in finding a home and supporting herself and the baby.

Each of these books is a romance, and the imminent demise of the protagonist adds both urgency and poignancy to the love story while freeing each protagonist from the usual real-life sequelae of falling in love at sixteen. They experience no censure of their juvenile sexuality; they deal with no STIs or unplanned pregnancy; they do not ever have to discover that first love generally does not last forever. They need never grow old or bored; they will never be divorced, middle-aged, single parents. These couples are, in short, Romeo and Juliet. The impending death of one or both is the tragic constraint on their love that also, conversely, frees them to experience passionate love and explore their sexuality.

Indisputably Dead

In these books, the protagonist is dead, even if she does not at first realize it. In most instances, she speaks for herself although hers might not be the only first-person voice narrating the book. I would suggest that Alice Sebold's *The Lovely Bones* (2002) was the originator of this entire genre. Although not the first story ever told by a posthumous narrator, and although not originally marketed as a YA book, it was the first of a growing number of books wherein a dead girl tells her story, specifically contemplating the circumstances of her life and death. *The Lovely Bones*, in which 14-year-old Susie has been sexually assaulted and brutally murdered, is, at least in part, about her desire to help her family solve the mystery of her death. Along the way, it is an observation of a family torn apart, and brought back together, by grief, and it is a portrayal of the pain of watching the living go on with their lives. It also captures the longing for what might have been missed; in Susie's case this is consensual sex with a boy she actually desires. Susie figures out how to achieve this by inhabiting the body of a girl who has been trying to channel her. There are some key themes here that appear across the genre.

Solving a Mystery

In Suzy Cox's *The Dead Girls Detective Agency* (2012), recently murdered Charlotte discovers that she must solve her own murder before being able to move onto whatever is next. The titular detective agency is composed of other dead teenage girls and one mysterious, brooding, and alluring teenage boy. Charlotte observes her own funeral, a common event in these books. She also learns how to manifest to the living and transport herself to places. She comes to realize that her boyfriend in life was not as great as she thought and that death might hold more promising romantic possibilities. This is also quite a common theme.

Jay Asher's *Thirteen Reasons Why* (2007) is not a mystery that Hannah, the dead girl, must solve, but is built around the question of why she killed herself. The other first-person narrator of this story is Clay, who has received a set of cassette tapes made by Hannah before her death. Over the course of a night Clay listens to the tapes in which Hannah explains the factors, including sexual victimization and bullying, that lead her to kill herself. She has asked that the tapes be passed along to each of the thirteen people she feels were in some way important to, or implicated in, her story. What sets this book apart is that Hannah is not dead when she is telling her story although she is dead when we (and Clay) are hearing it. Unlike other dead girls in these books, she cannot comment on the state of being dead itself; she is able only to comment on what is so unbearable about her life and why death might seem appealing. Her words seem to have an impact on the thirteen recipients of the tapes precisely because she has killed herself. The testimonials on the book cover, and inside the book, suggest that the readers have responded so strongly for the same reason; the story of victimization and bullying is more interesting, more compelling, perhaps even more valid, if the teller has killed herself.

In Jess Rothenberg's *The Catastrophic History of You and Me* (2012), 16-year-old Brie dies of heartbreak when her boyfriend, her first serious relationship, tells her that he does not love her. With the assistance of Patrick, an extremely attractive, mysterious, and sometimes brooding dead teenage boy, she works through the five stages of grief while trying to solve the mystery of what happened to bring about her ex-boyfriend's change of heart. She attends her own memorial service, learns how to manifest to the living, and how to zoom to various locations at will. Brie is at first convinced that her boyfriend had fallen in love with her best friend, so she haunts him and causes him to have an accident that destroys the collegiate athletic future that he had been working toward. She comes to realize, however, that he had only confided in her best friend, and that what he had confided was that he was gay. She watches as he writes his suicide note, because he knows his family will never accept this information, and he has lost his opportunity to get away from them. In her anguish about what she has done to him, she figures out a way to relive one day of her life and goes back to the day she died, when he tells her that he does not love her, this time giving him the chance to explain that he is gay and giving herself the chance to encourage him to be true to himself. Brie returns to death and to Patrick who, it turns out, is actually her true love. He was her teen love in a past life and has been waiting for her in death while she has lived another life in the meantime.

Death as a Do-over

This idea of going back and doing it over is the central premise of Lauren Oliver's *Before I Fall* (2011). In this book, Samantha dies in a horrible car accident but then awakes the next morning to relive her last day on earth. This happens six times, presumably until she can figure out what she needs to do to get it (her death) right. She learns that the car accident was caused by a young woman, the victim of bullying by Samantha herself and her friends, throwing herself in front of the car. In the course of a week, Samantha comes to comprehend that she cannot simply talk the girl out of killing herself. She never, however, tries to get her friends to stop bullying the girl. In the end, she pushes the girl out of the way and she dies instead. There is, however, also time in the week to realize that her boyfriend is a jerk and to fall in love with the sweet, geeky guy with whom she was friends in childhood. He is alive, however, and she is dead so, presumably, they will not be spending eternity together. This is not presented as a tragedy because she explains that their momentous kiss, the kiss of *true* love, was

> when I realized that time doesn't matter. That's when I realized that certain moments go on forever. Even after they're over, they still go on, even after you're dead and buried, those moments are lasting still, backward and forward, on into infinity. They are everything and everywhere all at once. (470)

In Gabrielle Zevin's *Elsewhere* (2005), 15-year-old Liz wakes on a boat without knowing that she died when a taxi knocked her off her bike. In the course of a seven-day journey, she makes some friends and figures out she is dead. The boat arrives at Elsewhere, where the dead live their lives in reverse. When they reach the age of seven days, they are put back in the water via which they will return to the living and be born again. She is greeted by the grandmother who died, at the age of 50, shortly before Liz was born. That grandmother is now 35. Liz learns how to observe the living, watching her own funeral, and spending many hours watching friends and family go about their lives. She also figures out how to contact the living, even though it is prohibited, and makes contact with her younger brother. She is required to get a job and she chooses to work with the dogs who have come to Elsewhere because, as it turns out, she can speak canine. She also meets and falls in love with Owen, a teenage boy, who must first get over the wife he left when he died several years before. The course of Liz and Owen's love is challenged when the wife dies and turns up in Elsewhere, but she is in her mid-30s while Owen is now in his mid-teens. She wishes the young lovers luck and pursues her own death away from them. Liz and Owen remain a couple, and then childhood friends, until, at the end of the book, the infant Liz is reborn in the land of the living.

Death is a Lot of Work

Like Liz in *Elsewhere*, 12-year-old Riley Bloom, in Alyson Noel's *Radiance* (2010) discovers that in the Here and Now that is death, she will have to have a job. The job she is assigned involves trying to convince reluctant dead souls to cross over to Here, rather than haunting the living. This is the first book in a series in which Riley, her dog, and her teacher and friend, the teenaged Bodhi, grapple with troublesome spirits. In addition to her dog, Riley's parents crossed over with her when the entire family was killed in a car accident. Her older sister went in a different, undead, direction that is explored in a separate series of books. Riley is the youngest of the dead girls in these books and the "Riley Bloom" series is specifically targeted at junior high students. Perhaps this is why Riley's parents are with her and she has not had to deal with the anguish of being separated from them or from her dog.

Death is not so Different, Not so Bad

In the "Riley Bloom" books, as well as several of the others, death, as a place or as a state of being, is portrayed as either not so very different from life or as not unappealing. Riley tells us that "the weirdest part about dying is that nothing really changed." She goes on to proclaim that "the moment I died I actually felt more alive than ever. I could jump higher—run faster—I could even walk through walls if I wanted" (Noel 2010: 3).

Similarly, in *Elsewhere*, Liz is disappointed to find that Elsewhere is just like the land of the living. We are told that

> Liz sees a place that looks like almost any other place on Earth. She thinks it is cruel how ordinary it is, how much it resembles real life. There are buildings, houses, stores, roads, cars, bridges, people, trees, flowers, grass, lakes, rivers,

beaches, air, stars, and skies. How entirely unremarkable, she thinks. Elsewhere could have been a walk to the next town, or an hour's ride in the car or an overnight plane trip. (Zevin 2005: 49)

Although some of the girls experience fear or anxiety upon realizing they are dead, in none of the books is death portrayed as a fearsome or horrific state in which to be. Adventures can happen here. Mysteries can be solved. Boys can be met and true love can blossom. The conflicts and tensions of one's life can be reappraised and reconciled. One can achieve distance, understanding, and peace in death. Oliver's Samantha assures readers:

> I am not scared, if that's what you're wondering. The moment of death is full of sound and warmth and light, so much light it fills me, absorbs me: a tunnel of light shooting away, arcing up and up and up, and if singing were a feeling it would be this, this light, this lifting, like laughing … The rest you have to find out for yourself. (2011: 470)

That, I would argue, could actually be interpreted as an invitation.

Girls' Relational Worlds

In all these books, regardless of any other obstacles to be overcome, or mysteries to be solved, three sets of relationships retain primacy in the stories and in the girls' lives and deaths. The first of these is with family.

Family

Although in the books in which the girls are dying there is room for familial conflict and ambivalence, in the books in which the girls are dead, it would appear that any familial conflict that might have existed disappears at the moment of death. Irritating siblings are forgiven and parents are remembered as loving, kind, fun people. Rothenberg's Brie, for example, offers an assessment of her life that does not significantly deviate from the types of sentimental tenderness with which families and loved ones are described in many other books of this genre.

> I had the perfect family: Mom, Dad, Jack, and Hamloaf (he's our basset hound). I had the perfect best friends: Sadie Russo, Emma Brewer, and Tess Hoffman. And I had the perfect boyfriend: track star, senior class vice president, Hottie McHotterson, Jacob Fischer. Before I died, I had everything and more. *I was happy*. (Rothenberg 2012: 4, italics in original)

It is perhaps not surprising then that many of the girls go through an initial grieving process. They grieve the loss of their lives and their life-based futures but, mostly, they grieve the loss of their families or they grieve the loss of themselves from their families. Many of the books feature the dead girl attending, or in some other way observing, her own funeral or memorial service. Although the protagonist is the one who is dead, she often experiences the event as if it were the others who are dead. Zevin (2005) captures this when she describes Liz's experience watching her own funeral: "In a way, it feels more like she is still alive and the only guest at the collective funeral for everyone she has ever known" (32). This might be an appealing notion to someone who is being relentlessly bullied.

Edna St. Vincent Millay's 1937 poem, "Childhood is the Kingdom where Nobody Dies," captures the cultural conviction that the intact simplicity of childhood ends when one experiences a significant death, such as that of one's parents. The characters experiencing their own funerals as the death of everyone else they love can be taken as a fairly straightforward metaphor for the familial separation processes that are a necessary part of most teen lives, even if the actual death of the teenager is an extreme form of separation. Nonetheless, their deaths generally provide these girls with the opportunity to reflect on their families and come to appreciate them in what might be considered more mature ways. In this sense, coming-to-death stories might be seen as a variant of coming-of-age stories.

Friends/Peers

The friendship worlds of these girls are absolutely central to their lives and thus might be massively missed in death. As important as friends in life are, so too might be those peers who are not friends, who might be enemies, bullies, or the victims of the protagonist's own bullying. Asher's (2007) Hannah, speaks solely to the peers who made her life so miserable that they apparently drove her to suicide. Oliver's (2011) Samantha relives the day of her death until she figures out how to prevent the suicide of the girl she and her friends bullied. She manages to do this without disrupting her relationship with her circle of best friends and without bringing up the topic of bullying with them.

While these dead girls often look upon their old friends with affection, finding forgiveness and understanding in death, if those relationships were not already perfect, they also look upon some of their other peers with bemusement. Several comment wryly on the attendance of peers they barely know at their funerals and memorial services. These memorial services, the scenes of such familial grief, are often also the places where they have their peers' attention to an unprecedented degree. Rothenberg's Brie describes her memorial.

For a second, it was kind of easy to forget this was a memorial service. It didn't *feel* like anyone had died. It wasn't morbid or depressing or creepy. It was actually kind of fun, hearing how much everyone liked me. I remember feeling silly that I'd been worried about it; for thinking it was going to be too hard to watch. But the mood was light. Like some sort of celebration or party. And this time, I was the *star*. (2012: 11, italics in original)

It is implied in many of these books that there is nothing quite like death for getting the attention, even admiration, of one's peers.

The importance of friends is never questioned so it is not surprising that many of the dead girls make new friends in death. Certainly, some appear to be alone in their experience of dying or of death, but most are able to either reconfigure their relationships with live friends, even though they are dead, or they make new friends in death (or both). This is very different from parents and siblings who cannot be replaced in death. Friends are important, even essential, but they can be replaced.

Romantic and/or Sexual Relationships

In most of these books, romance figures prominently. Any romance that actually occurs is heterosexual. There is almost no hint, in the vast majority of these books, that non-heterosexual identities or relationships are even a possibility.

As mentioned above, in books in which a girl's death is imminent, romance becomes the central concern, and what are thought of as ordinary rules often cease to apply. Dying girls can find true love before they die with boys who will love them tenderly to the point of death. They can have wonderful and fulfilling (and apparently unprotected) sex, with the blessing of their parents, and with no negative consequences.

In books in which the protagonist is dead, romance remains a central concern. It is quite common that, in death, these girls become disillusioned with the boyfriends they had in life. This is not problematic, however, because in death they often find the boy who is really their true love. If he is also dead, there is the suggestion that death might actually offer the opportunity to be together for eternity. The desire for a lifelong passionate romance comes to seem naïve (possibly even unambitious) in light of the possibility of this true, and infinite, love. Yes, dead love might be better than living love. Dead lovers, furthermore, apparently cannot get pregnant or acquire STIs. And they will remain teenagers forever, never aging and never, as it were, dying.

If the beloved boy is not dead, the protagonist is generally able to find a way to have at least one ecstatically romantic encounter with him. She might, for example, have the chance to return to life for a brief period, as in

Oliver's *Before I Fall* (2011), or she might have the ability to inhabit the body of a living girl and be with her boy that way, as in Sebold's *The Lovely Bones* (2002).

I would suggest that most of these books are actually thinly disguised, or not at all disguised, romances. This raises the question, once again, of how or why being dead can seem like a viable subject position for a teenage girl. What makes dead love so appealing?

Messages for Girls

A strong theme running through these books is that there is nothing like dying to boost your popularity. Whether it is the massive funereal crowds we see in most of the books, or the attention that is paid to Asher's (2007) Hannah solely because she has killed herself, the message seems to be quite clear: you matter when you are dead. It is here that I see troubling parallels with the media coverage of real-life teen suicides. I think, for example, of Canadian teen Amanda Todd, who was sexually victimized, then relentlessly bullied, and who then committed suicide after leaving a YouTube video in which she detailed the circumstances that had led to her feeling that she had no choice but to kill herself. It was abundantly clear that her death lent urgency and gravitas to the YouTube video that simply had not received the same kind or amount of attention when she was alive. She was by no means the first casualty of what has become known as bullycide and we have seen several well-publicized cases since, but her case marks a trend in increasing media coverage of such stories and demonstrates some of the ways in which social media platforms are being taken up by troubled teens.

An important difference between Amanda Todd (and many other real-life victims of bullycide) and Asher's fictional Hannah is that Hannah quite explicitly uses her suicide as a form of revenge against those she felt made her life so miserable. Orri et al. (2014) found that revenge is, in fact, sometimes a motive among teens who have attempted suicide. The suicide becomes a violent way of communicating their suffering to others and making those others suffer in retribution. But revenge is most satisfying when it can be savored. Describing their interview with one participant, Orri et al. observed that "it almost appears that she expects to be present to witness the scene" (6). The vast bulk of the dead girl books portray death as exactly that—the place from which they can witness the suffering and grief attending their death.

A further (explicit or implicit) message in many of these books is that death, and even impending death, can free girls from the life-bound constraints on their sexuality. In death, or impending death, they are free to find and express whatever counts to them as true love with absolutely none of the negative consequences, or serious implications that can attend sexual intimacy for living people of any age. Almost all these books are written by American authors and have living characters inhabiting the USA. Given the tremendous strictures American culture places on teen sexuality, discouraging it altogether, often refusing young people sex education or access to contraceptives, and being harshly condemnatory of teen pregnancy, it should perhaps come as no surprise that this genre has flourished in the USA. Being dead, or dying, becomes a viable subject position for girls who have no safe opportunities in life to realize their own sexuality. It is not necessary to have a parallel genre of dead boy books; teenage boys are not required to choose between virginity/purity/life, and sexuality/desire/death.

I would suggest that these books are a constitutive component of the larger cultural narrative that renders conceptually possible situations whereby teenage girls are sexually victimized and then bullied about their own victimization until they kill themselves. In these real-life instances a girl cannot survive being sexual, even when it has been against her will. To suggest that she consented or was complicit, is the ultimate, and unsurvivable, insult.

In a time when bullycide is either on the increase or is simply receiving increased media coverage, I find it troubling that a genre of books being marketed to teen girls presents death as both quite appealing and as the best way to have your friends and peers respect you, listen to you, and maybe even regret the way they treated you in life. Teens, of course, are not mindless dupes, and are able to engage critically with popular culture, although they might need to be educated in some of the ways of doing so. Teens are also the creators of their own stories although these are rarely published by mainstream publishers or turned into hit television series. My question is this: Why are adults telling girls this particular story?

I find it interesting, and somewhat alarming, that this genre has come into existence, and is gaining popularity, at a time when US culture appears to have become incapable of dealing sensibly with teenage girls' sexuality. It is a sorry comment on our cultural constructions of young womanhood when some of the most appealing romantic fantasies we can offer young women require them to relate to the subject position of someone who is dying or already dead. It strikes me as a failure of imagination, rather than a success, when we have to kill the young women in fiction in order to allow them freedom, agency, and sexuality.

In this sense, it is the culture that is toxic to young women. Of course, there are also many toxicities to masculinity. I would argue, however, that this particular phenomenon, the dead girl books, both reflects and reifies ongoing gender inequalities that affect girls and young women in particularly harmful ways. The solution is not censorship. We, the adults, are choosing to tell these stories to girls and are complicit in the mainstreaming of this narrative. Why? It behoves us to examine the personal and cultural costs and benefits of propagating this narrative of girlhood. Teens themselves should be invited into this conversation.

Acknowledgments

Sincere thanks to the two anonymous reviewers for their helpful suggestions and insights. I am also very grateful to Ann Smith for her careful reading and guidance.

FIONA NELSON is Department Head and Associate Professor in the Department of Sociology at the University of Calgary, Canada, where she has also worked with the Women's Studies Program. She is the author of two books on motherhood, *Lesbian Motherhood: An Exploration of Canadian Lesbian Families* (1996) and *In the Other Room: Entering the Culture of Motherhood* (2009). In the last few years she has begun studying and teaching in the area of gender and childhood/youth. She is currently involved in examining various subgenres of Young Adult literature, particularly the dead girl subgenre and the growing subgenre of LGBTQ+ literature.

Note

1. These are a sub-sample of the larger genre of dead girl books that includes the following themes: the possibly dying; the definitely dying; the possibly dead; the definitely dead (temporarily); the definitely dead (with a temporary reprieve); the definitely dead (forever); contemplating/attempting suicide; surviving a significant other's suicide; and non-fiction books by girls who have died. In the larger genre of dead teen books, there are also books about boys contemplating, attempting, or completing suicide, and about boys surviving the suicides of significant others. There are also apocalyptic books in which all the teens are on the brink of certain death. An examination of all these is clearly beyond the scope of this chapter.

References

Asher, Jay. 2007. *Thirteen Reasons Why*. New York: Razorbill.
Cox, Suzy. 2012. *The Dead Girls Detective Agency*. New York: HarperTeen.
Davies, Bronwyn. 2003. *Frogs and Snails and Feminist Tales: Preschool Children and Gender* (Revised ed.). New Jersey: Hampton Press, Inc.
Downham, Jenny. 2007. *Before I Die*. New York: Ember.
Gottschall, Jonathan. 2012. *The Storytelling Animal: How Stories Make us Human*. Boston, MA: Houghton Mifflin Harcourt.
Green, John. 2012. *The Fault in our Stars*. New York: Dutton Books.
Noel, Alyson. 2010. *Radiance*. New York: Square Fish.
Oliver, Lauren. 2011. *Before I Fall*. New York: Harpercollins Publishers.
Orri, Massimiliano, Matteo Paduanello, Jonathan Lachal, Bruno Falissard, Jordan Sibeoni, and Anne Revah-Levy. 2014. "Qualitative Approach to Attempted Suicide by Adolescents and Young Adults: the (Neglected) Role of Revenge." *PLOS One* 9 (5): 1–8.
Rothenberg, Jess. 2012. *The Catastrophic History of You and Me*. New York: Dial Books.
Sebold, Alice. 2002. *The Lovely Bones*. Boston, MA: Little, Brown and Company.
World Health Organization (2014). *Preventing Suicide: A Global Imperative*. http://www.who.int/mental_health/suicide-prevention/world_report_2014/en/ (accessed 27 February 2017).
Zevin, Gabrielle. 2005. *Elsewhere*. New York: Square Fish.

Filmography

Yorkey, Brian. 2017. *Thirteen Reasons Why*. USA.

CHAPTER 4

Girl Constructed in Two Nonfiction Texts
Sexual Subject? Desired Object?

Mary Ann Harlan

As Catherine Driscoll reminds us, "Girls are brought into existence in statements and knowledge" (2002: 5). In the United States, representations of girls in a wide variety of media shape our cultural knowledge about girlhood. These narratives about girls develop into what we might call cultural knowledge. This happens as independent narratives gain popular attention through research reports, news stories that can be positioned as demonstrating emerging trends, and fictional representation. Two examples of texts that present girlhood to adults and then, through adult interpretation, form narratives of girlhood come to mind. In the early 1990s the popularity of the text *Reviving Ophelia: Saving the Lives of Adolescent Girls* (Pipher 1994) led to subsequent cultural discussion focused on a narrative of girls at risk that then led to girl power programs (Currie et al. 2009; Ward and Benjamin 2004). In the early 2000s, this cycle repeated itself when *Queen Bees and Wannabees* (Wiseman 2002) was adapted into the film, *Mean Girls* (2004); this introduced a narrative that centered around mean girls and relational bullying.

In 2016, two nonfiction texts, written for an adult audience, Peggy Orenstein's *Girls and Sex: Navigating the Complicated New Landscape* (hereafter *Girls and Sex*) and Nancy Jo Sales's *American Girls: Social Media and the Secret Life of Teenagers* (hereafter *American Girls*) were published. These texts received media attention (Gross 2016a; Gross 2016b; Holbrook 2016; Levy 2016; North 2016) and articulated a narrative of girls navigating sexual activity in a manner that left them facing various forms of risk. In *Girls and Sex*, Orenstein explores how young women think about and engage in sexual activity; she weaves in research related to girls' sexual practices. Sales takes a different approach in *American Girls* in focusing on how girls represent themselves and communicate through social media, and emphasizing her interpretation of an online environment as being hypersexualized. The texts depict a girlhood dominated by sexism in which girls are sexual objects who practice complicity in their own objectification. However, a closer reading of what the girls themselves say in these texts indicates that they are aware of their own desires; they explore ways to control their own narratives, and struggle to do so in a culture that positions them as desired objects. However, the authors seem to ignore the ways in which the girls try to assert agency while being aware of the cultural forces that have an impact on them. The voices of the girls in the text provide a counterpoint to the authorial voices that presuppose the girls-at-risk narrative and, even worse, that the girls themselves are unaware of this narrative.

In this chapter, I examine both texts to identify how they construct girlhood. My purpose is to probe, on the one hand, how these two authorial perspectives critique the influence of American culture on girls' choices, and, on the other, the ways in which the girls' words present their own contrasting narrative. Since the emphasis of both texts is on sexual practices, I explore the narratives of girl as the desired object in Sales's *American Girls* in which, furthermore, her subjectivity is not explored or acknowledged as anything other than problematic, and as desiring subject in *Girls and Sex*, in which the girl is recognized as having the agency of desire. I attempt to identify how the texts construct girlhood within existing narratives related to girls' sexual behaviors.

Theoretical Perspective, Questions, and Analysis

Our beliefs about the development of knowledge and the objectivity of truth influence the questions we ask and the answers we develop. Joey Sprague points out that "abstract individuation creates systematic biases" (2005: 17). Therefore, it is imperative that we lay bare the epistemology that guides abstraction. Standpoint theory suggests that "knowledge is constructed in a specific matrix of physical location, history, culture, and interests" (41). It acknowledges and concerns itself with the "distortions created by power imbalances due to gender, race/ethnicity, class, and nation" (53). I ask questions grounded in a feminist standpoint that assumes that power guides what is valued as knowledge. Simply put, there are two assumptions regarding power that influence both how I ask the question and how I analyze the construction of girlhood. The first is that we live in a patriarchal culture in which power rests with men, allowing them to shape narratives through institutions. The second assumption is that age is a part of identity in which youth are outside power structures. In a patriarchal culture, gender-based power imbalances underlie the narratives of girlhood and these are further complicated by issues related to race and class (Currie et al. 2009; Driscoll 2002; Harris 2004). The implication of the second assumption is that a power imbalance exists when adults control and perpetuate structural institutions in a manner that others youth (Harris 2004; Woo 2012). I interrogate the framing of the two titles as one who is aware of these assumptions and their influence on both the questions I ask and the answers I construct.

Feminism and Girls

As mentioned above, girlhood is a constructed concept negotiated in particular moments and in particular cultures (Driscoll 2002; Griffin 2004). In US culture, girlhood is mediated through adults who have the power to constitute institutions and produce narrative through mass media (Griffei 2004; Lesko and Talburt 2012). Girlhood itself becomes an object of study, a product to sell, a narrative of other. Girls exist in this culture and shape their own subjectivity (Baumgardner and Richards 2004; Currie et al. 2009; Taft 2004). Therefore, feminist conversations regarding girlhood will influence girls' construction of their subjectivity while they are interacting with these narratives. As feminist conversations and the attendant backlash enter the mainstream through media landscapes girls must negotiate their own understanding of the emergent narratives of girlhood.

I consider the construction of girlhood in these texts, and the negotiation between object and subject as a cultural moment of postfeminism. Postfeminism is a contested concept; on the one hand it is represented by a critique of second wave feminism while constructing itself as feminist

(Sanders 2004) and, on the other, it is represented by the 1990s girl power movement in which the need for equality is self-evident (Griffin 2004), and is, therefore, a rejection of feminism. There is an interaction between the two representations in which feminism becomes the "depoliticization and reduction of [itself] to a justification for lifestyle, and commodification" (Lotz 2007: 79). The result is that currently girl power is built on the language of choice with a neoliberal focus on the individual for whom feminism is no longer necessary (Gill et al. 2009; Taft 2004). As the girl power movement of the 1990s was being commodified, packaged, and sold in popular culture, a girlish femininity emerged as a version of feminism that one chooses (Baumgardner and Richards 2004; Baumgardner and Waters 2014). Choice being the operative term, as Jennifer Baumgardner and Amy Richards write, "Feminine things weren't truly the problem; being forced to adopt them was" (2004: 61). In response, a critique regarding girls' agency about the commodification and selling of girl power and femininity emerged (Gill et al. 2009; Harris 2004; Taft 2004). Postfeminism's focus on choice, empowerment, and the agency of girls has particular import to girls as sexual subjects and/or desired objects since the so called depoliticization of feminism suggests that one's choice to present as a sexual object is a feminist act. This is evident in Orenstein's and Sales's text as girls use the language of choice and empowerment in speaking about their sexual subjectivity, and in recognizing their position as objects.

Sexual Subjects, Desired Objects

Historically, adults have concerned themselves with youth and sexuality, particularly in relation to girls (Driscoll 2002). Primarily, two narratives dominate: "sexuality as risk; and sexuality as resistance" (Kehily 2012: 226). When issues of desire and empowerment are at play, these two themes collide. For instance, Deborah Tolman (2002) writes that girls are presented as objects of male desire rather than as desiring subjects. She writes, "While sexualized images of adolescent girls are omnipresent, their sexual feelings are rarely if ever portrayed" (2002: 8). This affects how girls engage in sexual practices and how they understand their own desire.

As the commodification of girl power has promoted empowerment to young women regarding their sexual presentation and activities through images of women as sexy, a focus on the sexualization of girls has occurred (American Psychological Association 2008; Lamb and Peterson 2012; Tolman

2012). Rosalind Gill and colleagues highlight the sale of sexual subjectivity framed as "playfulness, freedom, and above all, choice" (2009: 148). This postfeminist girl power cooption has narrative consequences. For instance, Sharon Lamb and Zoe Peterson question whether "empowerment include[s] a subjective sense of efficacy, desire and pleasure" (2012: 704). When sexuality has been commodified and sold to girls, what is their agency? That Lamb and Peterson cannot find an answer indicates how complex the issue of agency is in a world that objectifies girls, and sells sexual freedom as an empowered choice. Tolman (2012) suggests that there may be more to the question: we need to interrogate young women's narratives of desire more deeply. The texts of Orenstein and Sales display the points that Lamb and Peterson make as central to the issue of empowerment as girls grapple with the pressure to be sexual subjects in a culture that positions them as desired objects.

American Cultural Narratives

As researchers interrogate issues of subjectivity common themes emerge in more popular media. One theme is the need to control how girls present themselves. From one perspective, we expect girls to present themselves as demure, but, conversely, there is pressure on them to be sexy. Currently the urge to control girls' presentation of self plays out at an institutional level through dress codes ranging from banning leggings to controlling the length of skirts and shorts, and the freedom to bare shoulders (Levy 2016; Needles 2017; Pearlman 2017) while the fashion industry sells *sexy* (American Psychological Association 2008; Gill et al. 2009). As is clear here, girls experience competing expectations of dressing in a demure manner that does not attract male attention as well as seeming sexy. Both these expectations are rooted in a narrative in which girls are sexual objects.

Another common theme in popular media is the need for young women to protect themselves from assault. In high profile sexual assault cases, focus has coalesced on the victim's actions, in particular, her sobriety. In Stuebenville, Ohio, a 16-year-old girl was assaulted and some in the community questioned her story because she had been drinking—despite many images of the assault appearing on social media shared in the community (Macur and Schweber 2012). Another case in Maryville, Kansas, involving a 14-year-old girl resulted in similar community backlash against the victim as reported by Dugan Arnett (2013). The Slutwalk movement began when Michael Sanguinetti, a Toronto police officer, made the infamous comment that "women should avoid dressing like sluts in order not to be victimized." This narrative constructs the girl as a slut responsible for her own assault (Arnett 2013; Macur and Schweber 2012). It uses the regulatory power of the term slut to control girls' sexual practices, thus placing them in a position that dictates that the only acceptable way to behave is as (sober) object without desire (Attwood 2007; Tolman 2012).

In examining the construction of girl by both Orenstein and Sales, I question whether the texts contribute to simplified narratives or more complex, nuanced understandings of girlhood. Do the authors construct girls as objects or as subjects?

Methodology

The popularity of the Orenstein (2016) and Sales (2016) texts ensures their contribution to cultural narratives related to girlhood. In my study, I used a modified qualitative content analysis to examine how these texts contribute to a specific narrative of girlhood in relation to sexual practices. Initially, I read the books to establish their broad themes and the relationship of themes to the sociocultural context from which the books arose. My second and third readings focused on how these themes were constructed and whether or not there was any nuance to the themes that challenged the dominant narratives of girlhood. I focused on the actual words of the girls quoted in the texts, and how the authors interpreted these words so as to construct girls. Emergent themes included the presentation of body, how expectations of prude and slut are navigated, the relationship between choice and risk, and the negotiation of a culture that sees girls as sexual objects while marketing representations of girls as sexual subjects.

Constructing Girls in *Girls and Sex* and *American Girls*

In *Girls and Sex* (2016) and *American Girls* (2016), the girl who emerges is one thoughtfully navigating a confusing world in which she is told to be sexy, not sexual. She feels empowered to have sex on her own terms, managing emotional and physical risk. She sees herself as the inheritor of a post-feminist culture, convinced that equality has been achieved. Meanwhile she accepts responsibility for traversing the patriarchal structures of institutions such as dress codes that focus on girls' clothing. She recognizes the role of the male gaze and discusses the influence of the rise of pornography on gendered relationships. However, the authors often present the girl as lacking the capacity or knowledge to enact power and agency in her sexual encounters. She claims agency in physical presentation, the loss of her virginity, and her choice of sexual practices. She is defiantly embarrassed when harassed by boys for what she wears, loses her virginity under the influence of alcohol, is at risk of sexual assault, and becomes labeled a thot (that ho over there) or a slut. She judges herself and others using markers familiar to women such as appearance and sexual partners. In short, the girl constructed by both Orenstein and Sales for adults is one simultaneously in control and confused while constructing her identity as a sexual subject.

Sexy not Sexual

The sexualization of girlhood is common throughout media (American Psychological Association 2008) but Kari Lerum and Shari Dworkin (2009) argue that sexualization does not equal objectification. Girls are commonly presented as objects of male desire in media (American Psychological Association 2008; Bae 2011; Gill et al. 2009; Tolman 2012), and yet girls coopt media images to present a self that is meant to evoke empowerment through choice (Bae 2011). This is grounded in the postfeminist narrative that the choice to be sexy is a feminist action (Baumgardner and Richards 2004). The girls in these two texts are conscious of inherent tensions in adopting a version of sexy that is based on male desire while being empowered to make that choice.

The girls in Orenstein's text use the language of empowerment in discussing their choices of presentation. For instance, Camilla speaks out in public regarding dress codes: "If I want to wear a tank top and shorts because it's hot, I should be able to do that and that has no correlation to how much 'respect' I hold for myself" (Orenstein 2016: 8). Camilla argues that she can choose how to dress without positioning herself as a sexual object. Sales introduces girls who discuss posting pictures of "butts and boobs in a bikini" and doing "all these thot poses" (67). The girls see physical presentation as branding themselves, and position themselves based on the likes that photos receive. In both texts, girls are clearly aware of the need to be sexy, and they suggest a power and confidence in their presentation of their physical selves, but also demonstrate an awareness of a complication in their presentation. Girls are clearly aware of the male gaze—"Sometimes I feel like all the posting is just for guys" (74). Camilla describes the experience this way: "I feel really hot and this is going to be a good day. Then as soon as I got to school I felt like … automatically I wasn't in control. People are staring at you, looking you up and down and saying things. … It was dehumanizing" (15). Camilla suggests that she was a victim of consistent harassment in stating, "Four out of five days I go to school I will be catcalled" (9). As a young woman, Camilla wants to dress in a way that she feels represents her confidence but her attire leads to her objectification by schoolmates and this makes her uncomfortable. She uses the language of empowerment but, in practice, she exists in a culture in which she lacks power; this leaves her confused.

Orenstein portrays girls as using the language of choice and girl power while struggling to negotiate a world that objectifies their bodies. She writes,

> The body as product however, is not the same as the body as subject. Nor is learning to be sexually desirable the same as exploring your own desire … It's not surprising that girls feel powerful when they feel 'hot': it's presented to them over and over as a precondition for success in any realm. (2016: 43)

Sales does not treat her girl with as much nuance. She writes, "It was perplexing to hear that, more than two decades since the 'girl power' movement, some American girls still felt this anxious need for male approval" (Sales 2016: 73). This suggests that the onus is not on the creators (including us) of the cultural messaging girls receive but on girls themselves to resist the messaging. Sales resists entirely the notion that branding one's self as a sexual being can be anything other than a need for male approval, despite the ways in which the girls themselves struggle with articulating their own discomfort with this notion.

Virginity

As a desired object, girls' virginity (and its status) has long been the subject and obsession of patriarchal institutions. Girls, as Driscoll proposes, "Come to be virgin" as a marker of adolescent femininity, thereby "designating girls' maturity as something gifted by men" (2002: 140–141). Adults expect girls to remain virgins, and policy and education have only emphasized this expectation. The emphasis on abstinence-based sex education as a governmental policy is one example of how this is culturally stressed. Another example is the purity movement that Orenstein explores. Society constructs the loss of virginity as a transformation into womanhood, and so girl has come to equal virgin. Virginity has a very specific definition in this narrative: the act of penis-to-vagina penetration causes the loss of virginity. This narrow definition fails to incorporate the many other sexual acts in which one might engage. More importantly, it codes the loss of virginity as a heterosexual rite of passage, disregarding, for example, homosexuality and its practices, and therefore silencing the experience of queer youth. This is true, too, for trans, bisexual, and asexual young people. Accepting this definition, the girls in Orenstein's and Sales's texts construct virginity as a significant marker and code the loss of virginity as a rite of passage, but one they control. One girl states, "I thought it would be like this whole new world after I had sex for the first time! … 'You have sex, you will be transformed'" (Orenstein 2016: 82). Girls suggest that the reality does not meet expectations. Brooke admitted that before she had sex she was "thinking more about what it would be like to remember it." She says, "The truth is losing your virginity is the least sexy sexual act there is" (80). Another girl states, "I am just afraid if I lose it to someone who doesn't really care, something bad will happen. Or it will just be so disappointing" (Sales 2016: 323). Since the loss of virginity is structured as transformative girls explicitly attempt to manage its loss either by trying to make a memorable experience of it or, conversely, wanting to "get it over with" (Orenstein 2016: 83). Girls are also aware of competing narratives related to virginity. One girl claims, "And you can be any sexuality you want to be, too, *except* for pure" (87). She was referring to a competing cultural message that says that one should not be a "prude" (Sales 2016: 53). Despite the competing pressure to not be sexy and not be a prude, the emphasis on virginity has led to narratives of "it just happened" (Tolman 2002: 2) and also sometimes to risky behavior as documented in these texts. Girls thoughtfully consider their identity as virgins, and their choices regarding virginity are embedded in cultural constructions emphasized in media and policy. Girls feel empowered by the choice, while the narratives of virginity still inhibit them.

Sluts, Thots, and Empowerment

Orenstein and Sales present girls as trying to manage their sexual activity. The authors frame sexual activity as primarily approached in a casual manner, often referred to as hooking up. The increased casual engagement in a variety of activities from kissing to engaging in oral sex has led to moral panics regarding hooking up and its relative dangers (Armstrong et al. 2010). The engagement in hooking up appears to threaten patriarchal norms regarding women's responsibility for remaining virgins, or, at the very least, having few sexual partners in the context of monogamous relationships. This focuses attention on the number of partners girls have as they navigate between being appropriately experienced, but not too experienced, while exercising their own sexual subjectivity.

Girls see themselves as empowered in their choices as sexual subjects. They might consciously make a choice "to get drunk and make out with someone" (Orenstein 2016: 123), adopting an "if you can't beat 'em, join 'em" attitude (Sales 2016: 123). This type of statement can lead to the cultural judgment of girls as naïve, as not understanding the risks (social, emotional, as well as physical) of casual sexual encounters. Both Orenstein and Sales participate in perpetuating this judgment. Sales argues that girls adopt a "hypermasculinity dressed up in a porn-star package … reflecting misogyny" (2016: 241). Her point seems to be that girls do not understand how a patriarchal culture is directing their choices, and that, therefore, the girls lack agency in their sexual practices. Orenstein suggests that girls do not examine how cultural structures related to patriarchy have an impact on behaviors while exploring how girls generally experience less physical satisfaction than boys, positing this as a double standard. They position girls as being unwitting participants adopting the façade of choice in a hypermasculine culture without any awareness of the implications of hooking up. One way in which girls navigate the double standard is by managing how many sexual partners they have. Brooke states, "I guess I would feel icky if my number started to climb into the double digits" (Orenstein 2016: 98). The concern over numbers does reflect the regulatory power the word slut still has on controlling girls' behaviors (Attwood 2007). Girls are clear that they are often called "thot, slut, whore" (Sales 2016: 150) as a way of denigrating them. By looking more closely at the girls' language one can see that they are not naïve. Rather, they are negotiating a double standard, however inexpertly.

A challenge to the narrative of the casual sexual encounter resulting solely in risk is that girls may see engaging in hooking up as a protective act. Hooking up is a way of avoiding the risk of rejection, loss, or heartbreak (Armstrong et al. 2010). Sarah clearly articulates this when she says, "I'm terrified about the idea of being exclusive with him" (Sales 2016: 346). Another girl specifically asks about "the fear of falling in love or being in love" (Orenstein 2016: 111), indicating that she avoids the possibility of love. Additionally, this attitude may allow girls to focus on personal ambition related to school, or on their female friendships. While Sales, in particular, in her relating that one girl looked "lost" (362) after discussing a hook up, suggests that girls face emotional risk through doing so, the girls themselves demonstrated many reasons for their choices. Additionally girls may adopt the persona of slut despite the regulatory power of the word (Attwood 2007) by constructing it as a positive, an answer to the double standard by self-labeling. One girl "gleefully" described herself as "the slutty friend" (Orenstein 2016: 124) suggesting that her behavior is liberating. Despite their adoption of the label for themselves, girls do not accept being called a slut or a thot by others. In both adopting and rejecting labels they display discomfort with them and their use in demarcating cultural sensibilities related to sexual activity, the number of partners one has, and the status of one's relationship to one's partners. In short, girls justify decisions in narratives related to hooking up and to the labels of slut and thot. This is problematic but one should not dismiss the problem as being a function of ignorance. These girls are negotiating the power of choice within the structures that still ascribe value to them as objects and that seek to constrain their behavior.

Girls at Risk

The narrative of girl at risk is not new, and therefore the need for protection has long historical roots (Driscoll 2002; Tolman 2002). However, with the recent attention on above mentioned cases in Ohio and Kansas, along with attention being paid to Title IX and to how universities handle rape allegations (Bazelon 2015; Koren 2016; Tracy and Barry 2017), a new conversation around consent has emerged, as Stephanie Auteri (2016) reminds us. Females aged between 16 and 19 are 4 times more likely than the general population to be victims of rape, attempted rape, or sexual assault (Rape, Abuse & Incest National Network (RAINN) 2016), and 58 percent of youth report never having had a conversation with their parents about the importance of "being a caring and respectful sexual partner" (Weissbound et al. 2017: 3). Girls, being aware of issues related to consent, recognize the risk of sexual assault but they still demonstrate confusion. In employing a narrative of accountability, they often take on responsibility for their own roles in being assaulted, rather than placing responsibility on the perpetrator of the assault. In these texts, girls often use the dominant narrative of the responsibility of girls to protect themselves. Holly said,

> I'd like to say he didn't know how drunk I was ... but I don't know. My friend who is in an organization that fights rape on campus said that by definition I couldn't consent, so I was raped. And I almost ... I guess I am fortunate that I don't remember. (Orenstein 2016: 132)

Another girl, Maddie, who had a similar experience said,

> Legally? ... Yes, I was [raped]. Asking for a condom doesn't imply consent. But the way everyone treated me afterward ... People would say 'Oh you had to switch schools because of *that?* That's *nothing.*' And guys are like, 'Oh that's not rape.' (Orenstein 2016: 204)

Both Holly and Maddie struggled to make sense of the narratives of consent and rape. Girls who have not experienced assault also struggle to make sense of the notion of consent and of naming an act as assault. For instance, one girl said, "Like running trains on people ... That's taking advantage of girls when they are drunk" (Sales 2016: 330). It is significant that the girl does not name the event as rape.

Sales, in particular, highlights risk to young women in regard to sexual assault, arguing that blame lies with the online porn culture as something she argues young people are emulating. Sales positions young women as ignorant not of the risk but of their own role in promoting risk through emulation. She tells stories of girls at Halloween dressing as "total sluts" (2016: 319) in costumes more suitable to pornographic texts. She follows girls on Spring Break who are aware of the risk of rape so take responsibility for their own drinks, but documents that they still become inebriated and use a language of passivity—"getting passed out" (312). She specifically ties this to emulating a porn culture. Sales seems to perpetuate the narrative of the responsibility girls have for protecting themselves in a hypersexualized culture. Orenstein tends to display more empathy while still constructing a narrative of girls willing to put themselves at risk so that they are liked or make a boy happy. While a superficial reading of Orenstein would lead one to think girls should take responsibility for their own protection, she more actively engages with the culture within which the girls exist and its impact on them. She advocates for a change in the approach we take towards sex education, asking for more openness that focuses on communication and, even, pleasure. She recognizes that we have raised "a generation of girls to have a voice, expect egalitarian treatment" (236) but that has not extended to how girls' sexual subjectivity is constructed.

Conclusion

Examining how girls are constructed in a text written by an adult for an adult audience also provides us with an opportunity to examine how a girl constructs herself through her own words. Both Orenstein and Sales position the girl as other, promoting a discourse of girls as becoming (Currie et al. 2009; Eisenhauer 2004). They display an authorial distance that suggests that, as adults, they know more, or better. This is true of Sales who finishes her book by musing on her past, and saying that she wants girls to "have this experience of feeling close to someone, feeling valued and loved" (375). This ignores the ways in which millions of girls were (and are) not valued. Orenstein has her girls look to a future that Anita Harris describes as a "keenly anticipated time when girls would enjoy greater freedom and opportunities." But Harris points out that although "we are [now] in such a moment, these experiences have not been straightforward" (2004: xx). Orenstein's and Sales's texts demonstrate that Harris's anticipation and this struggle still exist, not only for them as authors but also for the girls themselves. While Orenstein and Sales (in particular) frame girls as being at risk in their objectification of self, the girls themselves recognize that risk perhaps more than the authors realize. If we look closely at the girls' words we can see that they are not ignorant of the tensions between greater opportunities and a culture that still positions them as objects—either of desire or of fragility—in need of protection. We return to Camilla as she speaks out against a dress code that suggests that she is in need of protection, but still feels the pressure to be sexy and the objectification that brings. Or perhaps we can revisit the girls who adopt the language of choice and power while presenting themselves as objects of desire on social media, presenting themselves as they "need to be who [others] want [them] to be in order to get attention and likes." They know they are presenting a self, a self that might not be "who they really are" (Sales 2016: 114). It is not that they do not engage with this debate about power in adopting and using the ways in which women are objectified. The adult voice of these two authors in these texts leaves little room for this understanding; it contributes to the construction of girls as naïve others.

Acknowledgments

I acknowledge the valuable conversations with Danielle Lehman that had an impact on the development of this article, and the insight and constructive criticism of Dr. Cheryl Stenstrom. Thanks to the reviewers for their constructive criticism and the suggestions that helped me strengthen this chapter.

MARY ANN HARLAN, a former school librarian and professor of school librarianship, is an Assistant Professor in Library and Information Science at the School of Information at San Jose State University, California. Her research interest is in the information practices of adolescents, particularly in how they experience everyday information. Her current focus combines her expertise as a school librarian, in reading and interpreting Young Adult literature, and in information experience research as she investigates how Young Adult literature constructs the girl as an information source for adolescent readers with an emphasis on the information experience of the reader.

References

American Psychological Association. 2008. *Report of the APA Task Force on the Sexualization of Girls*. Washington, DC: American Psychological Association.

Armstrong, Elizabeth A, Laura Hamilton, and Paula England. 2010. "Is Hooking Up Bad for Young Women?" *Contexts* 9 (3): 22–27. https://doi.org/10.1525/ctx.2010.9.3.22.

Arnett, Dugan. 2013. "Nightmare in Maryville: Teens' Sexual Encounter Ignites a Firestorm against a Family." *Kansas City Star*, 12 October. http://www.kansascity.com/news/special-reports/maryville/article329412/Nightmare-in-Maryville-Teens%E2%80%99-sexual-encounter-ignites-a-firestorm-against-family.html (accessed 12 June 2017).

Attwood, Feona. 2007. "Sluts and Riot Grrrls: Female Identity and Sexual Agency." *Journal of Gender Studies* 16 (3): 233–247. doi: 10.1080/09589230701562921.

Auteri, Stephanie. 2016. "When Should Kids Start Learning about Sex and Consent?" *The Atlantic*, 28 April. https://www.theatlantic.com/education/archive/2016/04/when-should-kids-start-learning-about-sex-and-consent/480264/ (accessed 10 June 2017).

Bae, Michelle S. 2011. "Interrogating Girl Power: Girlhood, Popular Media, and Postfeminism." *Visual Arts Research* 37 (2): 28–40. doi: 10.5406/visuartsrese.37.2.0028.

Baumgardner, Jennifer, and Amy Richards. 2004. "Feminism and Femininity: Or How We Learned to Stop Worrying and Love the Thong." In *All About the Girl: Culture, Power, and Identity*, ed. Anita Harris, 59–67. New York: Routledge.

Bazelon, Emily. 2015. "Have We Learned Anything from the Columbia Rape Case?" *The New York Times*, 29 May. https://nyti.ms/2jVZcu3 (accessed 10 June 2017).

Currie, Dawn H., Deirdre M. Kelly, and Shauna Pomerantz. 2009. *Girl Power: Girls Reinventing Girlhood*. New York: Peter Lang.

Driscoll, Catherine. 2002. *Girls: Feminine Adolescence in Popular Culture and Cultural Theory*. New York: Columbia University Press.

Eisenhauer, Jennifer. 2004. "Mythic Figures and Lived Identities: Locating the 'Girl' in Feminist Discourse." In *All About the Girl: Culture, Power, and Identity*, ed. Anita Harris, 79–90. New York: Routledge.

Gill, Rosalind, Giovanni Porfido, and Róisín Ryan-Flood. 2009. "Beyond the 'Sexualization of Culture' Thesis: An Intersectional Analysis of 'Sixpacks', 'Midriffs' and 'Hot Lesbians' in Advertising." *Sexualities* 12 (2): 137–160. doi: 10.1177/1363460708100916.

Griffin, Christine. 2004. "Good Girls, Bad Girls: Anglocentrism and Diversity in the Constitution of Contemporary Girlhood." In *All About the Girl: Culture, Power, and Identity*, ed. Anita Harris, 29–44. New York: Routledge.

Gross, Terry. 2016a. "Teen Girls and Social Media: A Story of 'Secret Lives' and Misogyny." *Fresh Air*. National Public Radio. Washington D.C., 29 February.

Gross, Terry. 2016b."'Girls & Sex' and the Importance of Talking to Young Women About Pleasure." *Fresh Air*. National Public Radio, 29 March.

Harris, Anita. 2004. *All About the Girl: Culture, Power, and Identity*. New York Routledge.

Holbrook, Sharon. 2016. "Parents Need to Talk to Their Daughters About the Joys of Sex, Not Just the Dangers." *Washington Post*, 29 March. https://tinyurl.com/y82pspkj (accessed 12 June 2017).

Kehily, Mary Jane. 2012. "Sexuality." In *Keywords in Youth Studies: Tracing Affects, Movements, Knowledges*, ed. Nancy Lesko and Susan Talburt, 223–227. New York: Routledge.

Koren, Marina. 2016. "Telling the Story of the Stanford Rape Case." *The Atlantic*, 6 June. https://www.theatlantic.com/news/archive/2016/06/stanford-sexual-assault-letters/485837/ (accessed 12 June 2017).

Lamb, Sharon, and Zoë D. Peterson. 2012. "Adolescent Girls' Sexual Empowerment: Two Feminists Explore the Concept." *Sex Roles* 66, (11–12): 703–712. doi: 10.1007/s11199-011-9995-3.

Lerum, Kari, and Shari L. Dworkin. 2009. "'Bad Girls Rule': An Interdisciplinary Feminist Commentary on the Report of the APA Task Force on the Sexualization of Girls." *Journal of Sex Research* 46 (4): 250–263. doi: 10.1080/00224490903079542.

Lesko, Nancy, and Susan Talburt, eds. 2012. "A History of the Present of Youth Studies." In *Keywords in Youth Studies: Tracing Affects, Movements, Knowledges*, eds. Nancy Lesko and Susan Talburt, 11–24. New York: Routledge.

Levy, Laurie. 2016. "Teaching Body Shaming to Young Girls: School Dress Codes." *Chicago Now*, 16 August. http://www.chicagonow.com/still-advocating/2016/08/teaching-body-shaming-to-young-girls-school-dress-codes/ (accessed 10 June 2017).

Lotz, Amanda D. 2007. "Theorising the Intermezzo." In *Third Wave Feminism*, ed. Stacy Gillis, Gillian Howie and Rebecca Munford, 71–85. New York: Palgrave Macmillan.

Macur, Juliet, and Nate Schweber. 2012. "Rape Case Unfolds on Web and Splits City." *The New York Times*, 16 December. https://nyti.ms/2jMlCSf (accessed 12 June 2017).

Munford, Rebecca, and Melanie Waters. 2014. *Feminism and Popular Culture: Investigating the Postfeminist Mystique*. New Brunswick, NJ: Rutgers University Press.

Needles, Allison. 2017. "Claiming it's Sexist, Puyallup High School Students Protest Dress Code." *Seattle Times*, 17 May. http://www.seattletimes.com/seattle-news/claiming-its-sexist-puyallup-high-school-students-protest-dress-code/ (accessed 12 June 2017).

North, Anna. 2016. "'American Girls,' by Nancy Jo Sales." *New York Times*, 16 March. https://nyti.ms/2kpNJaX (accessed 12 June 2017).

Orenstein, Peggy. 2016. *Girls and Sex: Navigating the Complicated New Landscape*. New York: HarperCollins.

Pearlman, Catherine. 2017. "Invitation for Principal to Take My Daughter Shopping After Dress Code Violation." *Today Parenting Team*, 16 May. https://tinyurl.com/ycq4jbg7 (accessed 12 July 2017).

Pipher, Mary. 1994. *Reviving Ophelia: Saving the Lives of Adolescent Girls*. New York: Putnam Adult.

Rape, Abuse & Incest National Network. 2016. "Children and Teens: Statistics." https://www.rainn.org/statistics/children-and-teens (accessed 12 June 2017).

Sales, Nancy Jo. 2016. *American Girls: Social Media and the Secret Lives of Teenagers*. New York: Alfred A Knopf.

Sanders, Lise Shapiro. 2004. "'Feminists Love a Utopia': Collaboration, Conflict, and the Futures of Feminism." In *Third Wave Feminism*, ed. Stacy Gillis, Gillian Howie and Rebecca Munford, 49–59. New York: Palgrave Macmillan.

Sprague, Joey. 2005 *Feminist Methodologies for Critical Researchers: Bridging Differences*. Walnut Creek, CA: Rowman & Littlefield.

Taft, Jessica K. 2004. "Girl Power Politics: Pop-Culture Barriers and Organizational Resistance." In *All About the Girl: Culture, Power, and Identity*, ed. Anita Harris, 69–78. New York: Routledge.

Tolman, Deborah L. 2002. *Dilemmas of Desire: Teenage Girls Talk about Sexuality*. Cambridge, MA: Harvard University Press.

Tolman, Deborah L. 2012. "Female Adolescents, Sexual Empowerment and Desire: A Missing Discourse of Gender Inequity." *Sex Roles* 66 (11–12): 746–757. doi: 10.1007/s11199-012-0122-x.

Tracy, Marc, and Dan Barry. 2017. "The Rise, Then Shame, of Baylor Nation." *The New York Times*, 9 March. https://www.nytimes.com/2017/03/09/sports/baylor-football-sexual-assault.html (accessed 11 July 2017).

Ward, Janie Victoria, and Beth Cooper Benjamin. 2004. "Women, Girls, and the Unfinished Work of Connection: A Critical Review of American Girls' Studies." In *All About the Girl: Culture, Power, and Identity*, ed. Anita Harris, 15–28. New York: Routledge.

Weissbound, Richard, Trisha Ross Anderson, Alison Cashin, and Joe McIntyre. 2017. "The Talk: How Adults Can Promote Young People's Healthy Relationships and Prevent Misogyny and Sexual Harassment." *Making Caring Common Project*. Report to the Harvard Graduate School of Education, Cambridge, MA.

Wiseman, Rosalind. 2002. *Queen Bees & Wannabes: Helping Your Daughter Survive Cliques, Gossip, Boyfriends, and the New Realities of Girl World*. New York: Three Rivers Press.

Woo, Yen Yen. 2012. "Age." In *Keywords in Youth Studies: Tracing Affects, Movements, Knowledges*, ed. Nancy Lesko and Susan Talburt, 111–115. New York: Routledge.

Filmography

Waters, Mark. 2004. *Mean Girls*. USA.

Chapter 5

Perfect Love in a Better World
Same-Sex Attraction between Girls

Wendy L. Rouse

Margaret (Peggy) Spalding, the 17-year-old daughter of a Boston merchant, was one of the most popular girls[1] at Newton High School. As a cheer leader, class treasurer, and a member of the photograph and reception committee she was well-known for her enthusiastic personality and celebrated for her athletic abilities in dancing, basketball, and hockey. Spalding typically spent her summer vacations at Camp Quanset, a camp for girls on Cape Cod. The camp offered opportunities to enjoy the outdoors through swimming, canoeing, sailing, tennis, horseback riding, volleyball, and golf. Although Spalding had attended camp for several years, the summer of 1916 was different; she fell in love with Ethel Stanton.

Stanton was three years older than Spalding and much more reserved. Her family and friends described her as a generous, happy, and beautiful girl. She grew up in Los Angeles, later moving east to attend school. Perhaps inspired by a restless spirit, she had traveled the country extensively, visiting friends and studying at various universities. Stanton's travels eventually led her to Camp Quanset where she met Spalding. By the end of summer, the two girls had clearly developed a crush on each other.

Notes for this section can be found on page 91.

Spalding and Stanton's crush, however, was developing in a historical moment when perceptions of relationships between girls were shifting. In the nineteenth century same-sex crushes were seen as a normal and natural part of a girl's life. Since Victorians generally believed that females were passionless and devoid of sexual desire, same-sex crushes were considered mostly harmless. By the early twentieth century, however, views of female sexuality began to change as sexologists confirmed the existence of the female sex-drive and concluded that homosexuality was a naturally-occurring condition (Ellis 1901; Krafft-Ebing 1886). These sexologists' texts moved the discussion to a medical model that focused on diagnosing, preventing, and treating homosexuality as an illness. The conversation about romantic friendships began to shift as parents, teachers, and administrators worried about the sexual undertones of female relationships.

Previous scholars (Chauncey 1983; Faderman 1981; Rupp 1999; 2009) have noted the predominance of crushes and romantic friendships among girls in the nineteenth century and the decline of these relationships in the wake of the findings of sexologists in the early twentieth century. However, few have considered how the larger cultural paradigm shift that cast female relationships under intense scrutiny had life-changing implications for girls. The story of Spalding and Stanton illustrates the effects of changing scientific and cultural attitudes on young women who were coming of age during this shift. Girls who remained committed to their same-sex crush, as girls of previous eras had freely chosen to do, now faced intense pressure to conform to heterosexual norms. Spalding and Stanton's story, and others like it, would serve as moral lessons about the dangers of female love for successive generations of girls.

Two Lives Intersect

Perhaps it was their similar life experiences that first drew Spalding and Stanton together. Spalding was the daughter of Florence Atherton Faxon, a writer of music, and George Frederick Spalding, a Boston merchant. Stanton had a similar middle-class upbringing in Southern California as the daughter of Christobel M. Jones and Joseph L. Stanton, a passenger agent for a railroad company. Stanton's parents divorced and her mother then married Thomas Albert Snider, the founder of the Snider Preserve Company. After her mother and step-father died in a car accident, Stanton inherited a fortune that ensured her financial independence for life.

Shortly after meeting and falling in love with Spalding in the summer of 1916 at Camp Quanset, Stanton decided to enroll at the Garland School of Homemaking in Boston where Spalding was beginning the fall semester as a teacher-pupil in the physical culture department. Their emotional connection only deepened as they experienced the independence of college life.

Crushes

In the nineteenth century, same-sex crushes were recognized as a common part of school culture. A younger girl typically developed a crush on an older girl and would express her admiration with gifts, flowers, candy, poetry, and adoration. The older student could choose to reciprocate by inviting the younger student to luncheons, spreads, or sporting events. All-female dances further normalized romantic friendships on college campuses. Hugging, kissing, and cuddling were not uncommon between crushes. These relationships were a means of assimilating young women into the college culture. The relationship was generally viewed as mutually beneficial in helping girls to develop into more compassionate women (Faderman 1991; Inness 1995; Newman 2012; Smith-Rosenberg 1975).

The dominant perception of girls' sexuality was based on the belief that females felt little sexual desire. Intense emotional relationships between girls were therefore seen as innocent. School officials rarely interfered with schoolgirl crushes. Many female faculty had had similar relationships in their youth and some had even continued these relationships into their adult life forming what were known as Boston marriages in which college educated and professional women formed same-sex households. Influenced partly by economic necessity and a desire to pursue a professional career, many women formed committed and loving relationships with a life-long partner. Contemporaries assumed that these relationships were devoid of any sexual component and therefore viewed Boston marriages as acceptable forms of female friendship (Chauncey 1982–1983; Faderman 1981; Inness 1995, 1997; Newman 2012; Rupp 1999; Smith-Rosenberg 1975).

However, by the early twentieth century schoolgirl crushes and Boston marriages were increasingly scrutinized after sexologists revealed the existence of female sexual desire and the alleged causes of homosexuality. Richard von Krafft-Ebing, a Viennese psychiatrist, writing in the 1880s, defined same-sex desire as a symptom of sexual inversion, an inherited, congenital disease that he described as including a variety of sexual and non-sexual behaviors reflecting a complete inversion of gender norms. Through the book *Psychopathia Sexualis* (1886), Krafft-Ebing sought to document the range of human sexuality with extensive case studies. He concluded that homosexuality was a product of degeneration—a sort of physical, moral, and mental evolutionary deterioration resulting from widespread sexual immorality. Yet, Krafft-Ebing's initial rather negative view of inversion shifted over his lifetime to a more sympathetic portrayal of homosexuals as victims of nature. Identifying inversion as a condition existing prior to birth suggested that inverts did not have a choice over their behavior. Krafft-Ebing eventually concluded that homosexuality should not be viewed as criminal behavior requiring punishment but as a disease requiring treatment. Still, he defined homosexuality in opposition to heterosexuality in terms of normal versus abnormal. Krafft-Ebing also continued to espouse the Victorian notion that so-called normal women generally had less sexual desire than men and that therefore only inverted or sexually deviant women demonstrated sexual desire akin to men. In popular thought then, the female homosexual identified by Krafft-Ebing posed a new type of sexualized danger by preying on normal women. (Chauncey 1982; Faderman 1981; Oosterhuis 2000)

Havelock Ellis, a British sexologist, expanded on the ideas of Krafft-Ebing in both defining sexual inverts as abnormal and in recommending some degree of tolerance. Ellis's marriage to Edith Lees, who was a lesbian, may have motivated his desire to understand the range of human sexuality and perhaps to remove the stigma surrounding homosexuality. Ellis collected case studies of sexual inverts and published his findings in his 1897 book, *Sexual Inversion*. Significantly, Ellis published first-hand accounts from female homosexuals. Like Krafft-Ebing, Ellis believed that sexual inversion was a congenital abnormality. However, Ellis recognized a distinction in female inversion between what he defined as (typically more masculine) congenital inverts and those (typically more feminine) individuals with a predisposition to inversion whom he believed could be seduced by congenital inverts. Ellis therefore warned of the dangers of environments, such as all-female boarding schools, that allowed opportunities for same-sex relationships to flourish. In the 1901 version of this book Ellis explicitly linked school-girl crushes to homosexuality and argued that they were problematic since all crushes contained a sexual element even if there was no overt sexual activity. Historian Sherrie Inness noted that this was a dramatic shift from the nineteenth century view "that no crush has an erotic element to Ellis's understanding that all crushes contain a sexual component" (1995: 50).

In the early twentieth century, Sigmund Freud (1910) proposed a theory that homosexuality stemmed from a failure to resolve psychosexual issues in childhood, thus resulting in a sort of arrested development in adolescent years. Freud challenged the theory that homosexuality is congenital, arguing that it was more of a product of environment. Freud's research further cast suspicion on female crushes as evidence of lesbianism and emphasized the dangers of all-female environments in fostering homosexuality.

Despite their explicit intention of studying the range of human sexuality and demystifying the causes of homosexuality partly in an effort to dissociate it from its criminal or immoral taint, the sexologists had succeeded in implicitly associating same-sex love with disease and psychological abnormality. As this information filtered out to the public, people began to worry about the implications of the sexologists' findings. So called congenital inverts were portrayed sympathetically to some extent but they were also viewed suspiciously, giving rise to a fear of what came to be called the lesbian menace.[2] Romantic friendships between girls came under more scrutiny with revelations about the dangers of unrestrained female sexual desire and fears that homosexuals could seduce normally heterosexual girls in single-sex educational institutions. School administrators could no longer view same-sex crushes as normal or innocent (Inness 1997; Wilk 2004).

The textual discourse about same-sex love was changing. School officials began to actively discourage romantic friendships among students through lectures on hygiene and health, editorials in student newspapers, and shifts in school policies. Perhaps motivated by feelings of defensiveness, some female faculty sought to distinguish their own Boston marriages from those of so called real lesbians described as pathologically disordered in the sexologists' writings. They distanced themselves from the definition of homosexual even as they remained committed to their own female partners. This defensiveness helped shape their responses to crushes among students (Faderman 1981; Rupp 1999).

School policies were also influenced by increasing pressure from concerned parents. Popular magazines and newspapers disseminated the sexologists' theories and alerted parents to the possible dangers of certain types of romantic friendships. In 1898, Ruth Ashmore in the *Ladies Home Journal* condemned "overly romantic relationships" between girls insisting that there "is something wrong" with a girl who wants to spend her life with her "chum." Ashmore's writing also reflected popular fears that girl's education fostered a sense of independence that resulted in an unsexing or masculinization of girls and a growing antipathy for the male sex: "the ecstatic girl lover is invariably bitter against man. She regards him as her natural enemy" (20). The article's central premise was that romantic relationships distracted girls from pursuing heterosexual relationships.

The potentially devastating long-term effects of same-sex relationships became a common theme in advice columns and articles. In "Your Daughter: What Are Her Friendships?" a writer for *Harper's Bazaar* warned that a girl's crush on another girl should be taken very seriously since it had the potential to "mar if not ruin her whole future career, both physically and morally." The author placed responsibility on parents who neglected the development of their daughters and warned diligent parents to beware of the "mutual crush" where two girls tend to become obsessed with each other neglecting other friendships. The author warned that "a 'crush' of this kind frequently prevents a girl from marrying" (1913:16).

David Irving Steinhardt went even further by openly discussing the potential sexual aspects of female relationships. In *Ten Sex Talks to Girls*, Steinhardt focused on the sexual threat of romantic friendships, explicitly warning about the dangers of sharing a bed or cuddling with another girl: "Avoid the touching of sexual parts, including the breasts ... and let your conversation be of other topics than sexuality" (1914: 60). In Steinhardt's description, certain girls were portrayed as predatory sexual aggressors. This was a clear repudiation of earlier depictions of female sexuality that denied that females were even capable of sexual feelings; this new depiction was laden with fears about the need to contain female sexuality.

These fears regarding women's and girls' sexuality were not entirely unfounded, either. Later studies confirmed that sexual relationships between college girls were quite common during this era. As Sarah Stage (2013) reminds us, a study of female sexuality published in 1929 generated a scientific scandal by revealing the extent of sexual activity and especially homosexuality among so called good girls of the middle and upper classes. Katharine Bement Davis was a graduate of Vassar College who later earned a Ph.D. in political economy from the University of Chicago. Davis, as director of the Bureau of Social Hygiene, conducted a scientific study of female sexual behavior. She surveyed educated, middle-class women, asking frank questions about their sexuality in both their youth and in their adult life. Many of the 2,200 individuals surveyed had attended school during the same time period as Spalding and Stanton. Davis's findings revealed that girls had very active sexual desires and had engaged in extensive sexual activity. Davis's report (1929) also scandalously revealed that over 50 percent of the respondents reported having had intense emotional relations with other females in either their youth or adult life and in 26 percent of these cases the feelings were accompanied by sexual activity. Davis's research also shattered the idea that same-sex institutions alone were culpable in fostering an environment that led to homosexuality in girls since many of the respondents had attended coeducational institutions. Davis's conclusion that over 43.5 percent of the respondents had intense emotional relations with girls before college challenged the notion that universities were to blame for fostering homosexual thoughts and behavior.

The women interviewed in Davis's study revealed candid details about their relationships with girls in their youth. One interviewee explained that sexual relationships among girls were more common than people were willing to admit. Sharing her own experiences of multiple sexual encounters with girls in college, she explained that these practices frequently occurred among what she called nice girls from cultured homes. This woman expressed her opinion that there was nothing inherently wrong with homosexual acts per se. Her main concern was when physical attachments moved beyond merely sexual encounters into deeper emotional connections. Some sexologists agreed. Dr. Bernard Talmey succinctly expressed this view in 1908, arguing that the distinction was one of perversity versus perversion. Engaging in a homosexual act (a perversity) did not necessarily mean that an individual was or would become a homosexual (the perversion). Like previous sexologists, Talmey thus made a distinction between congenital homosexuality and acquired homosexuality. The dangers of schools as breeding grounds for homosexual activities therefore seemed obvious. The concern was less about isolated sexual acts and more about a pattern of behavior that might become permanent and a fear that girls might choose to commit their lives to each other and reject heterosexual marriage.

Devoted Companions

Classmates described Spalding and Stanton as inseparable, frequently walking arm-in-arm. Henrietta Case explained, "Their attachment for each other was so sudden and fervid that it caused much comment among the girls" (*Cincinnati Enquirer* 1917). Other classmates described them simply as devoted companions. Stanton was rooming at 48 West Cedar Street at the Garland School. Although Spalding lived with her parents, she often spent nights staying with Stanton. They clearly loved each other deeply and publicly expressed their desire to spend their future lives together.

Spalding and Stanton's social standing provided them with benefits available only to individuals of their class. However, their membership in this elite group also confined them to a strict set of social expectations that rigidly dictated the future course of their lives. This was especially true for Spalding who remained financially dependent on her parents. The expectations for Spalding's future were evident in the decision to attend the Garland School for Homemaking, a college for young women over eighteen. The school emphasized the central role of the homemaker in keeping the house and nurturing the family. Students took courses in household management, food, clothing, furnishing, and the family. Even traditionally academic subjects such as science, economics, and literature were focused on practical implications for the housewife. The mission of the school was to groom young women for their future roles as wives and mothers.

Fearing that their daughter's relationship with Stanton threatened her future, Spalding's parents began to object fervently to the girls' friendship. Publicly they expressed concern that Stanton's wealth and extravagant traits were a bad influence on Spalding and that the two girls were spending too much time together, thus excluding other friends. Spalding's parents were likely very aware of the warnings about dangerous types of relationships between girls; they must surely have feared that the relationship would prove a moral detriment or prevent their daughter from pursuing what they would have thought of as normal relationships with men.

Suddenly in early March 1917, Stanton transferred out of Garland, enrolling in Dana Hall at Wellesley. Administrators at Garland publicly stated that they had noticed nothing out of the ordinary in the relationship between Spalding and Stanton. Their private thoughts may have been different but these were not recorded. School officials said that Stanton had come to them "nervous and somewhat excited" seeking advice. Stanton suffered some "lung trouble" (*Cincinnati Enquirer* 1917) and they suggested fresh air to improve her health. Perhaps also succumbing to pressure from Spalding's parents, school administrators decided to recommend that Stanton transfer to Dana Hall. They immediately arranged lodging for Stanton in a private home in Wellesley. But the transfer out of Garland was clearly not entirely Stanton's choice.

Classmates at Dana Hall confirmed the story that Stanton came to Wellesley to be in the "country for better air." But they also noted that Stanton "was given to fits of melancholy that seemed to disappear only when she was in the company of Peggy Spalding." Against the wishes of her parents, Spalding frequently snuck away from Garland to see Stanton. When they parted, as students at Dana Hall noted, the two girls could barely handle the separation. They frequently overheard Stanton engaged in intense phone conversations pleading with Spalding to visit her. At one point, classmates heard Stanton begging Spalding to meet her: "I shall die if you don't come to me at once" (*Cincinnati Enquirer* 1917). The students at Dana Hall gossiped about the intense devotion between the two girls and this information spread to Spalding's parents.

The Reaction of Outsiders

Societal rejection of same-sex relationships and the responses of family, friends, educators, and doctors dramatically influence an individual's sense of identity and self-worth. Davis concluded in her 1920s study that public attitudes against homosexuality led some girls to feel abnormal or ashamed of their same-sex relationships. One interviewee described the intensity of affection and sexual attraction between her and her female partner. Yet, they were also ashamed of their feelings and tried, often unsuccessfully, to suppress their sexual expressions seeking to "overcome it ... without losing a sincere and genuine love for each other" (1929: 285). By projecting an image of respectability, rejecting their sexual desires, and embracing their love for each other they sought to distance themselves from the deviant label of homosexual and distinguish themselves from the mannish women whom they perceived as real lesbians (Rupp 1999).

Another woman who had engaged in same-sex relationships in college and who had by the mid-1920s adopted the increasingly common notion that such desires were not normal, looked back with regret. She warned that girls must "know that this thing exists and should guard against its faintest expression." She explained, "In my own case the strength of my love [for a woman] swept me off my feet, but I never believed that it was right or decent." The biggest negative impact she noted was her delaying marriage by tying herself emotionally to a woman whom she could never marry. She later married a man, conforming to societal expectations of "right and decent" (Davis 1929: 324)

However, not every woman abandoned her same-sex partner or viewed her relationship with shame. Some people embraced the new label of homosexual or regarded homosexual behaviors as harmless or even natural. Just as negative perceptions from outsiders could lead to negative feelings of self-worth, support from outsiders could lead to a positive sense of self and affirmation of one's homosexual identity. One anonymous woman interviewed by Davis explained how societal responses to her sexual preference affected her emotionally. She had had a variety of sexual and non-sexual relationships with females until the age of 25 when she began to have anxiety that her feelings were "out of the ordinary." She consulted a female physician who explained that it was all "quite natural with some people." This advice was comforting and allowed her to resume her life free from anxiety. Ten years later, she was in a happy committed relationship with a woman. She described it as a love that had made her "life inexpressibly richer and deeper" (1929: 283).

Unfortunately, Spalding and Stanton experienced little support for their relationship. Spalding's parents put increasing pressure on her to abandon the friendship. Echoing warnings heralded in the texts of popular magazines, they told her that Stanton was a bad influence and was monopolizing her time. The pressure to break off the friendship escalated even further when Spalding's older brother called Stanton on several occasions warning her to stay away from his sister. According to the *Cincinnati Enquirer* (1917), he told Stanton that the family did not want her to associate with his sister. Finally, Spalding's father ordered her to break off the friendship permanently and forbade her from seeing Stanton ever again.

A Portsmouth Cafe

These efforts to break apart the relationship drove the two girls to desperation. On 21 March 1917, Spalding and Stanton took a train to Portsmouth, New Hampshire, and checked into the Rockingham Hotel. The next evening they dined a block away from the hotel. Around 10:50 pm, two simultaneous shots rang out in the crowded cafe. A brief moment of chilling silence was quickly followed by frenzied chaos as people rushed to the booth. They discovered the bodies of the two young women, each with a self-inflicted bullet wound in her temple.

A note revealed the motive for their suicide: "We have experienced perfect love for each other and cannot bear the thought of separation. So we will end it all." They asked their parents to forgive them and not to be grief-stricken since "they would all be happy and peaceful when reunited in a better world." Their last request was that they be laid in the same grave, buried together as they would have chosen to live. An unfinished love poem composed by Spalding lay nearby. The family never revealed the full text of the poem (*Cincinnati Enquirer* 1917; *Oakland Tribune* 1917; *Portsmouth Herald* 1917).

The press immediately went on a search for answers. They attempted to explain Stanton's behavior by suggesting that she was not mentally well, describing her as "thin, somewhat anemic, evidently on the verge of nervous decline" (*Oakland Tribune* 1917) and having a "delicate constitution" (*New York Times* 1917). However, Stanton's close friends expressed shock at the suicide and repeatedly told the press that there was never any indication of any kind of mental illness. Judge Charles F. Malsbary, Stanton's attorney and friend, also told reporters that he never saw any sign of serious mental problems in Stanton. He said that the girl had suffered from some lung trouble but that she was overall happy and had no reason as far as he knew to kill herself. In other newspaper reports, Malsbary is reported to have concluded that Stanton's frail physical health was the most likely cause of her suicide (*Boston Herald* 1917).

Stanton's father confirmed that Ethel had struggled with health issues as a result of an earlier attack of typhoid fever (*Los Angeles Times*, p. 3). He explained that his daughter had a positive outlook on life and was rarely troubled: "She was not the type to take life seriously … she was of a happy disposition, studious, although not of robust health" (*Boston Globe* 1917: 14). Responding to pressure from the press to identify a cause for the suicide, he suggested that perhaps his normally happy daughter had fallen victim to a "temporary mental aberration brought on by over-study" (*Cincinnati Enquirer* 1917: 8). This statement echoed the sentiments of critics who decades earlier had opposed girls' education on the grounds that it was too taxing on girls. Education was often associated with a wide variety of conditions that were said to afflict females, including anxiety, depression, feminism, and lesbianism (Clarke 1884; Gordon 1987; Sahli 1979).

While Stanton's suicide was attributed to physical sickness, mental illness or over-study, there appeared to be no logical explanation for Spalding's. She was described as a young, healthy girl with a strong sense of independence. Sexologists tended to associate athleticism with lesbianism. Female congenital inverts were frequently described as mannish, displaying a preference for rough sports, male clothing, or masculine mannerisms. References to Spalding's athletic abilities in contemporary texts may have been an attempt to identify her as mannish. However, Spalding's family and friends countered those implications by emphasizing her striking feminine beauty and social grace. The *Boston Evening Globe* reported that Spalding "had innumerable friends, both boys and girls, and has always been very prominent in the younger social life of this city" (*Boston Evening Globe* 1917: 4). Whereas sexologists had defined the homosexual female as inherently unhappy, Spalding's closest friends described her as a joyful, socially well-adjusted girl.

Although they never explicitly said so, reporters clearly suspected that the relationship had sexual undertones. In response to apparent inquiries about Stanton's sexuality Malsbury commented, "I never knew her to consider the attentions of young men seriously" (*Cincinnati Enquirer* 1917). A reporter posed a similar question alluding to Stanton's sexuality to her father who said, "As far as I know she never had a love affair with any man." Perhaps out of fear that this would be taken as evidence that Stanton was a man-hater, he defensively added, "Although she seemed to enjoy men's company" (*Cincinnati Enquirer* 1917).

Unable to firmly categorize Spalding or Stanton as insane, masculinized, or man-hating sexual inverts, the press seemed at a loss to explain the double suicide. A reporter ultimately concluded that the motive was "family interference in the progress of the 'affair'" (*Cincinnati Enquirer* 1917). Their love for each other and the demand from Spalding's family that they stop seeing each other was too much for the young couple to handle. The Portsmouth Police officially concluded that the "fear that perhaps the family would finally succeed in separating them" compelled their suicides (*Boston Post* 1917). In the end, their love was labeled as aberrant and relegated to the margins of normality by the press who described it as "mystic" and "strange." One writer insisted that the "infatuation was strong as it was weird" dismissing it as "one of these strange and consuming attractions found weirdly scattered through the love history of the world" (*Oakland Tribune* 1917). Their dying wish to be together in death was ignored. Spalding was interred in Massachusetts and Stanton laid to rest in California.

A Better World

Intense societal pressure drove Spalding and Stanton to desperation. Their relationship was condemned not only by Spalding's family and school officials but by the larger community that labeled female romantic friendships abnormal. A schoolgirl crush that a few years earlier would have been seen as harmless was now deemed dangerous. Whereas in a previous generation women who chose to commit their lives to each other could form a Boston marriage without any suggestion that their relationship was abnormal, by 1917 the notion that Spalding and Stanton might choose to spend the rest of their lives together was viewed as deviant. Their story reflected fears of unrestrained female desires, of the extremes of sentimentality, and of female aspirations left unchecked. Despite all the advantages that education and financial independence afforded them, the two girls found themselves confined by the expectations imposed on young women of their social class. They felt trapped with only one choice—to abandon each other and conform to rigid heterosexual standards of acceptable female relationships.

To future generations of girls, Spalding and Stanton's suicide, along with other similarly ill-fated female relationships, served as a warning about the dangers of same-sex desire. One of the anonymous college graduates who responded to Davis's sex questionnaire in the 1920s admitted that she had a number of sexual relationships with other girls. Ultimately, however, she concluded that heterosexual marriage was the only "sane" option. She alluded to the case of Spalding and Stanton as proof, saying, "The girl I adored is still unmarried and still has her train of women adorers. Sometime one of them will blow out her own brains with a revolver, as two girls I know of did, for hopeless love of each other … I 'thought through' my experience to a sane conclusion; but not all women can" (Davis 1929: 322). Thus, Spalding and Stanton's sad story became an enduring moral lesson for this woman and countless others of her generation and beyond. Girls who loved girls were warned that their only logical option was to acquiesce to heterosexual marriage or fall victim to their own passions.

Spalding and Stanton's tragic story, and others like it, were dramatized in the press. In literature and film, the lives of real human beings were converted into characters and then into caricatures. A new trope of the unhappy suicidal lesbian entered the mainstream from the 1920s onward (Inness 1997). In Radclyffe Hall's *The Well of Loneliness* (1928) Jamie kills herself after her lover, Barbara, dies. In Mary Lapsley's *Parable of the Virgins* (1931) Mary Nugeon commits suicide after the school physician chastises her as an "immoral influence" and her girl lover abandons her. In Lillian Hellman's play, *The Children's Hour* (1934), Martha Dobie and Karen Wright, two teachers in a girls' boarding school are accused of lesbianism. Martha shamefully acknowledges that she does indeed have feelings for Karen and ends her humiliation by shooting herself in the head. The obscenity laws and censorship rules that regulated the content of literature and film (such as the 1930–1968 Motion Picture Production Code) mandated either the complete invisibility of same-sex relationships or the unsympathetic portrayal of suspected homosexuals and a condemnation of homosexual behaviors. This often resulted in stories that ended in the conversion, punishment, murder, or suicide of a homosexual character. The suicidal lesbian thus became a well-known fictional character in popular culture and has endured to the present day (Beirne 2012; Russo 1987).

Although Spalding and Stanton lived in a different era, the challenges they faced in loving each other are similar to issues faced by girls who love girls today. Their story reverberates through time, revealing the crippling impact of social pressure and the danger of stigmatizing homosexual relationships in both the past and present. Recent studies reveal that LGBTQ youth are at a higher risk for suicide. Rejection from family plays a significant role in those suicides (Centers for Disease Control and Prevention 2016; Ryan et al. 2009). In preventing the suicide of LGBTQ youth, family acceptance, supportive peer groups and school environments, and access to medical and mental health professionals are crucial. Positive representations of successful LGBTQ people and relationships in popular culture are also essential. In their 2017 report GLAAD (formerly the Gay and Lesbian Alliance Against Defamation) called for an end to the decades-long trend in television of killing off lesbian and bisexual characters insisting that these "harmful tropes" essentially "exploit an already marginalized community"(6). Scholars have noted that although we must acknowledge the reality of lesbian suicide among girls and continue to work to counteract it, the fictional suicidal lesbian character is especially dangerous in that it perpetuates a view of LGBTQ youth as abnormal in comparison to heterosexual youth. The stereotype, in ignoring the diversity of experience, casts LGBTQ youth as victims and denies them a sense of agency (Bryan and Mayock 2017).

So much has changed since Spalding and Stanton's suicides in 1917. The LGBTQ movement has achieved significant gains in the past century. Protests, marches, and legal challenges have expanded the visibility and political equality of LGBTQ people. Queer youth have access to a stronger social support network. Although there is still much work to do in moving toward full equality for LGBTQ people, the majority of Americans today support homosexual relationships and girls who fall in love may choose to spend their lives together and legally marry. Peggy Spalding and Ethel Stanton did not have that choice. Since they could not live together, they chose to die together. They hoped instead to meet again in a "better world" (*Oakland Tribune* 1917). We can continue to work together to build the better world that they were seeking.

WENDY L. ROUSE is an Associate Professor of history at San Jose State University, California, where she teaches courses in history and teacher preparation. Her research focuses on the history of women and children in the Progressive Era. Her first book, *The Children of Chinatown: Growing up Chinese American in San Francisco, 1850-1920* (2009) examines the experiences of Chinese American children facing segregation in Exclusion Era California and the most recent, *Her Own Hero: The Origins of the Women's Self-Defense Movement* (2017), traces the history of women studying self-defense for personal and political empowerment in the early twentieth century.

Notes

1. Although we would call her a young woman, an unmarried female was then described and regarded as being a girl.
2. Sherrie Inness used this phrase in the title of her 1997 book, *The Lesbian Menace: Ideology, Identity, and the Representation of Lesbian Life*.

References

Ashmore, Ruth. 1898. "The Intense Friendships of Girls." *The Ladies' Home Journal* 15 (8): 20.
Beirne, Rebecca. 2012. "Teen Lesbian Desires and Identities in International Cinema: 1931–2007." *Journal of Lesbian Studies* 16 (3): 258–272.
Boston Evening Globe. 1917. "Two Girls Preferred Death to Separation." 23 March.
Boston Globe. 1917. "Suicides Would Not Be Parted." 24 March.
Boston Herald. 1917. "Suicides Died Rather Than Be Parted." 24 March.
Boston Post. 1917. "Death Pact to Prevent Separation." 24 March.
Bryan, Audrey, and Paula Mayock. 2017. "Supporting LGBT Lives? Complicating the Suicide Consensus in LGBT Mental Health Research." *Sexualities* 20 (1–2): 65–85.
Centers for Disease Control and Prevention. U.S. Department of Health and Human Services. 2016. *Sexual Identity, Sex of Sexual Contacts, and Health-Related Behaviors Among Students in Grades 9–12: United States and Selected Sites. Morbidity and Mortality Weekly Report* 65 (9). https://www.cdc.gov/mmwr/volumes/65/ss/pdfs/ss6509.pdf (accessed 15 May 2017).
Chauncey, George. 1982. "From Sexual Inversion to Homosexuality: Medicine and the Changing Conceptualization of Female Deviance." *Salmagundi* 58–59: 114–146.

Cincinnati Enquirer. 1917. "Girls Die in Suicide Pact." 23 March.
Cincinnati Enquirer. 1917. "Flame of Perfect Love." 24 March.
Cincinnati Enquirer. 1917. "Solicitude." 25 March.
Clarke, Edward C. 1884. *Sex in Education or a Fair Chance for Girls.* Boston: Houghton, Mifflin.
Davis, Katharine Bement. 1929. *Factors in the Sex Life of Twenty-Two Hundred Women.* New York: Harper & Brothers.
Ellis, Havelock. 1901. *Studies in the Psychology of Sex: Sexual Inversion.* Philadelphia: F. A. Davis Company, Publishers.
Faderman, Lillian. 1981. *Surpassing the Love of Men: Romantic Friendship and Love Between Women from the Renaissance to the Present.* New York: William Morrow.
Faderman, Lillian. 1991. *Odd Girls and Twilight Lovers: A History of Lesbian Life in Twentieth-Century America.* New York: Columbia University Press.
Freud, Sigmund. 1910. *Three Contributions to the Sexual Theory.* Trans. A. A. Brill. New York: The Journal of Nervous and Mental Diseases Publishing Company.
GLAAD. "Where We Are on TV, '16–'17: GLAAD's Annual Report on LGBTQ Inclusion."
Gordon, Lynn D. 1987. "The Gibson Girl Goes to College: Popular Culture and Women's Higher Education in the Progressive Era, 1890–1920." *American Quarterly* 39 (2): 211–230.
Hall, Radclyffe. 1928. *The Well of Loneliness.* Garden City, NY: Sun Dial Press.
Harper's Bazaar. 1913. "Your Daughter: What Are Her Friendships?" 47 (10): 16.
Hellman, Lillian. 1934. *The Children's Hour.* New York: Alfred A. Knopf.
Inness, Sherrie A. 1995. *Intimate Communities: Representation and Social Transformation in Women's College Fiction, 1895–1910.* Bowling Green, OH: Bowling Green State University Popular Press.
Inness, Sherrie A. 1997. *The Lesbian Menace: Ideology, Identity, and the Representation of Lesbian Life.* Amherst: University of Massachusetts Press.
von Krafft-Ebing, Richard. 1906. *Psychopathia Sexualis.* Trans. 12th German Edition F. J. Rebman. New York: Rebman Company.
Lapsley, Mary. 1931. *Parable of the Virgins.* New York: R. R. Smith.
Los Angeles Times. 1917. "Love Given as Death Motive." 24 March.
New York Times. 1917. "Fear of Separation Impelled Suicides." 24 March.
Newman, Sally. 2012. "'The Freshman Malady': Rethinking the Ontology of the 'Crush.'" *Rethinking History* 16 (2): 279–301.
Oakland Tribune. 1917. "Mystic Love is Ended by Death Pact." 23 March.
Oosterhuis, Harry. 2000. *Stepchildren of Nature: Krafft-Ebing, Psychiatry and the Making of Sexual Identity.* University of Chicago Press.
Portsmouth Herald. 1917. "School Girl Love Ends in Suicide." 23 March.

Rupp, Leila J. 1999. *A Desired Past: A Short History of Same-Sex Love in America*. Chicago: University of Chicago Press.

Rupp, Leila J. 2009. *Sapphistries: A Global History of Love between Women*. New York: New York University Press.

Russo, Vito. 1987. *The Celluloid Closet: Homosexuality in Movies*. New York: Harper & Row, Publishers.

Ryan, Caitlin, David Huebner, Rafael M. Diaz, and Jorge Sanchez. 2009. "Family Rejection as a Predictor of Negative Health Outcomes in White and Latino Lesbian, Gay, and Bisexual Young Adults." *Pediatrics* 123 (1): 346–352.

Sahli, Nancy. 1979. "Smashing: Women's Relationships before the Fall." *Chrysalis* 8: 17–27.

Smith-Rosenberg, Carroll. 1975. "The Female World of Love and Ritual: Relationships Between Women in Nineteenth-Century America." *Signs* 1 (1): 1–29.

Stage, Sarah. 2013. "What 'Good Girls' Do: Katharine Bement Davis and the Moral Panic of the First U.S. Sexual Survey." In *The Moral Panics of Sexuality*, eds., Breanne Fahs, Mary L. Dudy and Sarah Stage, 151–163. Palgrave Macmillan.

Steinhardt, Irving David. 1914. *Ten Sex Talks to Girls*. Philadelphia: J. B. Lippincott Company.

Talmey, Bernard S. 1908. *Woman: A Treatise on the Normal and Pathological Emotions of Feminine Love*. New York: Practitioners' Publishing Company, Inc.

Wilk, Rona M. 2004. "What's a Crush? A Study of Crushes and Romantic Friendships at Barnard College, 1900-1920." *OAH Magazine of History* 18 (4): 20–22.

Chapter 6

Narrating Muslim Girlhood in the Pakistani Cityscape of Graphic Narratives

Tehmina Pirzada

In the United States, representations of Muslim girlhood[1] in comics such as Dust in *X-Men Comics* (1963–2014) and Kamala Khan in the *Ms. Marvel* (2014) series have offered Muslim girlhood much needed visibility. However, the representations of Muslimness and femininity in comics is sporadic and somewhat limited in nature. Dust, created in the post 9/11 era is a burka-clad Afghan girl who willfully dons the burka and uses her super powers to destroy her enemies. However, Dust still exists within a Western rescue narrative in which a white mutant, Wolverine, saves her (Dar 2008). In contrast to Dust, Kamala Khan is a fashionable 16-year-old Pakistani-American girl who combats crime, racism, and Islamophobia in Jersey City, New Jersey. Deploying her liminal position as a young Muslim girl, Khan defies both the patriarchal status quo of her own community and the hegemonic power of white masculinity (Khoja-Moolji and Niccolini 2015). However, the portrayal of Muslim girlhood in comics is not restricted to the United States, nor is it the sole creation of Marvel and DC comics. Graphic narratives like *Gogi* (1970–present) by Nigar Nazar and *Burka Avenger* (2013–present) by

---

Notes for this section can be found on page 108.

Haroon Rashid serve as an interesting counterpoint to the Western big budget productions. In my discussion of *Gogi*, I analyze the newly hosted website *Gogi by Nigar Nazar* as well as the book *Going Gogi* published in 2009. The *Gogi* narratives are fascinating because, unlike Western graphic novels, they do not exist in a cohesive volume. Instead, *Gogi* appears in several different media such as newspapers, printed books, television, and online resources to reach its desired audiences. In contrast to *Gogi*, *Burka Avenger* is an animated television show, of which many episodes are also available online at no charge. It is currently in its third season on the TV channel, Geo Taiz, but in this chapter, I will focus only on the first season.

I argue that *Gogi* and *Burka Avenger* are significant because they employ the format of what could be loosely termed a cartoon to portray Muslim girlhood,[2] while simultaneously drawing attention to the medium of the cartoon itself. Reviled by conservative Muslims for its perceived use as caricature but considered a form of liberal expression in the West, the cartoon signifies a polarized sociopolitical reality.[3] However, *Gogi* and *Burka Avenger* deviate from the binary us-versus-them way of thinking by transforming the cartoon into a graphic narrative that engages in a complex discussion of gender, adolescence, religion, and urban reality. Pramod K. Nayar considers graphic narrative as a "descriptor and label that references the visual 'graphic' composition of the medium and the crafting of the story or 'narrative'" (2016: 5).

In my discussion of graphic narratives, I draw on David Lewis's concept of "putting the hero back in the superhero" (2013: 34; see also Lewis 2014) to discuss the visibility that graphic narratives like *Gogi* and *Burka Avenger* offer Muslim girlhood. I argue that these narratives offer a layered verbal-visual aesthetic by synthesizing codes of realism with the artifice of the graphic medium, subsequently allowing their girl protagonists to oscillate between the tropes of heroism and superheroism. Joseph Campbell (1949) describes the (male) hero as an individual who represents the core values of his society, is first and foremost a winner, a successful warrior, and, second, refuses being defined by other persons. For Campbell, "A hero ventures forth from the world of common day into a region of supernatural wonder: fabulous forces are there encountered and a decisive victory is won: the hero comes back from this mysterious adventure with the power to bestow boons on his fellow men" (1949: 23). David Lewis (2013) argues that in contrast to Campbell's hero, the American superhero ventures on an adventure, achieves victory, but remains unchanged and immortal in the process. Therefore, superheroes, especially in the American context, overcome death and restore order by shifting the society to its unchanged previous position. However, for Lewis the concept of heroism as opposed to superheroism gets complicated when we analyze this from the standpoint of a Muslim superhero. Lewis argues that Muslim superheroes in comics like *The 99* actively try to change their communities, advocate for Islamic principles of self-sacrifice, and remain humbly human. As a result, they emerge as "misfits in the genre that mis-fits" (Lewis 2014:1).

Building on Lewis's concept of the Muslim superhero, I argue that the everyday heroism of Gogi and Jiya reframes the superhero trope by focusing more on the ordinary experiences of Muslim girlhood instead of emphasizing values of exceptionalism. In *Burka Avenger*, Jiya represents herself as the school teacher during the day and Burka Avenger at night, while in *Gogi* comics, Gogi is a powerful social activist, trendsetter, and conscientious citizen. In having these characters refer, for example, to girl activists such as Malala Yousafzai, their creators blur the boundaries between fiction and reality. The nuanced self-representation and social activism of the girls gives them a superheroic quality, and their day-to-day heroism foregrounds Pakistani cityscapes as familiar places rather than dangerous, unfamiliar, and othered spaces. Furthermore, Gogi and Jiya engage with the city in slightly different ways. Jiya's interaction with her city is more "panoramic" as she offers an overview of the city from the top, rendering the complexity of the city into a readable, stable function. In contrast to Jiya, Gogi prefers to walk in the city, thereby engaging with it in a more "ambulatory" (de Certeau 1984: 99) fashion. The girls' varied engagement with the city relies on what de Certeau calls "tactics" that allow the girls to assess their environments and challenge those in power by "seizing the opportunity" (33) thereby creating new opportunities for themselves. For de Certeau, tactics are practices that are not contained within institutional or spatial borders. Therefore, subaltern groups such as workers, migrants, ethnic minorities, and women usually employ tactics to transform everyday life practices into different forms of resistance. The use of tactics by the girls in *Gogi* and *Burka Avenger* allow for the girls' self-representation on their own terms in addition to providing them with heightened visibility.

School Teacher during the Day and Burka Avenger by Night

The creator of *Burka Avenger* (2013–present), Haroon Rashid, emphasizes Jiya's struggle to create a hybrid self-representational space. As a superhero,

Jiya dons a silken ninja-like burka different from the yards of bulky cloth that make up an actual burka. Further accentuating the power evident in Jiya's appearance is a provocative hip-hop song that is also a part of *Burka Avenger*'s opening credits. The lyrics of the song ominously warn her adversaries to be careful.

> A spirit so quick to deliver a beating
> To the enemies of peace, love, logic, and reason…
> The way it was, she'll be taking it back
> So tune in for the story of the lady in black (n.p.)

The lyrics of the song point to Jiya's role as a social justice warrior who refuses to fight her adversaries with violence. Instead, she chooses peace, love, logic, and reason as viable tactics to overcome her enemies. These tactics are particularly significant because they not only subvert the platitudinous stereotype about the Muslim community, especially Muslim men, as irrational and barbaric, but also celebrate logic and reason as feminine (and feminist) qualities. Confident in her abilities yet relaxed in her demeanor, Jiya moves between the light and shadows as she anonymously fights the tyrannical authority of adult men, especially the clerics, whom she feels have hijacked her Muslim faith.

Jiya's burka'ed persona, although pitched as a strategy of self-defense and anonymity, enters the broader discourse about veiling in Islam and its contentious position in feminist conversations. Sherry Rehman, a Pakistani lawyer, praised the concept of Jiya's story but disapproved of the burka. For her, "*Burka Avenger* is good, but I don't like the feudal stereotyping of the burqa" (quoted in Khazan 2013: n.p.). Rehman's critique is grounded in the equation of female modesty with social respectability in a country like Pakistan. Feminist blogger and writer, Bina Shah, expressed her concern in arguing that the burka, perceived as a symbol of female oppression, was not an ideal outfit for a Muslim superheroine. For Shah, the "burka in the series represented an indoctrination of the worst kind. Pakistani girls and women need to know that their natural state of being should not be hidden away to make their presence in society acceptable, safe, or halal" (quoted in Mahr 2013: n.p.). The journalist Mahvesh Murad disagreed with Shah, stating that Jiya had turned the burka into something spunky and adventurous. Murad remarked, "When Jiya takes back the power of the burka, she's taking back the power … of every woman" (quoted in Khazan 2013: n.p.). The show's creative team compared Jiya's burka to Superman's cape, arguing that if Superman's cape was never a cause of concern, Jiya's burka should also not evoke discomfort (quoted in Usmani 2013: n.p.).

I suggest, however, that Jiya wrests her self-narrative from the debate about the veil by describing her burka as a matter of individual choice. When Jiya works at the school, she chooses not to wear the burka, which is suggestive of her pluralistic professional persona as a teacher.

Illustration 6.1: Jiya and Burka Avenger in a *Burka Avenger* Poster (2012)

However, when Jiya dons the burka, she also wears makeup and nail varnish, two grooming details that are conspicuously absent from her ordinary persona. Jiya's glamorization of her burka'ed alter ego emphasizes her bodily autonomy; she rejects the modesty expected from a burka-clad girl in both appearance and action. She also rejects the male gaze by choosing to cover and reveal herself only on her own terms.

Jiya's trendy persona as a school teacher denies the austere conservatism and piety often expected from girls clad in burkas. She transforms the burka into a glamorous body suit and performs extraordinarily athletic actions such as flying, running, and kickboxing. Her performance is further complicated by her rejection of the hypersexualization that is mostly imposed on Western female superheroes like "big breasts and unrealistically accentuated bodies" (Rosenberg 2013:76), as well as the de-sexualization forcibly imposed on Muslim girls. Jiya's bodily autonomy, therefore, situates her burka as more than a tool of oppression since it advocates respect towards the varied sartorial choices of young girls.

Jiya's dual self-narration also reconceptualizes the trope of superheroism, juxtaposing the politically loaded burka with the Western pop cultural phenomenon of the avenger. Published in 1963 by Stan Lee and Jack Kirby, *The Avengers* is a "story of the Norse god Thor and his team of superheroes who fight to protect the planet Earth" (Darowski 2014: 93). Rooted in a Western epistemological framework, *The Avengers* celebrates white male power with its accompanying ideals of technological advancement, its investment in modern warfare, and its frequent desire for world domination (Dittmer 2013; Lawrence 2009). In his depiction of Jiya, Rashid imagines this trope of white male power by replacing the figure of the bulky, masculine Avenger with that of an ordinary, petite Muslim girl who is more diplomatic than vengeful in her approach towards her enemies. By uprooting both the burka and the avenger from their particular cultural schemas, Jiya subverts the cultural essentialism associated with both terms, thereby creating opportunities for renegotiation and hybrid self-representation.

Jiya foregrounds her hybrid self-identity as a tactic to undermine the patriarchal status quo. Dressed modestly in a *shalwar kameez*, Jiya refuses to follow prescribed ideals of beauty and, instead, inscribes her self-worth through abstract qualities such as kindness, congeniality, and patience. However, her kindness and congeniality, which are often perceived as feminine virtues, do not impede her from protecting her community from the nefarious plots of her adversaries. She also succeeds in winning the admiration of both her male and female students such as Ashu and Moli. These students look up to Jiya as a suitable role model, ask her questions, and share their educational concerns with her. Jiya protects the young boy Moli from communal estrangement because Moli and his family are perceived as looking different from the other inhabitants of Halwa Pur. By emphasizing the virtues of communal tolerance and cooperation, Jiya asserts herself as the leader of her community, thereby becoming a suitable role model for young girls and boys. In this way, she reinforces the overriding theme of female leadership in the series.

By celebrating Jiya's role as both a superhero and teacher, *Burka Avenger* implicitly honors the pursuit of leadership roles and professional careers by young women, especially in a country like Pakistan where women constitute only 25 percent of the labor force (The World Bank 2014). The focus on Jiya's ordinary job also sets her apart from the female characters in graphic narratives like *Superman* (1933) and *Wonder Woman* (1941) in which the day jobs of the "superheroes are a form of camouflage or a mundane aspect of the plot" (Yeffeth 2015: 93). Jiya takes her ordinary job seriously since it allows her to educate people about the social justice issues that she later fights for as the Burka Avenger. By constructing a healthy discourse around social and environmental issues, Rashid has Jiya highlight the role of both theory and praxis in her social activism. Her teaching along with her abilities as a superhero blur the fluid boundaries that exist between heroism and superheroism in addition to celebrating the struggle of both ordinary and exceptional girls.

Mirroring Malala's Story

Jiya's fight against patriarchy is particularly evident in the first episode of *Burka Avenger*, in which the fanatic Baba Bandook (whose name means an old man with a gun) along with his accomplice, the evil politician Wadero Pajero, lock the school. Jiya fights these men and rebukes them for oppressing young girls and boys. Jiya's struggle is particularly relevant to the Pakistani context where more than 3 million girls are out of school (UNESCO 2013). Jiya's fight against Baba Bandook and his cronies directly alludes to the story of Malala Yousafzai, Pakistan's renowned girl activist who was shot by the Taliban for protesting the ban on female education in the Swat Valley. The shooting of Malala generated a fierce debate on the status of women and girls in Pakistan that transformed her into a controversial figure. Lambasted by the conservative Pakistani Muslims, celebrated by the religiously moderate, and co-opted by the West in the name of female emancipation, Malala has emerged as an appropriate symbol for the rights of Muslim girls. What Malala engendered were "affects of pain, shock, pity, compassion, and hatred" (Khoja-Moolji 2015: 539) making her an evasive figure even in relation to the convenient victim/savior narrative of the West. Despite the controversy surrounding Malala, Jiya implicitly celebrates Malala's struggle. Her subtle allusion to Malala's story brings together graphic fiction and reality, enabling Jiya to highlight the unique challenges faced by Muslim girls in an effective manner for her implied audiences.

The Activist in Polka Dots

The creator of *Gogi* comics (1970–the present) offers a girl activist quite different from Jiya. Unlike Jiya, Gogi is not a superhero; her wit and intelligence situate her as an astute observer of Pakistani society. In her depiction of Gogi, Nazar offers her readers a realistic view of life as Gogi struggles to improve the existence of Pakistani men, women, and children. For her admirers, Gogi is the eternal girl, endearing to both children and adults. Gogi is painfully aware of the structural and social inequalities of her world yet she navigates these inequalities with optimism and laughter. With her friendly face, inviting demeanor, and brightly colored clothes, Gogi presents herself as a more confrontational and progressive Muslim girl who often tries to outsmart her peers with her great sense of humor. She is the girl-next-door who enjoys chatting with her girlfriends, shopping, wearing make-up, and occasionally skipping class. However, her desire to challenge the status quo that marginalizes people is what makes her extraordinary.

In *Going Gogi* (2009), we see Gogi working in a village and talking about the hard (often invisible) labor performed by the village women. Gogi emphasizes the lack of opportunities that the rural Pakistani women and girls experience in comparison to their urban peers. In a brightly colored panel, Nazar shows both Gogi and the village women who are working in the blinding sunshine and heat.

In the Pakistani context, this panel functions as a reminder of the stark urban/rural divide in this society. The composition of the panel resonates with Pramod K. Nayar's remark that the cultural markers in graphic narratives should not be regarded as "merely aesthetic or apolitical" (2016: 80). His comment is particularly relevant to this panel because on the surface the panel offers a romantic vision of rural life but a closer look reveals the exhaustion on the faces of the village women forced to carry large pitchers of water. In contrast to the village women, Gogi looks relaxed with a stack of books on her head, imitating their actions, yet starkly removed from the everyday reality of these women. The apparently innocuous but highly telling contrast is a frank acknowledgment of Gogi's class privilege that further emphasizes the fact that the urban dwellers often ignore the harsh reality of rural Pakistan. Gogi's presence here, therefore, highlights the needs to bridge the economic divide between the urban and rural areas. Gogi's appearance in the panel and her concern for the women becomes a plea for an intersectional feminism that advocates for female empowerment regardless of age given the discrepancies in class, geographical location, and economic status.

Illustration 6.2: Gogi in the village from the *Going Gogi* book (2009)

Mediating Feminist Reality

Gogi's feminist leanings are evident in many of her comics. Gogi situates herself as a traditional girl, respectful of her cultural heritage, but also unafraid to criticize certain aspects of her culture. She audaciously (and regularly) voices her opinions on feminist issues that plague Pakistani society like honor killings, street harassment, and violence against women. Moreover, her proficiency in both Urdu and English allows her to address these matters more effectively for both English- and Urdu-speaking audiences. For example, a comic strip published for Women's Day (and available on Nazar's website) shows Gogi fervently working on her computer while she overhears a conversation between Butt Bahee and his friend. Butt Bahee, an unemployed idler, complains that the girls have become fiercer after the Women's Day celebrations just as "their lipsticks have become a ferocious shade of red!" (2016: n.p.) Butt Bahee's placement in the forefront of the panel symbolizes the Pakistani patriarchal order that considers even the red lipstick worn by girls as a threat to male power. Moreover, Butt Bahee's comment is significant because Nazar portrays him as Gogi's potential suitor and friend whom she later rejects. Right behind Butt Bahee we see an amused Gogi laughing at his fear of feminism. Gogi's carefree body language and spatial positioning not only contrasts with the nervous demeanor of Butt Bahee, but also transforms the image into an overt celebration of women's rights. Gogi's defiant posture pushes against the desires and expectations of men like Butt Bahee, which, in turn, strengthens her position as a heroic young girl. Moreover, Butt Bahee's coded reference to bright lipsticks and Gogi's amused response draws attention to the argument that girls have the right to make their own choices regarding their appearance, bodies, and lifestyles without any fear. In this way, Gogi makes a powerful statement about feminism.

Navigating the Pakistani Cityscape

Gogi and Jiya are trailblazers because they audaciously advocate for female independence in a conservative society, all while situating themselves as individuals keen to fulfill their civic responsibilities. The personal and professional struggles of Gogi and Jiya as citizens and community leaders also offer them an insight into Pakistani cityscapes that they subsequently share with their audiences. Both Jiya and Gogi represent their respective cities as lively, familiar, and spectacular places worthy of exploration. Moreover, the girls intervene in the organization of their cities by visiting social spaces, an act generally considered taboo for young girls.

In *Burka Avenger*, the desire to fully explore the city compels Jiya to navigate Halwa Pur in her various avatars. Halwa Pur, a semi-fictional Pakistani city, possesses the liveliness of an urban center and the serenity of a rural landscape. Halwa Pur (that literally means the land of sweets in Urdu) becomes a utopian and therefore idyllic space for children. Halwa Pur's fictionality allows Rashid, through his characterization of Jiya, to construct a rich mythology about it. She introduces it to the audiences as "Mera Shehr" (my city), suggesting her strong affiliation with it. Besides expressing her love for Halwa Pur, Jiya reveals that she lost her parents in an accident in this city, thus linking it to her personal story. Despite this loss, she memorializes and celebrates this city.

The promotional images of *Burka Avenger* show Jiya hovering in the air in her black burka enjoying the skyline of Halwa Pur. Jiya's hovering presence lends an element of fantasy to urban reality, giving these promotional images a timeless quality. Jiya's vision of Halwa Pur resonates with what de Certeau calls the "panoramic view of the city" that allows us to observe "the city from the top, free from all its physical, mental, and political impurities" (1984: 110). Jiya's panoramic view, with its vibrant colors and surreal skyline of minarets and domes, situates Halwa Pur as a stereotypically Middle Eastern town and is reminiscent of the cityscape in the Disney movie *Aladdin*. However, unlike *Aladdin*, which attempts to portray the exoticism of the unknown and othered space, Jiya offers a more habitable view of the city, allowing the viewers to connect with the geographical and social realities within which she exists. Jiya not only looks at her city while she is flying, but also views it while playing on the rooftop of her house. In this way, her personal familiarity with the city is accentuated.

On the roof top, Jiya also practices *takht kabaddi,* an imaginary form of martial arts, which allows her to fight her enemies with books and pens. *Kabaddi* refers to a tag team sport popular in India and Pakistan. Joseph S. Alter argues that *Kabaddi* is "rooted in *Shakha*, a Hindu theological school of thought that focuses on self-discipline, games, devotional songs, and prayers" (2007: 18). Although young girls play *kabaddi* as part of their physical education curriculum, the sport remains traditionally masculine. By practicing a sport usually played by men, Jiya transforms the rooftop into a liminal, feminist zone, and in this way, subverts the patriarchal power that regularly surveils her and the other girls. Moreover, *takht* in *takht kabaddi* means throne as well as wooden board. In the remote areas of Pakistan, school children to this day use these small wooden boards for writing and calligraphy. Therefore, the reference to *takht* in Jiya's story implies her desire for both leadership and the dissemination of education.

While training on her rooftop, Jiya jumps from one roof to another thus demonstrating the interconnectedness of her cityscape. Her rooftop view also evokes the similarity that exists between Halwa Pur and the old walled city of Lahore with its intriguing architecture, close quarters, narrow alleys, and high roof tops suggestive of a well-knit community that enables social exchange between people, especially women, all year round. Jiya's presence on the rooftop resonates with Ruby Lal's point of view that the roofs provide a different, "not-quite-domestic" (2013: 169) space for South Asian girls. On rooftops, young girls find opportunities for adventure, experimentation, and physical transgression. According to Lal, rooftops often connect to other spaces, which make them ideal for friendships and romance. As a result, they offer new openings to young girls free from the intrusion of the adult world. Jiya's presence on the rooftop provides her with the freedom to understand her city and to later navigate it better. Still, certain parts of the city are inaccessible to her, such as the forest across the bridge from her school.

The narrative describes the forest as home to shady individuals who engage in nefarious activities. Baba Bandook and his followers often kidnap, terrorize, and imprison the school children in the forest. Jiya rescues these children and tries to reclaim the forest as a safe space. However, the children are deeply afraid of the forest and consider it haunted. Jiya tries to assuage their fear by telling them "there are [no ghosts] in the forest only people" (Rashid 2013: n.p.). Her statement emphasizes that although she perceives her opponents as threatening, she does not want the school children to live in constant fear of them and desires to reclaim the forest as a habitable space. Jiya's intervention in the forest often takes place with her wearing a burka. This makes the point that wearing the veil or the burka is sometimes necessary if young girls and women wish to break into taboo spaces in a conservative society.

Besides engaging with the difficulties of navigating cityscapes, *Burka Avenger* also engages with the harsh reality of terrorism. The series alludes to the precarity of life in a Pakistan city where terrorism has destroyed many lives, including those of school children. The show subtly hints at this frightening reality through Baba Bandook's statement, "*Akad Bakkd bombay bo bumb phattein gay pooray sau*" (Fee-fi-fo-fum. There are going to be 100 bomb blasts) (Rashid 2013: n.p.). This statement signifies Baba Bandook's desire to control Halwa Pur by evoking tyranny and fear, as well as altering the cityscape through violence.

Jiya persistently struggles to defeat Baba Bandook by highlighting the kindness, vibrancy, and optimism of Halwa Pur's community. She establishes this city's vitality by foregrounding the numerous festivals, events, and celebrations that take place in it. In the first episode, Jiya and her students celebrate their victory over Baba Bandook and Wadero Pajero by holding a musical show at the girls' school. Baba Bandook, who, as mentioned earlier, wishes to shut down the school, is infuriated when he sees young boys and girls singing and dancing in the school playground. He considers music inherently evil and decadent, whereas Jiya believes that music can unite the people of Halwa Pur. The school concert, organized by Jiya, incorporates the figure of Haroon Rashid, Pakistan's renowned pop singer and the creator of *Burka Avenger*, in animated form. Haroon's entry into Jiya's fictional world is, therefore, a judicious blending of fact and fiction as well as a clever example of metafictional awareness.

In comparison to *Burka Avenger*, the cityscape in *Gogi Comics* is much more realistic, allowing Gogi and her readers to immerse themselves in a Pakistani cityscape. Furthermore, Gogi, unlike Jiya, prefers to discover the city on foot. If Jiya's relationship with the city is panoramic, Gogi's connection with the Pakistani city is ambulatory. In her excursions, Gogi sees the city's landmarks, while hearing snatches of conversation. Her intimate connection with the city transforms it into an amorphous, uncontrollable, and strange entity, generating what de Certeau calls the "rhetoric of walking" (1984: 93). Gogi's movement through the city not only colors it with her individual perceptions, but also celebrates a teenage girl's wanderlust and curiosity. Nazar depicts Gogi and her surroundings in vibrant hues of yellow, gold, red, and blue, symbolizing the diversity of life around her. In many of her drawings, Nazar portrays Gogi as a participant or a witness in a highly dramatic situation advocating for social justice while navigating a variety of urban settings ranging from schools to hospitals, from roads to parks, and from libraries to rallies.

Gogi's urban interactions focus on creating an alternative temporality that physically and ideologically protects her position as a girl. In a 2015 comic available on her website, Nazar shows Gogi asking a Mullah questions about female education while standing right outside his house. The act of questioning the Mullah is daring by any standard, but Gogi engages in it fearlessly. When she questions the Mullah, he remarks that women's education should enable them only to read the Quran. When Gogi probes him further, he says, "They should also read religious books." When Gogi asks why he is opposed to formal female education he explains that women's education should be limited because they are more intelligent than men! Gogi's perplexed expressions and the sequential art emphasize both the irony and humor of the Mullah's statement. The discussion with the Mullah becomes a kind of intellectual and gender trespass, allowing Gogi to challenge the Mullah's authority on Islam, while advocating for her rights as a Muslim girl. By questioning the Mullah, Gogi also rejects the gendered expectation of feminine docility so often imposed on girls in the name of religion. Moreover, her conversation establishes the cityscape as a place of performance in which she demands both visibility and equal access.

To initiate change, Gogi focuses on the signs, slogans, speeches, banners, and posters that arrange and organize the city. She not only walks in the city but also intervenes in its organizational structure by observing, understanding, and occasionally criticizing the signs, engendering what de Certeau calls an "urban text" (1984: 110) that signifies the textual and kinesthetic connection that an individual has with a city. In Gogi's case, the urban text allows her to focus on vehicles causing pollution, criticize slogans that promote discrimination, and protest against huge billboards that are destroying the natural beauty of her city. Her tactful engagement also allows Gogi to be a part of real cities in the form of a giant-sized puppet that tours schools, villages, and the conflict ridden tribal areas of Pakistan. She also exists as a mural in Pakistan's largest children's hospital, which further corroborates her engagement with the city. Gogi's appearance in fictional and real cities transforms her into a distinct girl figure who advocates for the physical and social mobility of real girls in actual Pakistani cities.

Conclusion

Gogi and *Burka Avenger* offer a sophisticated understanding of Muslim girlhood for both local and foreign audiences. They not only critique the inherent otherness that haunts representation of Muslim girlhood in Western narratives, but they also address the age- and gender-based issues that Muslim girls experience. Gogi and Jiya share an emotional connection with the Pakistani cityscapes because they celebrate the unique cultural and social ethos of their respective cities, counteracting the political discourses that characterize their cities as inherently violent. Gogi and Jiya also employ tactics to break down the religiopatriarchal hegemonies of their cities. Inspiring other Muslim artists from Pakistan and around the world to share their girlhood stories, *Gogi* and *Burka Avenger* create awareness about a range of both local and transnational issues affecting Muslim girls in terms of their visibility, safety, and empowerment. Moreover, they present a nuanced picture of Muslim identities in a world plagued by Islamophobia, War on Terror, and the numerous militaristic conflicts that have left Muslim girls in highly precarious situations.

TEHMINA PIRZADA is an Assistant Professor of English at the Lahore School of Economics. Her areas of research are gender and adolescence, youth cultures, Pakistani popular culture, and postcolonial cinema. Her work has appeared in *Journal of Language, Literature and Cultural Studies*, *Girlhood Studies: An Interdisciplinary Journal*, *South Asian Popular Culture,* and *South Asian Review*.

Notes

1. Borrowing from Daniel Varisco's (2005) definition, I define Muslim as an individual who, implicitly or explicitly, associates herself with Islam. For the term girlhood, I borrow from Judith Butler who describes "girlhood as a set of identity statements that, at birth, enmesh us in the process of 'being girls.'" Butler's phrase, "being girled" (1993: 7) refers to the set of ideological perceptions, roles, and limitations imposed on girls from a very young age in every sociocultural framework. Therefore, the term Muslim girlhood emerges as a relatively underexplored category that demonstrates the need to construct a nuanced discourse about Muslim girls. By focusing on the representational practices of Muslim girls and their navigation of cityscapes, I create awareness about a range of transnational issues such as patriarchy, Islamophobia, and War on Terror, as well as local issues that concern female visibility, safety, and empowerment in local communities.
2. I use the term Muslim girlhood, instead of Pakistani girlhood, to describe girls like Gogi and Jiya because they exist within geographical, ethnic, racial, and social frameworks perceived as Muslim.
3. The genre of the cartoon has become particularly controversial, especially in the aftermath of the Charlie Hebdo attacks of 2015.

References

Alter, Joseph S. 2007. "Physical Education, Sport and the Intersection and Articulation of 'Modernities': The Hanuman Vyayam Prasarak Mandal." In *The Politics of Sport in South Asia*, ed. Subhas Ranjan Chakraborty, Shantanu Chakrabarti and Kingshuk Chatterjee, 8–23. New York: Routledge.

Butler, Judith. 1993. *Bodies That Matter: On the Discursive Limits of 'Sex.'* New York: Routledge.

Campbell, Joseph. [1949] 2016. *The Hero with a Thousand Faces*. Novato: New World Library.

Dar, Jehanzeb. 2008. "Female, Muslim and Mutant: Muslim Women in Comic Books." Broken Mystic. https://brokenmystic.wordpress.com/tag/muslim–women/ (accessed 10 March 2016).

Darowski, Joseph J. 2014. "The Earth's Mightiest Heroes and America's Post-Cold War." In *The Ages of the Avengers: Essays on the Earth's Mightiest Heroes in Changing Times*, ed Joseph J Darowski, 92–102. Jefferson: McFarland.

de Certeau, Michel. [1984] 2011. "Walking in the City." In *The Practice of Everyday Life*, ed. de Certeau, Michel, Trans. Steven Rendall, 99–111. Berkeley: University of California Press.

Dittmer, Jason. 2013. *Captain America and the Nationalist Superhero: Metaphors, Narratives, and Geopolitics*. Philadelphia: Temple University Press.

Khazan, Olga. 2013. "The Burka Avenger." The Atlantic. November. https://www.theatlantic.com/magazine/archive/2013/11/big-in-pakistan/309530/ (accessed 27 June 2017)

Khoja-Moolji, Shenila. 2015. "Reading Malala: (De)(Re)Territorialization of Muslim Collectivities." *Comparative Studies of South Asia, Africa and the Middle East* 35 (3): 539–556.

Khoja-Moolji, Shenila, and Alyssa D. Niccolini. 2015. "Comics as Public Pedagogy: Reading Muslim Masculinities through Muslim Femininities in Ms. Marvel." *Girlhood Studies: An Interdisciplinary Journal* 8 (3): 23–39.

Lal, Ruby. 2013. *Coming of Age in Nineteenth-Century India: The Girl-Child and the Art of Playfulness.* New York: Cambridge University Press.

Lawrence, John Shelton. 2009. "Foreword." In *Captain America and the Struggle of the Superhero: Critical Essays*, ed. Robert G. Weiner, 1–8. Jefferson: McFarland.

Lewis, A. David. 2013. "Save the Day." In *What Is a Superhero?* ed. Robin S. Rosenberg and Peter MacFarland Coogan, 31–42. Oxford: Oxford University Press.

Lewis, A. David. 2014. "The Muslim Superhero in Contemporary American Popular Culture." http://www.academia.edu/5280870/The_Muslim_Superhero_in_Contemporary_American_Popular_Culture (accessed 27 June 2017)

Mahr, Krista. 2013. "Burka Avenger: Conservative Pakistan's New Animated Liberal Superheroine." TIME. 1 August. http://world.time.com/2013/08/01/burka–avenger–conservative pakistans–new–animated–liberal–superheroine/ (accessed 15 July 2016)

Nayar, Pramod K. 2016. *The Indian Graphic Novel: Nation, History, and Critique.* New York: Routledge.

Nazar, Nigar. 2009. *Going Gogi.* Islamabad: Gogi Book Series.

Nazar, Nigar. 2015. "Gogi Talking to a Mullah," Gogi by Nigar Nazar. 11 December. http://www.gogistudios.com/comic/ (accessed 13 January 2017).

Nazar, Nigar. 2016. "Gogi celebrating Women's Day." Gogi by Nigar Nazar, 8 March. http://www.gogistudios.com/comic/ (accessed 8 August 2016)

Rosenberg, Robin S. 2013. *Our Superheroes, Ourselves.* Oxford: Oxford University Press.

The World Bank. 2014. "Labor Force Participation rate, Female (% of female population ages 15+) (modeled ILO estimate)." International Labour Organization. Key Indicators of the Labour Market Database http://data.worldbank.org/indicator/SL.TLF.CACT.FE.ZS (accessed 8 August 2016).

UNESCO. 2013. "Girls' Education—the Facts." *Education for All Monitoring Report.* http://en.unesco.org/gem–report/sites/gem–report/files/girls–factsheet-en.pdf. (accessed 8 August 2016)

Usmani, Basim. 2013. "The Burka Avenger's Creator Talks about the Pakistani Cartoon Haters." *VICE*. 8 Aug. http://www.vice.com/read/the-burka-avengers-creator-talks-about-the-pakistani-cartoons-haters (accessed 8 August 2016).

Varisco, Daniel. 2005. *Islam Obscured: The Rhetoric of Anthropological Representation*. New York: Palgrave Macmillan.

Yeffeth, Glenn. 2015. *The Man from Krypton: A Closer Look at Superman*. Dallas: BenBella Books.

Filmography

Clements Ron, and John Musker. 1992. *Aladdin*. USA.
Moulton, William, and Harry G. Peter. 1941. *Wonder Woman*. USA.
Nazar, Nigar. 1970–the present. *Gogi*. Pakistan.
Rashid, Haroon. 2013–the present. *Burka Avenger*. Pakistan.
Siegel, Jerry, and Joe Shuster. 1933. *Superman*. USA.

CHAPTER 7
Confronting Girl-bullying and Gaining Voice in Two Novels by Nicholasa Mohr

Barbara Roche Rico

In October 2015, the artists El Mac and Cero unveiled a mural of Nicholasa Mohr as a part of the International Monument Art Project on Lexington Avenue and 111th Street in East Harlem, New York. The mural, which covers the full side of a building, celebrates the work of the first Rican woman to have her work published in English by a major American publishing house (Acosta-Belén 1992). The writer of more than a dozen books, Mohr has been "recognized as a pioneer figure ... [with a] decisive role in the development of Latina narrative" (Moreno 2012: 23). Although praised by critics, who have said it "represents the strongest [Rican] woman's voice of [her] generation," (Torres-Padilla and Rivera 2008: 10) Mohr's writing has received a "surprisingly limited amount of scholarly attention" (Lomelí et al. 2016: 195) in mainstream academic journals. Of Mohr's novels, *Felita* and *Going Home* seem to be the least known. In this chapter I explore how both works examine the emergence of the female subject during times of intercultural tension. Among the elements not yet remarked upon is their sustained attention to the issue of bullying long before the topic became a popular one in young adult literature (Bennet 2011; Hillsberg and Spak 2006; Pytash et al. 2013; Young and Ward 2011). As I will show in this chapter, the novels raise important issues related to bullying, especially that which is practiced by girls.

Illustration 7.1: Mural featuring Nicholasa Mohr by El Mac and Cero. Photo by Ben Walton.

Felita (1979) and *Going Home* (1986) make use of a girl's first-person perspective to examine bullying and related issues in some detail. *Felita* examines how the exclusionary practices of one generation can lead to bullying by the next and how the objects of bullying can also turn a critical eye on themselves. *Felita*'s sequel *Going Home* (1986) also uses a first-person perspective to show how intercultural and intracultural tensions—which Mohr also examines in two of her essays—can lead to ethnic-based bullying (1986b, 1987). Both texts also explore the roles of adults in both enabling and counteracting bullying behavior. Moreover, the novels highlight the potential of art and of dialogue to promote the re-engagement of the girl who has been bullied.

As the literature suggests, the subject of bullying (once treated as an expected part of childhood and a normal initiation rite) is now recognized as a serious hazard to physical and psychological health. "Aggression is commonplace in U.S. schools: bullying and other forms of proactive aggression adversely affect 30 percent, or 5.7 million, American youth each school year" (Faris and Felmlee 2011: 48). Bullying research has expanded over the last half-century from articles published in isolated studies in small journals to global projects investigating both short-term and long-term effects on the perpetrator and the subject of the bullying, and the contexts in which bullying takes place. The roles of authority figures—parental, educative, and community-based—have also been studied, and preventative programs and legislative actions have been put into place at both local and national levels.

Bullying has been characterized as "a form of aggression that can be direct or indirect and includes physical, verbal, or psychological and relational acts, that is intentional and occurs in a relationship characterized by a power imbalance, and is repeated over time" (Mishna 2012: 5). Key research areas include direct and indirect forms of bullying, the roles of gender and ethnicity in determining who bullies and who is to be bullied, and the advantages of cognitive (as opposed to punitive) approaches in counteracting bullying behavior (Day et al. 2014; Jimerson and Huai 2010; Olweus 2010; Swearer and Espelage 2010).

The study of bullying is no doubt an especially complex one and Mohr's work should not be approached as a treatise. At the same time, it is especially noteworthy how many of the topics mentioned above in relation to bullying are explored in *Felita* and *Going Home*, the first of which reflects on the author's own experiences as a child who experienced bullying and who would later find herself a bystander to a bullying episode. Close readings of the two young adult novels demonstrate how the subject of bullying serves as a through-line in *Felita* and *Going Home*, and how the two novels model (in their storytelling and dialogue) ways in which tween readers and their mentors might approach this complex subject.

Background and Context

Even though it shares many of the elements of immigrant literature, that of Puerto Ricans living in the Continental United States is not the literature of immigrants since Puerto Ricans have been US citizens since 1917 (Stevens-Arroyo and Díaz-Ramírez 1982; López 1980; Wagenheim and de Wagenheim [1975]1988). In her preface to *El Bronx Remembered* (1975), Mohr suggests that while they "did not face immigration laws or quotas, [the migrants were nonetheless] strangers in their own country" (1975: n.p.). In the most general terms, Puerto Rico's history reveals a pattern of conquest and colonialism (from 1493 to 1897), a few months of some autonomy (1897 to 1898), and more than a century of American domination (beginning in 1898), which many consider another form of colonialism. After nearly 500 years of Spanish control, Puerto Rico became an American possession in 1898. Puerto Ricans were accorded American citizenship in 1917 (see Cabranes 1979; Carrión 1981, 1983).

It was not until the 1950s that Puerto Rico was permitted to write its first constitution since 1897. The Island's status as a free state associated with the United States had been supported in the plebiscites of 1967 and 1993. During periods of mainland prosperity, labor shortages in the US prompted Islanders to migrate north in record-numbers. In more recent years, periods of economic decline and industrial relocation in the Continental US have led to a deterioration of living conditions and an increase in revolving-door migration. Several decades ago, the US Civil Rights Commission found that the Puerto Ricans living in Continental US cities often experienced a low standard of living, discrimination, and limited educational opportunities—a situation described by others as a form of internal colonialism (Flores 1993; United States Commission on Civil Rights 1976). Recent work, focusing on "the advances that the community has made," has emphasized the importance of the cultural production of Diaspora writers to "fill a gap in US dominant narratives and ... provide a source of validation for the community" (Moreno 2012: 98).

Mohr's fiction can be read as a representation of the Diaspora during several important historical moments. *Nilda* (1973) uses the context of the 1940s to explore one girl's experiences as she takes on greater responsibility for her family. Both *El Bronx Remembered* (1975) and *In Nueva York* (1977) include interconnected stories about mainland Puerto Ricans who were part of the Great Migration from the Island from the 1940s to the mid-1960s. The novels *Felita* and *Going Home* address a girl's attempt to negotiate a bicultural identity within the cultures of her native New York City and the Puerto Rico of her ancestors. Two of Mohr's later works, *Rituals of Survival* (1985) and *A Matter of Pride and Other Stories* (1997), are set during the period after the Great Migration, when declining economic conditions made survival in an urban environment even more difficult. *A Matter of Pride and Other Stories* echoes concerns also addressed in Mohr's essays (1986b, 1987) related especially to tensions between the sensibilities of both the Continental US and the Island, as well as the roles of gender and custom. For if Mohr's earlier works (such as *Nilda*) look to the possibility of dialogue and exchange, her later works, beginning with *Felita* and *Going Home,* seem to stress its difficulty.

Affiliation and Bullying in *Felita*

Felita and *Going Home* were both published by Dial Books under the imprint of their Young Readers series. *Felita*, which was awarded the American Book Award in 1981, explores bullying from the perspectives of family aspirations and the proverbial good life. Indeed, *Felita* can also be read as using a girl's epistemological perspective to effect a systematic dismantling of clichés in American fiction—witness the ironic relationships between the received notions of a better neighborhood and the behavior of the self-appointed gatekeepers of these imagined communities (Anderson 1991). Like other works addressing mid-twentieth-century life in the United States, Mohr's story points to a tension between a neighborhood's appearance of clean streets and apparent respectability on the one hand and its adherence to exclusionary customs and beliefs on the other. Indeed, the novel links personal experience and social history by adapting episodes recounted in Mohr's 1994 memoir *Growing Up Inside the Sanctuary of My Imagination*. The fictional narrative explores more fully an episode (recounted in Mohr's memoir), when her family moved into a new neighborhood.

> Back then we [as Latinos] were conspicuous in *that* racially homogeneous surrounding, and unwelcome ... My first attempt to play with the children was quite successful ... But when I went down a second time, the grown-ups interfered ... I was verbally and physically abused in the presence of adults who joined in the name-calling. (50–51)

In adapting the event in *Felita* Mohr puts the bullying episode into a larger context by contrasting Felita's parents' expectations, with those of the girl herself. One notes the repeated contrasting of the "new place" (18) and "a way better neighborhood" (22) to the old one, and the parents' shared motivation to move to a district with "better schools" (25). In explaining and justifying the move, family members also minimize any possible inconvenience: Felita's elder brother states, for example, that the new neighborhood "ain't far" (22). Although her family seems to connect the move to perceived notions of upward mobility, Felita—who is more concerned with the loss of her old friends—does not. Moreover, as the narrative continues, the implied promises of a "cleaner and quieter" (29) (and by extension, safer) street take on an ironic cast.

The bullying episodes in both *Felita* and its sequel *Going Home* are structurally similar. In both novels, when a group invites Felita to join their game she agrees to do so but with some reluctance. The game first proceeds well, until one girl suddenly changes her affect; acting as a ringleader, she then turns the rest of the group against the newcomer who is seen to be challenging her authority.

Felita's first-person narrative shows the consequences of shunning and bullying through the point of view of the nine-year-old girl. The passage also juxtaposes phrases (and gestures) associated with the parents' optimism—and the girl's sense of apprehension—about the new neighborhood. In terms that are richly suggestive, Felita reports that her mother was "busy making curtains, matching appliance covers, and place mats," and that most of the furniture was "set in place" (28–29). Looking out onto the street, however, Felita assesses the new neighborhood with trepidation:

> I stood by the living-room window looking out. The day was warm and sunny. Below on the sidewalk a group of girls were playing rope—double dutch. Some of them were real good. The block was different from my old street. There were hardly any small stores. ... The street was cleaner and quieter. There were not as many people or kids outside.
>
> 'Go out and play, Felita. Why don't you go out and make friends?' Mami kept telling me this every day.
>
> ... 'Maybe tomorrow.' ... I was just scared to go out into that block with all those strange kids.
>
> ... 'Mi hijita [my daughter], please, por favor, give children a chance to know you.' (29–30)

As an incentive, her mother presents her with a new dress "like a sailor's suit ... [which] would be nice ... to wear on the first day you go out to meet our new neighbors." A bit more self-confident ("I looked nice, even pretty"), Felita makes her way to the stoop—occupying a liminal space as she witnesses the girls' gestures:

> I stood on the stoop, watching the group of girls I had seen from the Window ... One of them saw me, then whispered to the others. They all stopped playing and looked at me. Slowly I went down the steps to the sidewalk and leaned against the stoop railing. Then I walked toward them and stood only a few feet away. ... They were having a good time ... Hopscotch was a game I was really good at!
>
> 'Hi! Hey you!' a girl ... called out. "You wanna play with us?'
>
> 'Sure.' I walked over and waited my turn. (30–31)

In Mohr's story, the children first agree to invite Felita to join them. Soon, however, differences in the girls' proficiency at the game and their attitudes toward her emerge. As Felita reports, "We all played. When it was my turn, I got to play over and over because I was the best one" (32). Whereas two girls express welcome, two others assert their own sense of entitlement. Mary Beth states, "I've been living [here] all my life," and Thelma says she has lived on the block "since [she was] four" (33–34). The pattern highlighted here is related to two stages observed in ethnic-based discrimination described in Dale Nesdale's research that outlines a transition in some children from one of non-discrimination to an attitude of discrimination, based on a variety of factors. At first "playmate preferences [seem to be] unrelated to ethnic preferences or out-group stereotype responses," even if some of the girls see themselves as being a part of an in-group of residents (2004: 229).

The situation changes, however, after an adult intervenes: a parent, who has evidently been watching the children at play, calls her daughter Mary Beth over for a scolding. When Mary Beth returns, whatever welcome that was expressed is now forgotten. As the rest of the girls huddle together, Katherine—the first to welcome Felita—walks away. The text reflects Felita's epistemological stance:

> The other girls huddled together with the grown-ups. They all spoke in low voices … I smiled at them and waited, but there were no smiles for me … Katherine had already disappeared into her building. Suddenly I felt frightened and all alone. (34)

Following the second stage described in Nesdale's research one notes that Felita is now regarded as an "outgroup [member who is] despised or hated" (2004: 230). Social cognitive theory "proposes that children learn violence by watching others engage in violence" (Kuykendall 2012: 82). The same girls who invited Felita to play with them now block her way: "As I tried to get by … the girls ran up the stoop and formed a line across the building entrance" (35) while adults watched. In juxtaposing Felita's expectation with her experiences, the narrative draws attention to the effect of the sudden change.

Felita is then subjected to ethnic bullying. As onlookers encourage them, the children mouth insults they have evidently heard:

> 'She should stay in her own place, right, Mama?'
> 'Can't you answer? No speak the English no more?' The grownups laughed.
> (35)

After being pushed down the steps and punched, Felita then feels "a wall of arms [come] crashing down" (37). The back of Felita's new sailor suit, worn to create a good first impression, is torn. Because the author is describing something happening quickly to a character in a state of shock, the general anonymity of those who strike the blows and hurl the insults is retained. When someone uses the N-word to address Felita, an adult reacts, "Shh, don't say that" (35), as if more upset that the term is voiced in public than that one's child has used such words. Even as some try to end the episode, their language continues to reinforce an exclusionary message: "'Let her go,' a woman shouted. 'She knows now she's not wanted here'" (37). As the children repeat phrases they have evidently been taught, the adults' lesson has apparently achieved its desired outcome.

Focusing on the minor character Katherine, Mohr's novel then calls attention to the bystander's difficult position. Before the bullying begins, Katherine leaves abruptly. "'I gotta be getting on home,' she murmured" (34), perhaps anticipating the kind of episode she might have witnessed before. Since she does not live in the same building, Katherine has arguably not been indoctrinated as other children had and, thus, refused to follow the mob.

This episode also aligns with a bullying event described in Mohr's memoir, *Growing Up Inside the Sanctuary of My Imagination* (1994), this time focusing on her role as a bystander when a friend experienced religious bigotry:

> Then one afternoon I was walking with the four girls and we saw Marilyn returning from Hebrew school. "That's your friend, the Jew girl," one of them said. I remember wanting to join Marilyn but not daring to go ahead. … Marilyn's wide smile faded when she greeted me and saw my reluctance … But I just stood there, feeling mute and powerless. (87)

The text then relates the author's subsequent failed attempts to atone for her lack of courage. By linking fictional work and the memoir, Mohr suggests that an understanding of bullying must consider not only the perspectives of the bullied and the bully, but those of the bystander as well. Mohr concludes the section of the memoir by reporting her promise "never … to keep silent again" (89).

In positioning Felita as the observer, subsequent sections of *Felita* also echo Mohr's memoir by highlighting the effects of the culture of bullying on the rest of the family. Bullying that upsets one's routine existence can create a special vulnerability. "Routine activity theory proposes a model of victimization in which an individual's behavioral patterns affect his or her risk of victimization" (Popp and Peguero 2011: 2430). Felita's brother is jumped by several young men, the family's mailbox is broken into, and Felita's mother is doused with hot and cold water by an unseen mob when she attempts to bring home the family's groceries. Felita also observes how her relatives blame one another as well as themselves, for what has occurred.

New Lessons in Managing Conflict and Gaining Voice

Even as she observes her relatives' reactions, she also reports her own. Having kept her dignity intact as she forced her way through the angry mob of parents and children, and strangers who attacked her, Felita now contemplates revenge thus recasting her role from victim to avenger. Yet as she questions the girls' motivations ("I didn't know why they hated us or what we had done, except that we were Puerto Rican. Somehow that made them very angry" (51)), Felita also turns the lens back on herself. Her anger is now matched by self-loathing: "[I felt] bad … and like I can't stand up for myself" (58). The silence in effect prevents the person being bullied from escaping the stigma of abuse.

In coming to terms with this event, Felita needs to contextualize her inability to stand up for herself. In this context, her grandmother, Abuelita, herself a gifted storyteller, becomes crucial. Their dialogues not only provide antidotes to the despair and self-loathing that follow the bullying episode, but also allow an important re-framing of the event itself. Abuelita's advice is to reject the hatred based on the "nasty things about them and their families" (59), and the desire for revenge. Moreover, her stories recast Felita's role from victim to agent through her connection to the imaginative life; Abuelita recognizes in Felita a kindred spirit, and a fellow artist.

In offering a different sort of response to the bullying episode, Abuelita's stories call on social history as well as cultural myths and metaphors. Her images of Puerto Rico as a "garden" and "a rainbow of earth colors" (60) provide an opportunity for re-framing so that the girl will be better able to cope with other such events in the future. The child's reference to the flowers at the end of the story signals an affirmation of her identity with its acceptance of her grandmother's metaphor of a rainbow that reinforces a message of pluralism and tolerance, a message that will be recalled even after the grandmother has died.

In narrating Felita's involvement in a school pageant and the agency she exercises given her role as an artist in this project, the last chapters of *Felita* explore the restorative value of art. The Thanksgiving Pageant allows Felita not only to display her talent but also to learn to manage interpersonal conflicts more effectively. After auditioning for—but not being awarded—a speaking part in the pageant, Felita declines all non-speaking roles but agrees to paint the scenery when that job is offered to her. After first shunning the winner of the auditions, who was once her close friend, Felita discovers ways in which to examine her own motivation and those of her friend and to value the friendship they shared. The importance of dialogue, asserted by Abuelita, is realized in the reconciliation at the end of the narrative. As important as this reconciliation is, the episode complements the rest of the narrative in offering the girl more positive approaches to conflict management.

The Problematics of *Going Home*

The sequel to *Felita*, *Going Home* (1986), presents a more complex narrative whose very title points to a problematic aspect of home—the cognitive dissonance between the stories that migrants "had nostalgically presented to their displaced offspring" labeled by Mohr a "false legacy" (1987: 89), and the lack of welcome the offspring later encountered when visiting the Island. These tensions provide additional aspects of the contexts of this novel. Now two years older, Felita looks forward to a summer in Puerto Rico. In *Going Home*'s first-person narration, Mohr uses the child's visit to re-examine issues of affiliation and belonging. In so doing, she revisits and problematizes some of the key episodes first highlighted in *Felita*. The sequel also presents several episodes in which the girl needs to contend with bullies who threaten both her and those close to her. In so doing, the narrative examines Felita's experiences as both a victim and a witness and it also expands its range from girl-bullying to ethnic-based bullying, involving both boys and girls.

The novel's first episodes explore Felita's choices in the role as a witness to bullying when her friend Vinny, an immigrant from Colombia, is taunted because of his accent. The episode shares many characteristics with the sidewalk episode in *Felita* discussed above in which Felita as a newcomer is also bullied. Here evidently, the price of admission to this imagined community is to speak American slang. As an onlooker to bullying, Felita—unlike Katherine, the passive witness of the first novel—decides to help her friend. Having experienced bullying herself, Felita begins to teach Vinny English "just like all the other kids" after she learns that her friend would be teased "until he learns our ways" (33). The episode is, however, not without its own problems. Felita, who (in the first novel) suffered because of her perceived difference, now becomes an agent of assimilation, teaching Vinny to use colloquial expressions so as to prevent his being bullied again.

In both *Felita* and *Going Home* issues of bullying also relate to larger questions of personal dignity that Felita learns to define as a freedom to develop one's talents and individual traits separate from the imposed views of others. If her grandmother's stories in the first novel emphasize the common human experience, the girl's own experience in the second book focuses on gender equality. If in the first novel the girl encounters ethnic prejudice, in *Going Home* she also witnesses cultural and gender bias both within and beyond her own family. Felita must, for example, react to her brother's assertion that it is a "law of nature" (20) that girls should not be allowed to have much freedom. As the narrative develops, she counteracts this prejudice, both by what she does and what she refuses to do. Her actions (such as reaching out to a marginalized classmate) earn her the respect of a brother whose routine actions typically demeaned her. Moreover, accepting such a mentoring role enhances Felita's sense of self-esteem in allowing her to fashion her own response to her brothers' patronizing challenge: "Since when have you become an English teacher!" (42). By engaging in dialogue she helps her brother understand her position while beginning to appreciate his resentment of their parents' insistence on the family's cultural norms such as the need to chaperone his sister.

Felita becomes a witness to bullying once again when her family visits the Island and her brothers are bullied by their male cousins. Here, too, affiliative claims are linked to language use. Here, too, an elder relative's comments trigger bullying behavior: after an uncle criticizes Felita's brothers' Spanish, they are mocked by the relatives who are hosting them. The episode might be read as recalling Mohr's view that Islanders at times "show disdain and contempt for [her] community," mocking their dialect, and categorizing them as "outsiders ... and newyoricans" (Mohr 1987: 90–91).

In outline, the third bullying episode—this time involving Felita—follows familiar patterns. The girl experiences the newcomer's marginalization when she attempts to join a social club. Once again, issues of competence are pitted against assumptions about affiliation and entitlement. After Felita establishes her competence at play, the games become increasingly exclusionary: the next one involves Spanish tongue-twisters, evidently designed just for her. As in the earlier sidewalk episode, Felita takes part though reluctantly: "I really didn't want to play this game, but I also didn't want to be left out, so I agreed" (1986: 117). Like her friend Vinny, Felita soon discovers that she is vulnerable to the ridicule of others when her answers are judged as being "too slow" (118). When told that she would go last next (which would force her "to [speak] faster than anyone else") Felita declines, only to be taunted as a "sensitive Yankee," a "gringita," and "Ms. Nuyorican ... too good to play with us" (118–119). Issues related to affiliation and entitlement emerge here as well. Ignoring Felita's logic—her suggestion that if the situation were reversed, others might stumble—the ringleader asserts that Felita is "not Puerto Rican," because she was "not born here" (120). Although Felita responds directly to these insults, her actions give her little satisfaction and much self-doubt:

> All my life I've been Puerto Rican, now I'm told I'm not, that I'm a *gringa*. Two years ago, I got beaten up by a bunch of mean girls when we had moved to an all-white neighborhood ... They just hated me because I was Puerto Rican ... How

could [Anita] say those things to me? Even today, back home when anybody tries to make us ashamed of being Puerto Rican, we all stand up to them ... At home I get called a 'spick' and here I'm a Nuyorican. (122)

She finds cold comfort when told that the bullies like "to tease and act smart when anyone from the States comes here" (118). Although in Mohr's first novel, Felita took consolation from her connection with her family and its history, in the second her memories of her grandmother's stories seem, at least temporarily, to have disappeared. Instead, when she returns to her relatives' home, after having been taunted, Felita lashes out at the relatives who are hosting her, and contemplates leaving the Island.

As in the first novel, Felita's reemergence is affected when she is able to exercise her agency as an artist. Her demonstrable talent allows her to thrive, even in a hostile environment. After a period of competitive appraisal, Felita (even though she is a newcomer) is put in charge of the club's large art project—a mural which will provide the backdrop for a pageant to be staged that summer. The art project also allows Felita to gain a deeper understanding of the history that has informed the Puerto Rican culture that she has inherited.

Bullying has been defined as any aggressive activity that damages a child's self-esteem. Even after she has been asked to supervise the mural project, Felita experiences forms of indirect bullying that threaten the project's success. Not only is Felita undermined by one of the other students working on the project, but the materials needed to complete the mural are stolen days before a key deadline. Moreover, on the day before the pageant is to begin, Felita discovers that her mural has been defaced with the words, "GRINGITA GO HOME" (167).

A key difference between how bullying is treated in the two novels, however, lies in the authority figures' response to it. Unlike *Felita*'s authority figures, who shirked their responsibilities, the program directors in *Going Home* address the situation immediately by interviewing the key suspects (and their families). Once guilt is determined, the bullies who tried to exclude the newcomer are themselves banished from the community. As the novel ends, Felita returns to her home with a new sense of satisfaction about what she has achieved in defying the biases of others, and asserting her own agency.

The Role of Art

In her memoir, *Growing Up Inside the Sanctuary of My Imagination* (1994), Nicholasa Mohr reflects on the intersection between the bullying episode in *Felita* and episodes in her own life. In *Felita* and *Going Home* we see Felita overcoming the biases of others to accomplish her goals. Not surprisingly, the girl's ambition involves the visual arts for Mohr was herself an artist and print-maker before she became a novelist, and her initial experiments in writing began as ways to annotate and contextualize her prints. For Mohr's characters (in *Nilda* (1973) and several of her short stories, as well as the two novels analyzed here) the artistic space often provides a quiet retreat from the world and a restorative journey into the self.

In the two young adult novels discussed above, the retreat into art is not simply a private journey but an opportunity for the child to exercise her agency. Her role is not simply to decorate the stage but to construct an imagistic backdrop for all the actors who would stand before it. In the first book, *Felita*, the role is more mediated: the character is an assistant, and thus takes orders from others. Limited satisfaction and limited agency are shown. In the case of *Going Home*, however, Felita is put in charge of the scenery, but not before she has proven herself as an artist and has made herself a student of the historical and cultural context that is at the center of the story.

If in *Going Home*, Felita begins as an informal language tutor (and an ad hoc expert on North American slang) she also shows herself to be a serious student of her own cultural history—a history that was largely ignored in her schools back home. With her mural completed, Felita silences the bullies and gains respect from those who would doubt her. Her art grants her the perspective to see the world in rich images and metaphors and with the wisdom of one who understands both the difficulty and the necessity of going home.

Acknowledgments

I acknowledge the assistance of Teah Goldberg, and Rains Research Fellows Morika Fields, Elizabeth Rahe, and Katherine Vermillion.

BARBARA ROCHE RICO is Professor and Chair of English at Loyola Marymount University. Her research interests include work on Nicholasa Mohr, Judith Ortíz Cofer, and other writers of the Puerto Rican Diaspora. Her publications include *American Mosaic: Multicultural Readings in Context* (1990, 1995, 2000), co-edited with Sandra Mano, and articles in *Frontiers: A Journal of Women's Studies* reprinted in *Latino/a Writing* (2014) and in *Short Fiction in Theory and Practice* (2011) as well as in several edited collections of essays. She serves as a member of the National Networking Board of the Lilly Fellows Program.

References

Acosta-Belén, Edna. 1992. "Beyond Island Boundaries: Ethnicity, Gender, and Cultural Revitalization in Nuyorican Literature." *Callaloo* 15 (4): 979–998.

Anderson, Benedict. 1991. *Imagined Communities: Reflections on the Origin and the Spread of Nationalism*. London: Verso.

Bennet, Jessica. 2011. "What Makes Mean Girls Tick." *The Daily Beast*, 11 October.

Cabranes, José A. 1979. *Citizenship and the American Empire: Notes on the Legislative History of the United States Citizenship of Puerto Rico*. New Haven: Yale.

Carrión, Arturo Morales. 1981. "Puerto Rico and the United States: A Historian's Perspective." *Revista del Colegio de Abogados de Puerto Rico* 42 (4):585–603.

Carrión, Arturo Morales 1983. *Puerto Rico: A Political and Cultural History*. New York: Norton.

Day, Kristen R., Ann Marie Popp, Anthony A. Peguero, and Lindsay L. Kahle. 2014. "Gender, Bullying Victimization, and Education." *Violence and Victims* 29 (5): 843–856.

Faris, Robert, and Diane Felmlee. 2011. "Status Struggles: Network Centrality and Gender Segregation in Same- and Cross-Gender Aggression." *American Sociological Review* 76 (1): 48–73.

Flores, Juan. 1993. "'Qué assimilated, brother, yo soy asimilao': The Structuring of Puerto Rican Identity." In *Divided Borders: Essays on Puerto Rican Identity*, 182–198. (2nd ed.) Houston: Arte Publico.

Hillsberg, Carol, and Helene Spak. 2006. "Young Adult Literature as the Centerpiece of an Anti-Bullying Program in Middle School." *Middle School Journal* 38 (2): 23–28.

Jimerson, Shane R., and Nan Huai. 2010. "Perspectives on Bullying Prevention and Intervention." In *Handbook of Bullying in Schools: An International Perspective*, ed. Shane R. Jimerson, Susan M. Swearer and Dorothy L. Espelage, 571–590. New York: Routledge.

Kuykendall, Sally. 2012. *Bullying*. New York: Greenwood.
Lomelí, Francisco A., Donaldo W. Urioste, and Maria Joaquina Villaseñor. 2016. *Historical Dictionary of US Latino Literature*. Lanham, MD: Rowman and Littlefield Publishers.
López, Adalberto, ed. 1980. *The Puerto Ricans: Their History, Culture, and Society*. Cambridge: Schenkman Publishing Company.
Mishna, Faye. 2012. *Bullying: A Guide to Research, Intervention, and Prevention*. New York: Oxford.
Mohr, Nicholasa. 1973. *Nilda*. New York: Harper.
Mohr, Nicholasa. 1975. *El Bronx Remembered*. New York: Harper.
Mohr, Nicholasa. 1977. *In Nueva York*. New York: Dial.
Mohr, Nicholasa. 1979. *Felita*. New York: Dial.
Mohr, Nicholasa. 1985. *Rituals of Survival*. Houston: Arte Publico.
Mohr, Nicholasa. 1986. *Going Home*. New York: Dial.
Mohr, Nicholasa. 1986b. "On Being Authentic." *Americas Review* 14 (3–4): 106–109.
Mohr, Nicholasa. 1987. "Puerto Rican Writers in the U.S., Puerto Rican Writers in Puerto Rico: A Separation beyond Language." *Americas Review* 15 (2): 87–92.
Mohr, Nicholasa. 1994. *Growing Up Inside the Sanctuary of My Imagination*. New York: Messner.
Mohr, Nicholasa. 1997. *A Matter of Pride and Other Stories*. Houston: Arte Publico.
Moreno, Marisel. 2012. *Family Matters: Puerto Rican Women on the Island and the Mainland*. Charlottesville: University of Virginia Press.
Nesdale, Dale. 2004. "Social Identity and Children's Ethnic Prejudice." In *The Development of the Social Self*, ed. Mark Bennett and Fabio Sani, 219–246. New York: Psychology Press.
Olweus, Dan. 2010. "Understanding and Researching Bullying: Some Critical Issues." In *Handbook of Bullying in Schools: An International Perspective*, ed. Shane Jimerson, Susan M. Swearer and Dorothy L. Espelage, 9–35. New York: Routledge.
Popp, Ann Marie, and Anthony A. Peguero. 2011. "Routine Activities and Victimization at School: The Significance of Gender." *Journal of Interpersonal Violence* 26 (12): 2413–2436.
Pytash, Kristine E., Denise N. Morgan, and Katherine E. Batchelor. 2013. "Recognize the Signs: Reading Young Adult Literature to Address Bullying." *Voices from the Middle* 20 (3): 15–20.
Rivera, Carmen H. 2002. *Kissing the Mango Tree: Puerto Rican Women Rewriting American Literature*. Houston: Arte Publico.
Stevens-Arroyo, Anthony M., and Ana Maria Díaz-Ramírez. 1982. "Puerto Ricans in the United States: A Struggle for Identity." In *The Minority Report:*

An Introduction to Racial, Ethnic, and Gender Relations, ed. Anthony Gary Dworkin and Rosalind J. Dworkin, 196–232. New York: Holt.

Swearer, Susan M., and Dorothy L. Espelage. 2010. "A Socio-ecological Model for Bullying Prevention and Intervention: Understanding the Impact of Adults in the Social Ecology of Youngsters." In *Handbook of Bullying in Schools: An International Perspective*, ed. Shane R. Jimerson, Susan M. Swearer and Dorothy L. Espelage, 61–72. New York: Routledge.

Swearer, Susan M., and Dorothy L. Espelage. 2012. *The Handbook of School Violence and School Safety: From Research to Practice*. New York: Routledge.

Torres-Padilla, José L., and Carmen Haydee Rivera. 2008. *Writing off the Hyphen: New Perspectives on the Literature of the Puerto Rican Diaspora*. Seattle: University of Washington Press.

Young, Terrell A., and Barbara A. Ward. 2011. "Bullies in Recent Books for Children and Young Adults." *Reading Horizons* 51 (1): 81–92.

United States Commission on Civil Rights. 1976. *Puerto Ricans in the Continental United States: An Uncertain Future*. Washington, DC: Commission on Civil Rights.

Wagenheim, Kal, and Olga Jimenez de Wagenheim, eds. [1975]1988. *The Puerto Ricans: A Documentary History*. Maplewood: Waterfront.

CHAPTER 8
"Like Alice, I was Brave"
The Girl in the Text in Olemaun's Residential School Narratives

Roxanne Harde

Over the first five years of this decade, Margaret (Olemaun) Pokiak-Fenton, with her daughter-in-law, Christy Jordan-Fenton, published two sets of paired chapter books and picturebooks that narrate Pokiak-Fenton's childhood experiences at a Catholic residential school (*Fatty Legs* (2010) and *When I Was Eight* (2013)) and the difficulties she encountered upon her return to her family and community (*A Stranger at Home* (2011) and *Not My Girl* (2014)). Set in the early 1940s, in the middle of the long period during which the Canadian government systematically removed Indigenous children from their homes and communities, these texts differ from most personal narratives about residential schools in that Olemaun chose—indeed she begged—to go to school. While these books, particularly the chapter books, make clear that Olemaun wanted to go to school because of a girl in a text—*Alice in Wonderland*—they also show the authors' placement of an Indigenous girl in the text as a model of resistance (and, therefore, an agent of decolonization), and it seems no accident that they were published during the years that Canada's Truth and Reconciliation Commission (TRC) convened.

The picturebooks were published after the chapter books; the first of them, *When I Was Eight* (2013) outlines Olemaun's determination to become literate: she pesters her father—a former mission school student and avid reader—into sending her to the school in Aklavik and refuses to let an abusive nun get the better of her. *Not My Girl* (2014), the second picturebook, frames her return home and the difficulties she has in re-assimilating into her family and culture. As she tells the longer version of her story to older readers in *Fatty Legs* (2010) and *A Stranger at Home* (2011), which are also illustrated and which include informative notes about the schools and photographs from her scrapbooks alongside detailed explanations of customs, tools, peoples, and the natural world, Olemaun engages in a discursive and material struggle that also becomes political action. While struggling to relearn *Inuvialuktun* and reclaim her cultural traditions, Olemaun offers a running critique of the institutions that attempted to steal her girlhood and identity even as they afforded what she desperately wanted—the ability to read about Alice for herself. Arguing that these books focus on the girl in the text as a way of demonstrating Indigenous resiliency and resistance to colonialism to their young readers, in this chapter I analyze the authors' depictions of Olemaun and the girls who matter to her.

Girlhood and Colonization

Since they tell these stories for young audiences, the Fentons appropriately craft the books with these audiences in mind: the language of each is at a suitable level, the more painful or graphic elements of residential school experience are veiled, and both sets of texts have beautiful illustrations. Political issues are not foregrounded, although they are present in explanatory notes and photographs in the picturebooks, and detailed in the chapter books through photographs, notes, and afterwords. In addition, the authors end the second book in each pair, *A Stranger at Home* (2011) and *Not My Girl* (2014) with acknowledgments of the TRC, dedicate the former to the TRC's commissioner, Justice Murray Sinclair, and list the TRC as one of the ways in which Canada and First Nations are working to address the trauma and loss resulting from the residential school system in the latter.

The TRC devotes the first two volumes of its multivolume report to residential schools and their impact on Indigenous, and, therefore, Canadian, society. The TRC notes that more than 150,000 Indigenous and Métis children were removed between the early 1800s and 1996. In dedicating the second volume to northern First Peoples, the TRC delineates differences dictated by cultures and geographies; these differences are the focus of Keavy Martin's (2011) study of Inuit writing, storytelling, and performance as an autonomous literary tradition. Martin attends to the ways in which Inuit narratives connect language, form, and context to satisfy both aesthetic and political agendas; these connections are subtle though meaningful in the Fentons' books. Olemaun's unwavering resistance to colonial oppression and her will to recover from the trauma she suffers in the Catholic school in Aklavik offer young readers ways in which to think about opposing the dominant settler discourse and decolonizing their world views.

There are, as Renate Eigenbrod has noted, many ways to narrate the traumas caused by the residential school system, including silences, and indirect forms of expression. Reading various texts about childhood in residential schools, Eigenbrod argues that narratives seemingly about victimization evoke, instead, "survival, resistance, and continuance of cultures against colonial policies aimed at their annihilation" (2012: 278). In terms of literature for children, narratives such as those by Shirley Sterling (Interior Salish), Ruby Slipperjack (Anishinaabe), and Nicola Campbell (Interior Salish), generally offer similar outlines: children forcibly removed from their homes to boarding schools where they face cruel members of religious orders; policies meant to negate their histories, traditions, and cultures; inadequate food and poor education; and violence and suffering. In each narrative, the author counters these colonial oppressions with the child protagonist's methods of resistance. Sterling's personal narrative, *My Name is Seepeetza* (1998), shows how summers and holidays at home strengthen and culturally renew Seepeetza. In Slipperjack's novel, *These Are My Words: The Residential School Diary of Violet Pesheens* (2016), the eponymous protagonist keeps a journal that helps her retain her language and traditions. Campbell's picturebooks, *Shi-shi-etko* (2005) and *Shin-chi's Canoe* (2008) feature a young girl and her little brother using mementos and memories from home to help them retain their culture and customs. The texts illustrate the resilience of Indigenous children as being limited only by their imaginations.

In the case of Olemaun, the Fentons' texts tacitly suggest that focusing on girls might be an important means of enacting decolonization; they are replete with girls: Alice, who captures, Olemaun's imagination; Olemaun as a compelling narrative center; her best friend Agnes, another residential school inmate; her mother, as one of the women who rejects the outsiders and their ways (although she, too, hungers to read and write); and her little sisters who will follow her to school. Male characters are fewer in number and mostly undeveloped: Olemaun's father, another residential school survivor, plays an important role, but all other male characters—Olemaun's little brother; a frightening monk; and a shadowy trapper of African descent—make the briefest of appearances. The plethora of girls in these texts insists that they have something profound to say about the realities of Indigenous childhood.

In a study of Aboriginal girls in Australian boarding schools, Christine Cheater points out that girls were targeted in far greater numbers than boys because of "anxieties about the girls' sexual behavior and demands for cheap domestic servants" (2010: 251). These schools taught only basic skills, she notes, and no "practical information on how to survive in white society" (263). However, Cheater also delineates the ways in which girls resisted by "forming bonds with one another and taking advantage of opportunities to be themselves" (251) and creating support networks that enabled them to "reestablish contact with Aboriginal communities" (264). In another qualitative study of Aboriginal girls, Pamela Downie looks at Canada's persistent colonial ideology that sees these girls as exploitable and dispensable, but she also sees the ways in which they resist. As she notes, the lived history of these girls "is also characterized by an intergenerational strength that is too often overlooked in depictions of gender- and culture-based violation and abuse." In her focus on gender and indigeneity, Downie juxtaposes stories about "the suffering and hardships faced by Aboriginal girls and women through the years" with "the equally powerful stories of survival and determination that are also told" (2006: 3). Similarly, in the Fentons' hands, Inuvialuit girlhood is not constituted exclusively by displacement and oppression but also by determination, innovation, and cultural survival.

As the focal point of these books, Olemaun is notable for her courage and intelligence but she is not the only girl who resists governmental and religious institutions that would rob her of her community, traditions, and cultural practices. Every girl in these books claims her agency in some way, from the fictional Alice who does as she pleases to the autobiographical Olemaun and her sisters and friends who counter colonization with strategies that range from talking back to engaging in subversive actions to running away. The Fentons' choice to identify her as Olemaun—even though she uses the name Margaret, given her by the nuns, as an adult—makes clear this girl's grounding in her culture even as her willingness to *be* Margaret demonstrates her ability to thrive in settler society. Contending that Aboriginal people have been reclaiming their cultures steadily as a means of unifying and healing their communities, the Fentons end both books with notes that outline the horrific experiences of Indigenous children in Canada's residential schools, and discuss efforts to reclaim traditional languages, foodways, oral traditions, and cultural practices. Their endnote to *Fatty Legs* (2010) points out that these schools were meant to strip generations of First Peoples of their culture and skills even as they prepared them for menial jobs while neglecting to teach them how to thrive in a colonized world. They conclude their endnote in *A Stranger at Home* by tying their work closely to that of the TRC: "The feelings of shame that have kept so many survivors on the outside of their own communities are being lifted through Truth and Reconciliation Commission national events, where experiences can be shared in a supportive setting, and through the work of brave survivors ... who have told their stories in all forms of art and media—including books like this one" (2011: 109). Decolonization through writing for girls seems an appropriate method, one that speaks to adults as well as children, and Olemaun Pokiak stands as an especially brave survivor.

Following Alice

In an essay on the legacy of residential schools and decolonization, Cynthia Wesley-Esquimaux (Chippewa) argues that First Nations people must resist the marginalization of their communities by moving "into the structured world of formal mainstream schooling" in order to "direct the transition and ultimate transformation of our families and communities" (2009: 28). Long before Wesley-Esquimaux contended that Indigenous participation in settler educational systems was one way to reinvent colonialism and change it into a forum where Indigenous people could thrive, a little Inuvialuit girl embraced that very idea. Early in *Fatty Legs* Olemaun emphasizes her fascination with the nuns she sees when she accompanies her father to Aklavik, because they "held the key to the greatest of the outsiders' mysteries—reading" (2010: 4). While Olemaun's older half-sister Ayouniq/Rosie refuses to discuss the school, she does read to Olemaun from the beautifully illustrated books their father had given her, particularly *Alice's Adventures in Wonderland*. "The stories were precious treasures to be enjoyed in the well-lit, toasty warmth of our smoke-scented tent, as the darkness of winter was constant, and the temperatures outside cold enough to freeze bare skin in seconds," Olemaun notes, but the "books were written in English, so I understood very little of them. I was always left with unanswered questions" (2010: 4). Rosie explains that Alice's Rabbit is "like a hare," to which Olemaun replies,

"Why did Alice follow it down the hole? To hunt it?" We read that Rosie gave her "a funny look" and replied. "No, Olemaun. She followed it because she was curious" (2010: 5). Olemaun quickly matches Alice's curiosity with her own as she questions Rosie about the school. The older girl refuses to discuss what must be painful memories; she exclaims that "[t]hey want all of your time for chores and for kneeling on your knees to ask forgiveness. … They take everything" (6). Aside from Olemaun's equation of Alice's rabbit with an Inuvialuit source of fur and food, the girls illustrate the tensions being faced by Indigenous families as increasing numbers of settlers entered their homelands, bringing with them their churches and schools, different technologies and materials, much of which these families find compelling and attractive. While the Inuvialuit, like other First Peoples, are willing to welcome and work with the settlers, to incorporate their innovations into traditional lifeways, they were and are not interested in giving up their own culture and traditions. Rosie, like her father before her, has learned the costs that come with acquiring the things the settlers can offer.

As Olemaun approaches her eighth birthday, she spends a good deal of time trying to convince her father to let her go to the school, pondering the book, and poring over John Tenniel's illustrations: "I still did not know what happened to her at the end of the burrow. Did she catch the hare?" (2010: 10). The images of Alice's adventures—bodily changes, encounters with strange creatures, conflicts with enemies—inspire her to badger her father to send her to the Catholic residential school in Aklavik, where he spent many years although he refused to speak "of the school and would never tell me of the wonderful things I could learn there. He was a smart man who loved to read, but he put little value in the outsider's learning compared to the things that our people knew" (8). When she asks again, he responds that the outsiders will not teach her necessary survival skills and that they will exploit her skills for their profit. "They feed you cabbage soup and porridge. They do not teach you how to make parkas and kamik. … They make you wear their scratchy outsiders' clothes, which keep out neither mosquitoes nor the cold. They teach you their songs and dances instead of your own. And they tell you that the spirit inside of you is bad and needs their forgiveness." Her response is confident: she already knows about hunting and trapping and curing foods; she will need to learn to sew anyway and she thinks the music she had heard resonating from the church in Tuktoyaktuk is beautiful. She confidently claims that "[t]hey would see that my spirit was good" (11). Just as her sister told her that the school would take everything, Olemaun's father explains that the school will wear her down the way the ocean wears a rock down into a small, smooth pebble. Her desire for literacy remains strong: she responds that the stone is still inside the pebble, and he agrees to send her. Her tenacity certainly does not wear away; her traditions and culture form the rock-solid foundation that allows Olemaun to layer settler education over the knowledge given her by her family and community.

At the school, the children spend far more hours working than learning, and Olemaun observes, "My stomach ached with hunger and my mind ached for knowledge" (2010: 41). In *When I was Eight*, she responds to every incident of cruelty by clinging to the "beautiful book my sister read me about a girl named Alice. I hugged it to my chest and tried to be brave like the girl in the story" (2013: n.p.). Olemaun learns quickly, however, repeatedly describing in *Fatty Legs* the means she found to practice reading and writing even as she followed the nuns' orders, noting that while "my schoolmates played cards and made dolls during recreation, I chose to read" (2010: 52). While working long hours in the hospital during an epidemic, she notes, "I could only find a moment's peace to read very late in the evening" (56). One nun in particular—whom Olemaun calls the Raven, in contrast to a kind nun she characterizes as the Swan while the children are wrens, small and clever—treats her with continual and extreme cruelty. As she gains literacy, Olemaun gains confidence, and after an especially miserable incident with the Raven, she notes, "I wasn't sure what she meant to teach me, but I had something to teach her about the spirit of us Inuvialuit" (49). Throughout, Olemuan responds to every incident of cruelty with a reference to reading, specifically reading about Alice. Immediately after a terrible encounter with one of the monks (she has been told to call them brothers, but notes that they are not family) who frightens her into soiling herself, she notes, "I had read *Alice's Adventures in Wonderland* four times. Rosie had been telling the truth: Alice had not been hunting the rabbit at all. I would have brought its pelt back for my father" (60). While she clearly gains comfort from her favorite book, Olemaun's comment demonstrates resistance: British Alice may just follow a rabbit to see where it takes her but Inuvialuit Olemaun will track and trap a hare, and make use of both its meat and its pelt. She offers young readers strategies of decolonization as she comes to understand the benefits and dangers of following a rabbit down its hole. She pays dearly for her literacy, but never loses the cultural autonomy that enables her to skin the hare.

The picturebook, *When I Was Eight* (2013), also offers scenes of cruelty, though these are even more circumscribed for a younger audience. After a series of incidents in which she defies the nuns, the Raven locks her in the cellar. "I descended each step deliberately, hiding my fear. My hands quickly found a cabbage in the shadows and I scurried up the stairs. But she slammed the door, shutting out all the light. I pulled the handle. It was locked. A scream build in my chest, but I held it in. I closed my eyes, pulled up my stockings, and breathed deeply. ... I spelled my Inuit name. ... I spelled many things from home and was starting on the title of my book—A—L—I—when the door opened" (2013: n.p.). In *Fatty Legs*, Olemaun continually comforts herself with the book, aligning herself with Alice and the nuns with the villains. "I pulled my favorite book from underneath my pillow and imagined the Raven in the role of the Queen of Hearts" (2010: 67). In both picturebook, *When I Was Eight* (2013) and novel, *Fatty Legs* (2010), she follows the story of the red stockings by noting that she feels just "like Alice after a bite of magic cake—as large as the entire room" (2013: n.p.). The narrative ties every victory to Alice, and when Olemaun triumphantly reads out loud in class to end *When I Was Eight*, she says, "I was Olemaun, conqueror of evil, reader of books. I was a girl who traveled to a strange and faraway land to stand against a tyrant, like Alice. And like Alice, I was brave, clever, and as unyielding as the strong stone that sharpens an *ulu*" (2013: n.p.). *Fatty Legs* ends with reference to Alice as well. When she finally goes home after two years at the school, Olemaun reads from Alice to her family and we read, "She crawled under the warm hides, gazed at the glow of the embers from my father's pipe, and drifted off to sleep. My curiosity had led me far away, and now here I was, after two years, satisfied that I now knew what happened to girls who went down rabbit holes" (2010: 82). Throughout, she responds to colonization as an agent, making her voice matter as she negotiates the most patriarchal of social institutions.

The second novel, *A Stranger at Home* (2011) and picturebook, *Not My Girl* (2014) involve Alice less, though Olemaun finds refuge in the English novel when things go badly, which they often do as she works to relearn her language and cultural practices. She continually retreats "into a corner of the tent [to hide] in [her] favorite book" (2014: n.p.). Moreover, on her first night home, after her mother fails to recognize her and she cannot eat her food, the family gathers around while Olemaun reads to them about Alice, her little brother sitting on her lap looking at Tenniel's pictures. *A Stranger at Home* demonstrates the whole family's pride in and fascination with Olemaun's accomplishment, but even so, she notes that while she has lost her language, her friend Agnes can still speak *Inuvialuktun*; because of Alice, she says, "I had been so eager to learn the new ways, I had not thought to hold on to the old ones" (2011: 53). She finally reflects on the differences between western culture and her own, considering both literacy and religion: "I understood from the elders that they had their own stories to give them guidance, stories that were handed down instead of being written" (83). Olemaun may have begun this rumination in concern for her family's souls, as the nuns have taught her is necessary, but she comes to understand the power of the traditional stories of the Inuvialuit because of the ways in which Alice has inspired, strengthened, and comforted her. In part, the power of Alice's story enables Olemaun to relearn the power of the oral traditions of her people and see how Catholic dogma provides an irrelevant substitute.

Finding Agnes

Olemaun's friend, Agnes, also inhabits these texts, moving in and out of them, teaching Olemaun important lessons, but not all the lessons she needs to learn. Although they were best friends on Banks Island, because of her mother's illness, Agnes's family relocates to Tuktoyaktuk and, because she is two years older than Olemaun, Agnes enters the school in Aklavik a few years before Olemaun does. Therefore, when Olemaun's mother warns her, in *Fatty Legs* (2010) that the strangers "will not be kind to you. They are not your family, and they are not like us," Olemaun declares, "I will have Agnes. I will be fine" (19). However, Agnes is not there when Olemaun expects her to be as she enters the school, although she shows up when the girls are having their hair cut and being given new clothes, and she helps Olemaun put on her uniform. Through the course of the chapter books, Agnes often whispers helpful translations in *Inuvialuktun* of the nuns' orders, demonstrates acceptable behavior to Olemaun, and explains the school's rhythms. For example, she tells Olemaun that she will get used to the food, and that classes will not begin until fall, so they will spend the summer doing chores and gardening. Even so, Agnes cannot rescue Olemaun during her most traumatic experiences at the school that include having the cruel nun, the Raven, make her work long hours in the hospital without a break, and then punish her for soiling herself after the frightening (and possibly veiled) encounter with a monk, as mentioned above, locking her in a dark cellar and making her do extra chores, and giving her ugly red stockings while all the other girls get lovely black or grey ones. When Olemaun is teased by the other girls about the red stockings, Agnes is bullied too, called "Skinny Legs" to Olemaun's "Fatty Legs," and Agnes does not help her. "For the very first time, Agnes did not pick me first to be on her team at recreation time" (2010: 69). While she makes clear that her feelings are hurt, Olemaun refuses to blame or condemn Agnes. Rather, she takes matters into her own hands and waits for an opportunity (while doing extra work in the laundry) to burn the hated stockings to ashes.

Adding Agnes to these texts allows the Fentons to model for children some of the various methods First Nations people employed to negotiate colonialism. Very much like the stone (after which she is named) that Inuvialuit women use to sharpen their *ulus* (stone blades), Olemaun deals with injustice in a straightforward manner while Agnes offers a model of passive endurance and resistance. *A Stranger at Home* (2011) begins with the girls' journey home to Tuktoyaktuk, where Olemaun's family now lives, since her father has been recognized for his skills and offered steady government employment. Because of a short summer, Olemaun has not seen her family for two years, and her anticipation almost overwhelms her. Agnes, however, remembers how difficult the transition from school to home can be. When they arrive, as her mother declares that she is "not my girl" over and over, Olemaun finally understands Agnes's stoic demeanor. Now that both girls live in the same community again, Olemaun, faced with her mother's anguish at the changes in her daughter, and unable to eat the food or speak her language, is cheered at the "thought of seeing [Agnes] every day" (29). However, Agnes's mother hisses "no English" every time she sees Olemaun, and she then forbids Agnes to play with Olemaun, because Olemaun has forgotten how to be part of her community and culture. Agnes again explains things to Olemaun in whispers during a chance encounter at the Hudson's Bay Company store. "My mother and father say I am an outsider now. ... They do not want me playing with children like you—children from the school. They don't want me speaking English, or praying, or doing anything like a white person" (53). While Agnes is absent from *When I Was Eight* (2013) the Fentons repeat this scene almost verbatim in the picturebook *Not My Girl* (2014) thereby emphasizing Agnes's acquiescence and Olemaun's near complete isolation and her ostracization from her community.

Agnes eventually informs Olemaun in *A Stranger at Home* (2011) that when she was at school, she practiced "conversations in her head in [their] native language. Because of this she had not forgotten how to speak [their] language" (53). Agnes's quiet resistance serves her well when, because of her mother's illness, she is to be sent back to the school. Instead, she disappears, later telling Olemaun that she ran hard for a full day and then took two days to walk back home. By that time, the ship had sailed and she was left alone, a trick Agnes repeats a year later when Olemaun returns to the school to protect her little sisters. The narrative offers a telling scene when Olemaun, mourning the loss of her friend and feeling betrayed, has a terrible nightmare, one she had had when she was at school. "I dreamed that I was back at the outsiders' school, locked inside the skirt of one of the nuns' habits. The nun told me that she would let me out if I could remember my name and if my mother could recognize me. ... Agnes knew where the key was to free me, but in the distance I could see her aboard the *North Star*, sailing away to Banks Island without me" (57–58). If Olemaun refused to blame Agnes for not supporting or saving her at the school, she clearly feels abandoned by her friend as she faces the difficulties of re-assimilating into Inuvialuit culture. At the same time, her dream links Agnes and the key to freedom that Olemaun will need to use in the future. When she returns to the school in order to take care of her sisters, who now are being forced to go, she will teach them Agnes's methods for maintaining their language. Wesley-Esquimaux emphasizes the need for education "in the more remote areas of central and northern Canada," as a necessary support for social action, and she argues that First Nations girls and women need to work together and prioritize all educational experiences, inside and outside of the classroom to help "stem the tide of dropping out of school and life" (2009: 29). The relationships Olemaun builds with Agnes and her sisters, before and through their schooling, strengthen them and enable them to make their communities resilient. The books emphasize their closeness as girls and now as elderly women.

Leading her Sisters

The Fentons end both novels, *Fatty Legs* (2010) and *A Stranger at Home* (2011), with scenes explaining that Olemaun will return to the school in order to protect her sisters. *Fatty Legs* concludes with a chapter titled "After the Story," in which Olemaun notes that the year following her return home was one of the happiest of her life, but "my three younger sisters grew curious. After they pestered my father non-stop, and the government made school attendance a condition for receiving child benefits, he gave in" (83–84). *A Stranger at Home* offers more detail. Her father asks her to return to Aklavik with her sisters, and he begins his request by foregrounding the necessity for the Inuvialuit to become educated in the outsiders' language and culture. He notes, on the one hand, that the government is making education mandatory and, on the other that "[m]ore of them will be coming. Without learning their language and how to read and write it, we won't survive" (95). In so doing, he shows that he fully understands what Olemaun has faced and must face again at the school, and that she will need to be even stronger in order to protect her sisters.

Julia Emberley examines the impact of colonial cultural practices on the everyday lives of Indigenous women, youth, and children, and the ways in which Indigenous writers confound these practices by deploying Aboriginality as a complex and enabling sign of social, cultural, and political transformation. Both *Not My Girl* (2014) and *A Stranger at Home* (2011) detail a scene that explains Olemaun's experiences as a sister. On the one hand, in *Not My Girl*, on Christmas morning, there are dolls for the little girls and a train for Olemaun's brother. Although these dolls look nothing like Inuvialuit girls, Olemaun cries in disappointment at not being given one. On the other hand, the gift she does receive makes up for the lack of a doll and comes directly from Inuvialuit traditions: her father gives her her own dogsled and team. The picturebook ends with Olemaun speeding past Agnes, who waves and cheers, and her mother, who proudly shouts, "My girl" (2014: n.p.). The novel offers more detail, but like the picturebook describes the scene in which Olemaun's father teases her for crying by asking if she is not "too grown up for dolls" (2011: 87; 2014: n.p.). Before the scene moves to her being given the dog team and sled, Olemaun explains that the "dolls we had made out of scraps at the outsider's school were clumsy, with lopsided or missing faces" (87). Like many little girls, she wants a beautiful doll, but like any child who has faced attempts to steal her childhood, she also wants to reclaim what girlhood she can. At the same time, both texts dim the shine of those settler-society dolls as they feature the girl-sized dogsled and team.

The day after Christmas and after her triumphant ride in her dogsled under the Northern Lights, her father takes Olemaun to the Hudson's Bay Company where he buys her both books and a doll. The next scene is incredibly poignant and pointed. Olemaun plays with her sisters and their dolls, fashioning little beds for their "children" and pretending "they were three sisters who did everything together." However, when the younger girls want to pretend that the dolls are going away to the outsiders' school, Olemaun refuses to play: "I didn't tell Mabel and Elizabeth that the nuns would chop off their dolls' pretty ringlets and make them wear shabby clothes that didn't fit properly. I didn't think anyone needed to know about that" (91). She thus emphasizes her desire to protect them even before her father asks her to accompany them to the school. When he does, they cry together as she understands and agrees to return to the school, but she notes, "I didn't cry again after that. ... I needed to start preparing myself to go back. I had to teach myself not to cry anymore" (97). Just as Rosie tried to shield her, she attempts to shield them from the knowledge that girls' well-being matters profoundly to the Inuvialuit but not at all to the Catholic Church. The narrative concludes with a note explaining that she knew "how the school worked and what to do to stay out of the nuns' way, and I made sure my sisters knew as well" (105). She details the difficulties they faced—the long hours of work and the homesickness—which she counters by letting them sleep with her even though she is punished when caught. She also remembers the lesson Agnes taught her. "I would whisper stories or sing them songs in *Inuvialuktun* until they fell asleep" (106). Her conclusion affirms the strength of Inuvialuit culture and their ability to excel in the Euro-western milieu: "as awful as it was, my sisters remained true Pokiaks: strong-willed and determined. Mabel did so well in school that she went on to high school in Yellowknife and eventually became a nurse" (106). Olemaun's pride in her sisters, in family, and community, affirms the role of education in Inuvialuit girls' lives. If education served as an agent of the state and a tool of colonialism, then at the same time it empowered girls to shape their own worlds, identities, and destinies.

Conclusion: Telling Her Story

As noted by Cheater and Downie above, the stories of girls' residential school experiences—whether through academic study and interview, or fictional and personal narrative—consistently allow for the misery of the experience, the empowerment of the education, and the victory of survival. Linda Tuhiwai Smith similarly discusses Indigenous resistance to colonization, noting that the politics of the everyday life of the Indigenous person is reflected in "stories which tell of what it means, what it feels like, to be present while your history is erased before your eyes" (2012: 31). Marie Battiste (2013) documents the nature of Eurocentric models of education and their devastating impacts on Indigenous knowledge, and argues for the repositioning of Indigenous knowledge systems. One method of enacting the foregrounding of Indigenous ways of knowing is through stories for young readers, like those by the Fentons. Wesley-Esquimaux also affirms the necessity for Native storytellers to tell all the stories. "Instead of telling only the stories about trauma and victimization and pain, let us talk about our survival and our undeniable strengths. It is essential for us to articulate the strengths that we have, not only in a way that validates our survival, but in a way that validates and 'victorizes' our ability to take control of our lives" (2009: 28). The Fentons offer their young readers all the aspects of the stories desired by Smith, Battiste, and Wesley-Esquimaux. Olemaun draws strength from Alice, but she receives as much inspiration from Agnes as she does from Alice; her sisters' needs necessitate but also enable Olemaun's return to the school, and the school in turn enables their success in the dominant culture while they determine their ability to thrive in their own communities and traditions. Wesley-Esquimaux looks for ways to show how Indigenous people can decolonize their homes: she suggests "talking to our children ... telling them about historic and personal lives and about the beauty of our cultural and social truths ... as the ancestors used to do, before contact and the subjugation of women, before religious guilt and patriarchy took over, before ... the dominant culture took over" (2009: 30). Overall, in telling Olemaun's story—and those of her sisters and friend, and her retelling of Alice—in texts for pre- and adolescent girls, Pokiak-Fenton and Jordan-Fenton employ the girl in the text as a means of offering young people an understanding of both colonial practices and methods of resisting them, of prioritizing their own culture and thereby decolonizing their world views.

Acknowledgments

I wish to thank the peer reviewers for their exceedingly helpful comments on this article, and Ann Smith, whose editorial work also made it much stronger than it might have been.

This work has been supported by a Killam Grant as administered by the University of Alberta.

ROXANNE HARDE is Professor of English at the University of Alberta's Augustana Faculty, where she also serves as Associate Dean, Research. A Fulbright Scholar, she researches and teaches American literature and culture, focusing on children's literature, popular culture, women's writing, and Indigenous literature. Her most recent book is *The Embodied Child*, coedited with Lydia Kokkola (2017). She has published articles in *The Lion and the Unicorn*, *Mosaic*, *Critique*, *Jeunesse*, and *IRCL*, and chapters in more than twenty collections of essays. An award-winning teacher, Roxanne has presented teaching workshops in Canada and Europe, and has published several pedagogical essays.

References

Battiste, Marie. 2013. *Decolonizing Education: Nourishing the Learning Spirit*. Saskatoon: Purich Publishing.

Campbell, Nicola I. 2005. *Shi-shi-etko*. Illus. Kim LaFave. Toronto: Groundwood.

Campbell, Nicola I. 2008. *Shin-chi's Canoe*. Illus. Kim LaFave. Toronto: Groundwood.

Cheater, Christine. 2010. "Stolen Girlhood: Australia's Assimilation Policies and Aboriginal Girls." In *Girlhood: A Global History*, ed. Jennifer Helgren and Colleen A. Vasconcellos, 250–267. New Brunswick, NJ: Rutgers University Press.

Downie, Pamela J. 2006. "Aboriginal Girls in Canada: Living Histories of Dislocation, Exploitation and Strength." In *Girlhood: Redefining the Limits*, ed. Jasmin Jiwani, Candis Steenbergen and Claudia Mitchell, 2–14. Montreal, OR: Black Rose Books.

Eigenbrod, Renate. 2012. "'For the Child Taken, for the Parent Left Behind': Residential School Narratives as Acts of 'Survivance'." *English Studies in Canada* 38 (3–4): 277–297.

Jordan-Fenton, Christy, and Margaret Pokiak-Fenton. 2010. *Fatty Legs*. Illus. Liz Amini-Holmes. Toronto: Annick.

Jordan-Fenton, Christy, and Margaret Pokiak-Fenton. 2011. *A Stranger at Home*. Illus. Liz Amini-Holmes. Toronto: Annick.

Jordan-Fenton, Christy, and Margaret Pokiak-Fenton. 2013. *When I Was Eight*. Illus. Gabrielle Grimard. Toronto: Annick.

Jordan-Fenton, Christy, and Margaret Pokiak-Fenton. 2014. *Not My Girl*. Illus. Gabrielle Grimard. Toronto: Annick.

Martin, Keavy. 2011. *Stories in a New Skin: Approaches to Inuit Literature*. Winnipeg: University of Manitoba Press.

Slipperjack, Ruby. 2016. *These Are My Words: The Residential School Diary of Violet Pesheens*. Dear Canada Series. Toronto: Scholastic.

Smith, Linda Tuhiwai. 2012. *Decolonizing Methodologies: Research and Indigenous Peoples*. (2nd ed.) London: Zed.

Sterling, Shirley. 1998. *My Name is Seepeetza*. Toronto: Groundwood.

Truth and Reconciliation Commission of Canada. 2015. *Canada's Residential Schools: The History*. Montreal: McGill-Queen's University Press.

Truth and Reconciliation Commission of Canada. 2015. *Canada's Residential Schools: The Inuit and Northern Experience*. Montreal: McGill-Queen's University Press.

Wesley-Esquimaux, Cynthia C. 2009. "Trauma to Resilience: Notes on Decolonization." In *Restoring the Balance: First Nations Women, Community, and Culture*, ed. Gail Guthrie Valaskakis, Madeleine Dion Stout and Eric Guimond, 13–34. Winnipeg: University of Manitoba Press.

CHAPTER 9

Girl, Interrupted and Continued
Rethinking the Influence of Elena Fortún's Celia

Ana Puchau de Lecea

In late 1920s Spain, Elena Fortún (pseudonym of Encarnación Aragoneses, 1886–1952) introduced the character of Celia Gálvez de Montalbán, a seven-year-old girl from a middle-class family in Madrid. She presented Celia as a girl who encouraged children to wonder why grown-ups have to be right even in the most illogical of circumstances. The construction of Celia's childhood innocence allowed Fortún to promote non-conformist messages directed at all members of society, starting with little girls and then their mothers. Although Celia's world reflects a hierarchy in which adults dominate children, she found a way to ask her readers to consider the fairness of given situations. In doing so, Fortún encouraged girls to be critical of their own world during the Second Republic (1931–1939), a period of social progress that preceded the Spanish Civil War (1936–1939).

Although progressive elements were silenced under Francisco Franco's dictatorship (1939–1975) in the decades to follow, Fortún continued adding titles to the series from her exile in Argentina. Her young readers could continue appreciating Celia's ability to disclose how things are not always the way adults say they are, even during a period of suppressed freedom. During the 1940s and 1950s, while the final stories in the series,

---

Notes for this section can be found on page 156.

Celia institutriz (Celia governess) (1944) and *Celia se casa* (Celia gets married) (1950), were being published some of her early readers began their own careers as writers. *Nada* (Nothing) (1944), by 23-year-old Carmen Laforet, initiated a boom of autobiographical novels written by women that featured adolescents. These *bildungsroman* show the characteristic stifling context of post-war Spain, represented through an unstable family atmosphere. These young characters, as reflected in the works of Carmen Laforet (1921–2004), were modelled on Celia and the novels written in emulation of Fortún's literary style. Appreciating her influence on different occasions, writer and critic Carmen Martín Gaite pointed out that "a rigorous study of the work of Elena Fortún, which all writers of the fifties enjoyed in childhood, will explain what the principles of 'social realism' of the mid-century novel were" (1993: 37).[1]

I consider Fortún as a harbinger of girls' power in the 1920s and seek to discuss how she, as a literary figure, served as a precursor to authors of the 1950s in Spain. In the first section I consider the creation and impact of Celia as an alternative character in children's literature in the context of the role of women and girls in society in the 1920s. The second section turns to the reaction of Franco's censorship corps to these books and their underlying ideology and considers the reception among members of the next generation of writers and the impact of these books on them. Through different examples, I demonstrate that Celia was not always the rebellious girl depicted in the first volumes, and I show how she transitioned into a misfit or what would later be called *La chica rara* (the weird girl) in an essay thus named by Martín Gaite in 1987. (I will return to this presently.)

Since the 1920s, Fortún's stories have continued to be republished, and Celia's adventures have been enjoyed by generations of girls. After a hiatus in the publication of the series during the Francoist censorship period, the discovery of the unpublished manuscript of *Celia en la revolución* (Celia in the revolution) (1943) at the end of the 1980s by researcher Marisol Dorao spurred interest in not only Celia but also in Fortún, and the writer's works were published again. In 1992, film director José Luis Borau produced a television adaptation of the first volumes of "Celia and Her World," with Martín Gaite collaborating on the screenplay. The recent re-editing of some of Fortún's books and the publication of what is now thought of as her secret novel, *Oculto sendero* (Hidden path) (2016)[2] have brought Fortún back to the forefront of the Spanish literary scene.

The Problem of the Modern Woman

Fortún's biography (Dorao 2001) illustrates the many lives lived by the author of "Celia and Her World," her constant pursuit of peace, happiness, and identity, and her personal struggle to remain true to her feminist values without neglecting her writing career while trying to be a virtuous mother and wife. Fortún's role as a mother and wife was troubled given the death of her youngest child, Manuel (Bolín), at the age of ten. Furthermore, this was not the only unexpected death in the family. Her husband Eusebio Gorbea, struggling with depression, committed suicide in 1948 in Argentina, where they had lived in exile for almost ten years because of his allegiance to and service with the Republican faction during the war. In 1951, months before her death, she wrote to her friends Inés Field and Mercedes Hernández regretting the "nonsense" (Dorao 2001: 73) of getting married and, later, not getting divorced, and explaining that she had never enjoyed motherhood.

It was Hernández's children, her daughter Florinda especially, who inspired Celia's adventures. However, as Martín Gaite has pointed out, it is unlikely that Fortún would have written these stories if she had not met other intellectuals at the Feminine Lyceum Club in Madrid, a socially progressive, cultural institution where women could organize and collaborate on intellectual events (1993).[3]

At different points throughout "Celia and Her World," Fortún's biographical details are recognizable through the words of her protagonist. In this way, Fortún explores the creative subjectivity of women and the problematic role of motherhood in a society that is beginning to discuss the emancipation of women and the importance of education as a means to regenerate the nation and the individual (Capdevila-Argüelles 2009). As an example of the faithful portrayal of the society of the time depicted in the stories about Celia, Fortún introduces Celia's mother as a member of the Lyceum. In a scene from *Celia, lo que dice* (What Celia says) (1929), Celia's mother cannot stay and play with her daughter because she has many things to do: "Paying the cook, writing two or three letters and going out at six to have tea with my friends from the Lyceum" (64). If the girl reader was not familiar with such a modern institution as the Lyceum, she would learn about it from Celia. In this subtle way, Fortún spread the idea of a progressive society.

One of the most interesting relationships in the books is that between Celia and her mother. Pilar de Montalbán is educated and spends a lot of time away from home and from her daughter. This relationship illustrates the role of women in the Spain of the 1920s and the uncertain role that motherhood had in the life of the new modern woman. Celia's mother represents a desire to be active outside of the home, to have a life separate from her family duties, and independent of her husband; she shares these desires with Fortún. As a consequence, Celia is left with Miss Nelly, her English nanny, who embodies traditional education. She is used by Fortún as a way of criticizing and exploring different forms of pedagogy.

Aligned with the philosophy of the *Institución Libre de Enseñanza* (The Free Educational Institution) (1876–1936), a significant educational project based on the ideas of Krausism, Fortún followed its guidelines and collaborated with their mission in different ways.[4] At an institutional conference Fortún read about the importance of telling stories to children and worried about how little time mothers were spending at home and their lack of contribution to their children's education. She wrote, "It would be desirable for it to be the mother who told the first stories because the faculty of attention is acquired in the first years of life ... but in modern times the mother is too busy ... or infinitely unoccupied, and either way she does not have time to tell stories to her children" ([1946] 2008: 19). Fortún knew about the importance of nurturing and the benefits that children receive from having a close relationship with their mother; she herself was dealing with a problematic relationship with motherhood. She presents Pilar de Montalbán as a modern woman combining motherhood with the development of her social and independent self. In contrast to the role of the domestic angel praised by conservative elements of society, Celia and her father respect and admire the kind of independent woman she is but at the same time they feel her abandonment of them. In this way Fortún shows the tension between children's emotional needs and the pull of female emancipation.

However, Celia's father is generally more sympathetic to her, and their relationship is very close since they find common ground in missing Celia's mother when she is away. Interestingly enough, it is Celia's father who presents her with a notebook so she can begin writing down her fantasies and become a novelist. This gesture is especially representative of Fortún's modern spirit since the father not only gives the girl permission to have her own ideas and a space in which to write about them, but he also encourages her to do so. Writing is considered a transgressive act since it fosters autonomy and individuality and can be used to create alternative realities. In contrast to the depicted support of Celia's father, Fortún had to start writing secretly to avoid disturbing her husband who was fairly well known as a writer and who did not take it well that she was becoming more successful than him (Dorao 2001).

Alternative Femininities

> I want to be a Greta Garbo ... or the cook, or a witch, but not a daughter.
> (Fortún [1929]1993: 69)

During the 1920s and 1930s, when the "Celia and Her World" stories were published, children's literature was being consolidated as a genre in itself. Public initiatives such as the National Book Festival in 1926 under Primo de Rivera proclaimed the advantages that the promotion of reading in children would bring to the publishing business. The commercial strategy devised in Spain during this period shows how children's literature could be lucrative given the collective will to spread reading practices among the young. The instating of the Second Republic in 1931 confirmed and accelerated the process of promoting reading since the potential to educate Spanish citizens was a key element of the Republic. Developing a love of books from childhood was fundamental to creating future readers who could become educated adults and it contributed at the same time to the increasing marketability of commodities targeted at children. This social and political aim overlapped with a period of creativity and renewal of literature in general in which children's literature and Celia the character were fully immersed. Manuel Aguilar, who founded his publishing company in 1923, discovered the stories in *Gente Menuda* (Little people), the weekly children's supplement to the journal *Blanco y Negro* (Black and White), part of the *ABC* newspaper, and decided to publish them in the form of books. The first compilation, *Celia, lo que dice* (1929) consisted of eighteen stories and was the first in the series "Celia and Her World." They were considered to be the best children's books of the time[5] (Escobar 1990; Sánchez 2001).

Fortún was also influenced by pedagogy and a great part of her success as an author was closely related to her education in the newest pedagogical strategies. Instead of providing a lesson in her stories, Fortún used children's logic to raise questions about socially acceptable concepts or institutions and to denounce the belief that logic and normality were relative concepts rarely shared among children and adults. With the reader, Celia shares her view of the world in which she grows up and she demonstrates her (and Fortún's) great social commitment represented in a responsibility to share with the less privileged. According to Fortún, stories awaken children's attention and imagination, and their intellectual and (possibly) moral future depend on them ([1946] 2008). Her presentation of Celia in first person narration as the voice of the author herself enables her to take sides among adults and children and allows her to refer to the silence always demanded of the latter.

In this way, she contests the restraints of her age and gender; she creates her own spaces and has her own opinions.

In Fortún's writing, the role of readers is an active one; they complete the written story by building on it as they read. Throughout this series, the character presents her readers with familiar dialogues and an evaluative conclusion of what has just happened. For example, in the story "El modelo de París" (The outfit from Paris), Celia argues with her mother because she does not want to wear a blue dress.

> 'Girls shut up.'
> 'Ok, girls shut up, but I say that this dress is ugly, and old, and it's not mine.'
> 'Can you shut up?' – said mum, very angry. … 'Shut up, my head is aching!'
> Grown-ups always have headaches when you want to tell them something. Mum went out to buy I don't know what; Juana went to the kitchen, to tell stories to the cook, who never has headaches, and I stayed in my room looking terrible in the blue dress. (Fortún [1929]1993: 88–89)

In this example, Fortún uses a variety of strategies such as different kinds of perspectivation (first person dialogue and narration), a topic of interest for children, and an evaluation of the scene after an unsuccessful interaction with a grown-up. The child reader can react to the passage by recognizing the context and the role of the characters but also by empathizing with Celia's evaluative use of reported speech as a conclusion to the scene. Fortún felt that individuals are more persuasive when they tell stories. In many scenes, she portrays Celia along with her mother as a representation of an old system that needs to be revised. Celia is aware that the role of the daughter in that relationship is terribly underestimated so she will avoid being in that position as much as she can. The scene while playing in her friend María Teresa's house in *Celia, lo que dice* provides an amusing example of this. In this passage, Celia refuses to play the character of the daughter, usually a passive personality condescended to by her mother (according to María Teresa, she would be taken, taught, and probably beaten). Instead, Celia suggests three interesting female characters: Hollywood star and *femme fatale* archetype Greta Garbo, who was a questionable model for a little girl; a cook, a submissive servant and representative of the role she is supposed to play later in life; and a witch, practically the opposite of the conservative ideal of the domestic angel. In this way, Fortún, through Celia, proposes different types of femininity for her readers, and, moreover, shows that she prefers other options over the one that she is expected to uphold.

The effect of the girl's voice in these stories is reinforced throughout the series by her asking the readers direct questions that invoke a sense of confidentiality and intimacy. In *Celia, lo que dice*, Fortún deliberately considers the reader as part of the plot and addresses her in the feminine: "*Tú, lectora, lo comprenderás mejor*" ("You, reader, will understand it better") (1993: 53), "*Presta atención, lectora*" ("Pay attention, reader") (70). With this inclusive formula the author directly challenges the child, and the reader approaches this incomplete text that must be built as it is being read. These two examples of interaction are offered at the beginning of the book and give the impression that the author/character is reading her story to the audience, inviting the participants to give their opinion. By using children as her main protagonists and focusing on their seemingly naive point of view, Fortún offered new visions of Spanish society and social change and established a dialogue with her audience, rather than writing books to be read without interrogation.

Girls under Dictatorship

Obedience, Submission, and Censorship

> And the tone they use! 'When adults speak, children must be quiet'. 'You should never contradict an adult'.
> At the table: 'Eat and be silent'. I don't know where things would end up if we always had to shut up. (Fortún [1929]1993: 42)

After being lauded in the 1930s, Celia's naturally rebellious personality did not escape Francoist censorship. As opposed to the guidelines of the *Institución Libre de Enseñanza*, Franco imposed a model of compliance and domestic education for girls based on the conservative norms of the *Sección Femenina* (Women's Section), a branch of the fascist political party Falange, which appeared in 1934 as a reaction to the modern woman. Girls were now considered only in their future roles as mothers and nurturers, and the principal features of national Catholic women were chastity, submission to men, and lack of rationality (Craig 1998). Far from these requirements, Fortún's early books advocate for the liberation of girls and women and question patriarchy and authority in general. Celia's rebellion represented a threat to the Francoist understanding of feminine submission and Fortún was in a dire situation in the new circumstances in which her books were published: she was a woman (dealing with the prejudices about what kind of literature women should write); she portrayed a girl protagonist behaving contrary to the official model and showing initiative; and she presented contemporary Spain as the context for her stories—the same context as that of the child reader (1998). The fact that the readers could relate a fictional story to their immediate environment, therefore acknowledging different ways to build their identity was a dangerous idea in the eyes of the censors.

Francoism celebrated obedience as virtue. In a society in which men should obey their superiors, children should obey adults and show respect by self-censoring their words. A woman's role as housewife, mother, and supporter of the husband erased the advances won by the feminists during the Republic (Bravo-Guerreira and Maharg-Bravo 2003). In contrast, the stories about Celia that had been in circulation since 1929 offered an opposing model of behavior with a protagonist who questions the authority of grown-ups, shows a lack of conformity, and confronts the adults with a child's logic. In contradiction to the lack of rationality projected by the Falangist prototype for girls, Celia's opinions are reasonable if they are heard. The imposition of silence among children was one of the abuses Fortún had denounced in "Celia and Her World" from the beginning, and this now also challenged Francoist precepts. Celia rebels against the continued burden of silence and feels frustrated when her complaints are not heard and she is not allowed to negotiate a new situation. In this way Fortún does not appear to be indoctrinating, but encouraging a critical perspective for the child reader.

Not surprisingly, there was some difficulty getting some of these books published and even reprinted under the dictatorship. The figure of Elena Fortún was suspect, a feminist writing in exile under a pseudonym, and married to a Republican. Ian Craig (1998) provides evidence of a letter from Aguilar in 1943, in which after being asked about Fortún's political tendencies, he would try to describe her as a modern woman who would never have included "antifascist" (73) content in her stories. Two years later, *Celia institutriz* (Celia governess) (1944) was censored, as well as the rest of Fortún's works. Fortún showed her surprise and indignation regarding this decision and resolved to change her strategy for the next book, *El cuaderno de Celia* (Celia's notebook) (1947), an odd novel in which Celia goes back to being her nine-year-old self and displays submissive behavior. Months later, the ban on *Celia institutriz* was lifted, but the book would be considered suitable only for adults, and the rest of the stories were censored.

However, *Celia en el colegio* (Celia at school), originally published in 1932, would be denied publication on several occasions and finally rated as appropriate only for readers older than 16 (Craig 1998). The importance of silence and obedience is manifest in many books in this series, but perhaps more importantly in this one. Respecting the *silencio mayor* (great silence) was a disciplinary measure at the Catholic boarding school Celia attended, where students had to remain silent in order to allow for reflection and prayer. The school as a social institution served as a site of traditional female socialization. Beatriz Caamaño (2007) explores the influence of religion and traditional education in the construction of femininity in "Celia and Her World." The model promoted by the *Institución Libre de Enseñanza*, followed and practiced by Fortún, was an instruction based on communication between student and teacher, with the objective of raising children capable of critical thinking who deciphered reality on their own terms. Instead, traditional education denied children's agency and trained them to adapt to oppression. This model is depicted in *Celia en el colegio* (1932), in which the nuns deprive girls of their individuality and educate them in submission and domesticity. Celia, who represents the new woman, experiences many difficulties in enduring the physical and behavioral limitations forced upon her by her superiors. Rigid timetabling and having to walk in line contradicts her desire for independence and her resistance to indoctrination is continually juxtaposed with what is expected of her. According to the censorship report in 1956, the book was "anti-pedagogical by continuous disobedience [and] disrespect," and the over patience and tolerance of the nuns with the "rebellious" (Craig 1998: 74) girl put discipline at risk.

According to Martín Gaite (1993) and María Jesús Fraga (2013), the point of view of the girl was incorporated by Fortún to criticize society through the use of naivety and irony. However, Francoist censorship did not forgive the lack of childlike innocence in Celia so some books were banned or altered. In her study of the tradition of novels written for girls, Ana Díaz-Plaja explicitly mentions Celia as an inquisitive heroine who "glimpse[s] some alternative path to the traditional role of women" (2011: 392). Moreover, the figure of the adolescent who wants to become a writer is particularly interesting, just as in *Celia, novelista* (Celia, novelist) (1934) since here she wants to be the writer and protagonist of her own adventures and this ensures her independence. Although Díaz-Plaja warns that novels written for girls are hardly valued in the literary canon, the truth is that "Celia and Her World" was acknowledged by writers like Laforet and Martín Gaite in the 1940s and 1950s.

In fact, the series stands out because of the complex construction of characters that displays their evolution or their regression. In the first book, *Celia, lo que dice* (1929), she is naughty and rebellious, while the orphaned *Celia, madrecita* (Celia, little mother) (1939) realizes her responsibilities in life and abandons her dream of being a writer. Pilar de Montalbán dies giving birth to Mila, and at fourteen, Celia takes responsibility for raising her little sisters. The problematic role of motherhood for Pilar is, in the end, symbolically lethal, and this role is then prematurely passed on to the next female character in the family, Celia. Her father, who once was her ally in her dream to become a writer, is now a limiting and discouraging figure who needs her at home and has come to represent a patriarchal force of submission.

This change in Celia's behavior is incomprehensible for Ana María Moix (1976) and it also disappointed María del Prado Escobar who explained this dramatic change by asserting that "after the Civil War came other stories, although in the latter the meaning of the *fortunian* creation is completely distorted, and Celia, who is older, appears to be a vulgar female hero from a *novela rosa* (romance novel)" (1990: 328). However, in *Celia, madrecita,* Fortún finds a way to criticize the genre of the romance novel in the words of one of Celia's friends, who dislikes "the engineer who marries the little duchess" (1941: 40). Progressive girls refused this kind of literature, which was consumed in vast quantities after the war, and fought against by the *chicas raras* (weird girls). Moreover, Celia's orphanhood links the character with the teenage girls Andrea and Natalia in the 1940s and 1950s *bildungsroman* created by Laforet and Martín Gaite.

In contrast with the first novels, where the free and naughty character of Celia was revolutionary, *Celia, madrecita* presents a regression by Celia's taking part in the patriarchal family by assuming the role of the mother. Although her transition from girlhood to womanhood is abrupt and traumatic, she understands that she is not allowed to rebel against this new situation by showing resilience. The stories of these two Celias coexisted under dictatorship and depicted contradictory roles—active and passive, inquisitive and submissive—of femininity, showing how the historical context and Fortún's personal experiences interfered in the building of Celia's identity.

The Rise of the Weird Girls

In 1944, Carmen Laforet, who had read the "Celia and Her World" stories as a young girl, continued the tradition with a misfit character in her novel *Nada*, the story of teenaged Andrea who witnesses the misery and the suffocating atmosphere of post-war Spain. At 23 years of age, Laforet won the Nadal literature prize and emerged as one of the most important writers in Spain, challenging the conventions of the popular romance novel and reincorporating the figure of the marginalized girl whom Fortún had portrayed in her stories. In contrast to the first Celia, Andrea does not feel free to speak for herself and is trapped in silence. Her apparent lack of agency dealing with problematic relationships with family and friends during her time in Barcelona invokes the notion of nothingness. *Nada* was the first of a series of novels by Laforet and others that portrayed teenagers who could not adapt to the society of their time, thus encouraging girls' defiance.

In her 1987 essay "*La chica rara*" (The weird girl), Spanish writer and critic Martín Gaite coined the term to refer to the protagonists of the postwar novels like Laforet's Andrea and her own Natalia, from her 1957 novel *Entre visillos* (Behind the curtains) and those of Ana María Matute and Dolores Medio. The orphan Natalia in *Entre visillos* is depicted as a misfit by her own actions; she is not willing to attend parties with her girlfriends and sister, and feels out of place among girls her age. She rejects social hypocrisy, tediousness, and conventions such as the way she is supposed to dress, and she gets bored during conversations about clothes and fiancés. As pointed out by Nuria Capdevila-Argüelles (2009), orphanhood is a common feature among the weird girls and it is also shared with later representations of Celia. The lack of the mother as a feminine model forces the protagonists to figure things out on their own by fleeing their claustrophobic households and rejecting the patterns of the romance novel. In the words of Martín Gaite, "They want to go out, simply, to breathe, to distance themselves from what is inside by looking at it from the outside ... to sidestep their point of view and expand it" (1987: 113). It is no coincidence that both Andrea and Natalia are presented arriving on a train at a destination where no one is waiting for them. The sense of loneliness and adventure is reflected at the beginning of *Nada*: "It was the first time I had traveled alone, but I wasn't frightened; on the contrary, this profound freedom at night seemed like an agreeable and exciting adventure to me" (Laforet [1944] 2008: 3). Living their girlhood in a post-conflict scenario, these characters are marked by marginalization and violence. However, they question the normalcy of domestic conduct and construct strong responses through their non-conformist behavior, challenging both the expectations that society has over them, and the rules of the romance novel.

Both Laforet and Martín Gaite read "Celia and Her World" in their childhood and acknowledged the decisive impact Fortún had had on their writing. Moreover, Martín Gaite wrote the prologue for the reprinted works of Fortún in the 1990s, vindicating the influential figure that Fortún represented for writers in the 1950s. She also studied the figure of Celia and her author (2002, 2006) and was in charge of the screenplays for the adaptation of "Celia and Her World" for television (1992).[6] Laforet was also a great enthusiast of Fortún's works and shared correspondence with her.[7] Their relationship of mutual admiration provides evidence of the trace of Fortún's children's books in the history of Spanish Literature. After receiving the Nadal prize for *Nada*, Laforet wrote a letter to Fortún to share the award with her since she had learned how to write by reading about Celia, to which Fortún reacted with pride and surprise and expressed her admiration for "the best Spanish writer!" (Laforet and Fortún 2016: 29). Moreover, Patricia Molins (2012) considers Andrea as a continuation of Celia, whose stories offered a *bildungsroman* of the modern woman, trapped between her will for independence and the restrictive familiar circumstances. Celia would then be a rebel girl who transformed into the first weird girl in whom authors like Laforet and Martín Gaite found inspiration.

Fortún's and Laforet's works overlapped in time, and *Nada* was published the same year as *Celia institutriz* (1944), which, in the line of *Celia, madrecita* (1939), portrays a Celia who finally had to adjust to the world of adults. Fortún's and Laforet's books share the literary strategy of using childhood to express a deep sense of isolation and lack of understanding of the world that the child reader could understand easily thanks to her or his viewpoint. In some way, both protagonists show a lack of intellectual freedom, childlike at the beginning of the "Celia and Her World" series, and totalitarian at the end as in the case of Laforet. At the beginning, Celia is a freethinking girl who introduces radical thoughts into a conservative society, and Andrea is a girl who somatizes trauma through silence in post-war Spain. The will of the characters to disobey social representations is often misunderstood and punished by adults relating to an oversimplified vision of the nature of girlhood and an authoritarian reaction by grown-ups and educational or religious institutions towards personal empowerment.

Conclusion

Seen in its historical context, Elena Fortún's "Celia and Her World" remains a unique and entertaining children's book series which should be explored through a feminist lens. The story of Celia sheds light on the pre-war era in Spain, but also on the period during and after the conflict. For the contemporary reader, it also provides an important vision on how historic and cultural events such as war or death can change the life of a child. Read as a character study of the protagonist the books are essentially stories about resolution in which Celia is an example of someone who uses the events of her own life to create her future and overcome oppression, thus encouraging agency in her readers. However, the character created during the liberal period as an emancipatory figure undergoes a regression as she grows older from book to book because of personal events in Fortún's life (her exile) as well as historical ones like the Civil War and the state's system of repression through censorship. Although there is a tendency to recall the non-conformist girl created before the Civil War, this is not the same Celia in later volumes. In these stories, the adolescent is an aberration of the original and is forced to conform as she grows up in an increasingly hostile world. The historical, social, and cultural circumstances in which the stories are written shape their characters who show themselves not only as dynamic psychological entities, but also as dynamic entities located within that particular social and cultural context.

Fortún's work led to the creation of the weird girls in Spanish literature of the 1940s and 1950s. The style of her dialogues, the social commitment, the point of view of children, and, most importantly, the point of view of the girl and the empowering messages of independence emerge years later in literature for and by female youth who refuse to watch the world from behind the curtains. Based on girls' and women's participation, not marginalization, Fortún's literary corpus is not only essential to understanding the history of children's literature in Spain, but also post-war Spanish literature. The fact that Celia was the first weird girl even before Laforet's Andrea, offers us the opportunity to observe changes in the social construction of girlhood through time and space. The point of view of the girl as a non-conformist subject is used as a mirror of what took place in Spain before, during, and after the Spanish Civil War and reflects literary continuity, instead of abrupt change. Moreover, the continuous, and yet shifting, presence of weird girls in twentieth-century Spanish literature encloses the concept of girlhood as a historical and social construction. Often classified as rebellious, nonconformist or non-submissive misfits, Celia, Andrea and Natalia emerge as characters as they construct their own individual experiences as a way to position themselves in relation to social and cultural expectations.

ANA PUCHAU DE LECEA is a Ph.D. Candidate and Teaching Associate at the University of Melbourne. Her background in Hispanic Studies and Childhood Studies reflects her interest in, and research into, the representation of girlhood in twentieth-century Spanish literature. In 2014, she was awarded the Villanova University Graduate Student Summer Research Grant for the project that became the basis of her dissertation on the impact of Elena Fortún's literary series, *Celia*, on the Spanish women writers of the 1950s. In 2018, she received the Arts Graduate Research International Grant to conduct archival research on Fortún's writing during her exile in Argentina.

Notes

1. I have translated all the extracts from "Celia and Her World" and all quotations from secondary literature published in Spanish.
2. David William Foster (1999) mentions Fortún among "a number of modern writers, lesbian or bisexual" who explored sexual identity in their writing. He also introduces Spain's hidden homosexual tradition, "the hidden path" (18). Fortún's *Oculto Sendero* (2016) about a woman's discovery of her true sexuality is probably related to this tradition.
3. Juan Aguilera (2011) explores feminism and female activism in 1920s Spain when intellectual and politician Clara Campoamor (1888–1972) advocated for women's rights and suffrage. The Lyceum connected Fortún with the writer María Lejárraga and Matilde Ras, a graphologist with whom she allegedly had a relationship, and a study of whose correspondence can be found in *El camino es nuestro* (The way is ours) (Fortún and Ras 2015).
4. Fortún studied library science and taught storytelling at the *Residencia de señoritas*, directed by pedagogue and founder of the Lyceum, María de Maeztu. Her son, Luis, attended the *Instituto-Escuela*.
5. For the complete list of titles in "Celia and Her World" see Capdevila-Argüelles (2009). For a complete list of Fortún's publications and journalistic collaborations, see Fraga (2013).
6. For studies on the adaptation of *Celia* for television, see Harvey (2011) and Vernon (2015).
7. This has been published recently in *De corazón y alma* (Of heart and soul) (2017).

References

Aguilera Sastre, Juan. 2011. "Las fundadoras del Lyceum Club Femenino español." *Brocar* 35: 65–90.

Bravo-Guerreira, María Elena, and Fiona Maharg-Bravo. 2003. "De niñas a mujeres: Elena Fortún como semilla de feminismo en la literatura infantil de la postguerra española." *Hispania* 86 (2): 201–208.

Caamaño Alegre, Beatriz. 2007. "Cosas de niñas: la construcción de la feminidad en la serie infantil de Celia, de Elena Fortún." *AnMal ELectrónica* 23: 35–59.

Capdevila-Argüelles, Nuria. 2009. *Autoras inciertas. Voces olvidadas de nuestro feminismo*. Madrid: horas y HORAS.

Craig, Ian. 1998. "La censura franquista en la literatura para niñas: *Celia* y *Antoñita la fantástica* bajo el caudillo." *Actas del XIII Congreso de La Asociación Internacional de Hispanistas* 4: 69–78.

Díaz-Plaja Taboada, Ana. 2011. *Escrito y leído en femenino: Novelas para niñas*. Cuenca: Ediciones de la Universidad de Castilla-La Mancha.

Dorao, Marisol. 2001. *Los mil sueños de Elena Fortún*. Cádiz: Alboroque Ediciones.

Escobar, Mª del Prado. 1990. "Un aspecto poco estudiado de la literatura española anterior a 1936: Narrativa para niños." *El Guiniguada* 1: 323–336.
Fortún, Elena. [1929] 1993. *Celia, lo que dice*. Madrid: América Ibérica.
Fortún, Elena. [1932] 1993. *Celia en el colegio*. Madrid: Alianza.
Fortún, Elena. [1939] 1941. *Celia madrecita*. Madrid: Aguilar.
Fortún, Elena. [1947] 2008. *El arte de contar cuentos a los niños*. Sevilla: Espuela de Plata.
Fortún, Elena. 1947. *El cuaderno de Celia*. Madrid: Aguilar.
Fortún, Elena, and Matilde Ras. 2015. *El camino es nuestro*, ed. Nuria Capdevila-Argüelles and María Jesús Fraga. Madrid: Fundación Banco de Santander.
Foster, David William. 1999. *Spanish Writers on Gay and Lesbian Themes. A Bio-Critical Sourcebook*. Westport, CT: Greenwood Press.
Fraga, María Jesús. 2013. *Elena Fortún, periodista*. Madrid: Editorial Pliegos.
Harvey, Jessamy. 2011. "Moving Beyond Identification: Carmen Martín Gaite, from Passionate Reader to Co-Scriptwriter on RTVE's Celia (1993)." In *Beyond the Back Room: New Perspectives on Carmen Martín Gaite*, ed. M. Womack and J. Wood, 35–47. Bern: Peter Lang.
Laforet, Carmen. [1944] 2008. *Nada*. Trans. Edith Grossman. New York: Random House Books.
Laforet, Carmen, and Elena Fortún. 2016. *De corazón y alma (1947–1952)*, ed. Nuria Capdevila-Argüelles and María Jesús Fraga. Madrid: Fundación Banco de Santander.
Martín Gaite, Carmen. 1957. *Entre visillos*. Barcelona: Destino.
Martín Gaite, Carmen. 1987. *Desde la ventana*. Madrid: Espasa Calpe.
Martín Gaite, Carmen. 1993. "Pesquisa tardía de Elena Fortún." In *Celia, lo que dice*, 7–37. Madrid: América Ibérica.
Martín Gaite, Carmen. 2002. *Pido la palabra*. Barcelona: Anagrama.
Martín Gaite, Carmen. 2006. *Tirando del hilo (artículos 1949-2000)*, ed. José Teruel. Madrid: Ediciones Siruela.
Moix, Ana María. 1976. "Érase una vez… La literatura infantil a partir de los años 40." *Vindicación Feminista* 5: 28–39.
Molins, Patricia. 2012. "La heterogeneidad como estrategia de afirmación. La construcción de una mirada femenina antes y después de la Guerra Civil." *Desacuerdos* 7: 64–145.
Sánchez García, Raquel. 2001. "Diversas formas para nuevos públicos." In *Historia de la edición en España, 1836–1936*, ed. Jesús A. Martínez, 241–268. Madrid: Marcial Pons Historia.
Vernon, Kathleen M. 2015. "'Niña somebody': Bringing Elena Fortún's *Celia* to Spanish television." *Studies in Spanish and Latin American Cinemas* 12 (1): 93–104.

CHAPTER 10
Lolita Speaks
Disrupting Nabokov's "Aesthetic Bliss"

Michele Meek

Dating back several centuries (recall Samuel Richardson's *Pamela* in 1740), the trope of the sexual encounter between the young girl and her benevolent and/or malevolent father figure has epitomized a tangle of consent, agency, and coercion for the girl. As the quintessential twentieth-century text in this genre, Vladimir Nabokov's *Lolita* (1955) has inspired abundant scholarly analyses, popular cultural critiques, and numerous novels, films, and other creative works. *Lolita* has also continued to evoke debate on how to read the text—both aesthetically and ethically. Although *Lolita* has been read as a "love story" (Patnoe 1995: 83), many feminist scholars have urged readers to reconsider the text from the perspective of Lolita, as a child incest victim. In this chapter, I examine several revisionary texts that present Lolita's voice as a first person narrator, such as Kim Morrissey's *Poems for Men Who Dream of Lolita* (1992); Pia Pera's *Lo's Diary* (published in Italian in 1995 and translated into English in 1999); and Emily Prager's *Roger Fishbite* (1999). I argue that these texts emphasize an ethical reading of *Lolita* by drawing attention to the girl's victimization while, nonetheless, retaining notable ambiguities that acknowledge the girl's sexual desire and agency.

Aesthetics or Ethics?

In his 1959 essay, "On a Book Entitled *Lolita*," Nabokov argues that the sole purpose of *Lolita* is "aesthetic bliss," which he defines as "a sense of being somehow, somewhere, connected with other states of being where art (curiosity, tenderness, kindness, ecstasy) is the norm" (314–315). Nabokov states, "*Lolita* has no moral in tow." The novel, he argues, does not exist for any ethical purpose, but simply an aesthetic one. He describes himself as "neither a reader nor a writer of didactic fiction," and states bluntly, "I detest symbols and allegories" (314). Here, Nabokov directly contests the novel's foreword by John Ray, the imagined psychologist who introduces *Lolita* as a factual account. Ray insists that the book is first and foremost ethical; he writes, "Still more important to us than scientific significance and literary worth, is the *ethical* impact the book should have on the serious reader" (4–5, emphasis added). Ray also describes the book's aesthetic "magic," but unlike Nabokov, Ray argues that it connects directly to the ethical impact of the text: "How magically his singing violin can conjure up a *tendresse*, a compassion for Lolita that makes us entranced with the book while abhorring its author!" (5). Quite clearly, Ray argues that his publishing the "case study" (4) of Lolita is ethical because, despite Nabokov's claim, there is in fact a "moral in tow" for readers who appreciate both the ethics and aesthetics of the text.

Feminist criticism of *Lolita* in the 1980s and 1990s initially argued that Nabokov's "declared dedication to 'aesthetic bliss'" proved that "the novel's design encourages readers to sympathize with the protagonist and artist-figure, Humbert Humbert, to the detriment of the child" (Pifer 2005: 186). Linda Kauffman articulated the feminist academic debate about the novel in her essay, "Framing Lolita: Is There a Woman in the Text?" as she considers *Lolita*'s erasure of its titular character, in particular how "through a variety of narrative strategies … the inscription of the father's body in the text obliterates the daughter's" ([1989]1992: 131). Kauffman suggests that Nabokov's "aesthetic bliss" is a "trap"—an ethical trap, perhaps—for "sophisticated readers of *Lolita*," who tend to sympathize with Humbert while "ignoring the pathos of Lolita's predicament" (138–139). Kauffman argues that critics and readers "fail to notice that Humbert is not only a notoriously unreliable narrator but that he is an unreliable reader too" (135), especially of Lolita, whom he has not only "'solipsized' but annihilated" (136). In urging feminist scholars to "read against the text by resisting the father's seductions," Kauffman challenges feminist readers to understand "what [Lolita's] victimization is like" (133). She insists that a feminist reading of *Lolita* must acknowledge that the novel is "not about love, but about incest" (131) and that Lolita is not a seductress or even a willing participant in Humbert's executed fantasy. Similarly, Elizabeth Patnoe, in her essay "Lolita Misrepresented, Lolita Reclaimed: Disclosing the Doubles" locates the "problem" in widespread "misreadings" of the novel that have "embrace[d] what they consider the book's pleasures" while "almost always skirt[ing] its pains—Lolita's pains, as well as the readerly traumas associated with this novel" (1995: 116). Patnoe suggests that to read the text pleasurably through Humbert's myopic vision is to fail to acknowledge how that pleasure comes at the expense of trauma to a girl child and how it derives from a culture that "violates and punishes women, that denies, trivializes, and fragments the female personal—especially trauma—while hegemonically advancing the male personal—especially pleasure" (120). The challenge put forth by scholars like Kauffman and Patnoe is thus to re-read the novel from Lolita's point of view with the girl's victimization in mind.

Rewriting *Lolita* in her own Words

Perhaps recognizing this urgency to unearth a voice for Lolita, several writers in the 1990s reimagined Nabokov's novel through Lolita's voice. As Naomi Wolf notes in *Promiscuities*, "Lolita is created and re-created by men, but she rarely writes her own account of events" (1997: xx). Perhaps unsurprisingly, many of these texts emphasize Lolita's victimization. In an interview with Camile Paglia, Morrissey stated that her motivation for *Poems for Men Who Dream of Lolita* (1992) was for "people to *never* be able to say the word 'Lolita' again and use it in the clichéd way that we have" (157, emphasis in original). Similarly, as Timothy McCracken points out, Prager's "political agenda" for *Roger Fishbite* (1999) appears "quite clear beginning with her dedication: 'To all the little girls I've met who have started out in desperate circumstances' and through her numerous references to child abuse and the sexual slavery of children" (2001: 137). Even Pera's *Lo's Diary* (1999), which Julia Vaingurt has argued was "not motivated by feminist critique" (2005: 20), took as her impetus the voiceless, and imprisoned Lolita. Pera explained in an interview with Alexandra Gill, "She was a little girl trapped in a cage. I wanted to see if she could write" (1999: D4).

In each of these texts, Lolita articulates her physical and emotional violation. In Morrissey's poem, "stepfather," Humbert's violence and Lolita's visceral disgust become apparent:

> I am holding my tongue like a fist
> pressed hard against teeth
> the smell of stale blood in my throat
> as you breathe through my mouth (1992: 15)

Lolita's recurrent horror of this old wound with its "stale blood" also emerges in the next poem, "sometimes I dream he's my mother." Here, she says she wakes "dreaming blood" (17), which evokes Humbert's molestation of her:

> I wake to the wet slap of sweat
> moving skin against skin (19)

Sex is repeatedly depicted as an injury or a nightmare, and Morrissey's poems stress Lolita's youth, with the opening untitled poem reminding us that she is twelve "and almost a quarter" (3) and the title of the poem, "stepfather," emphasizing the incest and child abuse inherent in their relationship. Through the poems' chronicling of sex with Humbert, we do not experience any sense of her desire, pleasure, or consent; Morrissey's rewriting underlines their interaction as being purely a violation. Later, in "stepfather," Lolita stomachs sex with Humbert by reimagining the flavors of her reality:

> think of lollipops
> not mouldy socks
> close your eyes
> tight, think sour cream
>
> don't think cheese, don't
> see raw sausage left too long
> in the heat
>
> think ice cream (16)

The imagery here reminds us of Lolita's status as a child and evokes her apparent disgust with the sights and smells of sex with Humbert, rendering it impossible to read this sexual interaction as anything but nonconsensual.

Prager's *Roger Fishbite* also accentuates Lolita's victimization. The narrator, Lucky Linderhof, has murdered her adult lover, Roger Fishbite, and now recounts and interprets her affair with him. The initial sexual encounter between Lucky and Fishbite is described as a clear violation of parental rights. In the hotel bed, Lucky snuggles up to her adoptive father, and then he makes his move: "He felt warm and good and I was very happy. I was just about to say 'I'm glad to have you for my dad' when I felt his fingers play across my nipple." To accentuate the nonconsent of their sexual relationship, Lucky narrates her subsequent detachment from her body and compares herself to "little slaves in Thailand" (1999: 85). In this moment,

Lucky finds Fishbite "blissfully unaware of possible trauma" (86) that he imposes on her in this situation. After this "psychic shift" Lucky becomes "once removed" or disembodied, stating that "as they say in juvenile detention, there are infinite degrees of casualty" (85). Furthermore, when Fishbite wants to "show [her] something else," Lucky clearly says "No" several times, until Fishbite pleads, "Can I show you later?" to which she responds, "Maybe … Maybe not" (86). At this point, Lucky has already irrevocably changed. When she cries and exclaims, "I want my mommy," Fishbite tells her that her mother is already dead, propelling her deeper into a "shock" of "sorrow and aloneness" (89). Later, Fishbite remains "blissfully unaware" as he begins to molest her again and asks her if she is okay. She recalls, "I didn't answer. I wasn't okay, of course. I would never be okay. It was astounding how self-centered he was" (92). Like Morrissey, Prager leaves no room here for an interpretation in which Lolita is the sexual aggressor, and, rather, represents her clearly as a victim of child abuse.

Pera's novel, however, depicts Lolita's sexual agency, illustrating what no feminist scholar today would be likely to argue—the validity of Humbert's "very strange" assertion that "it was she who seduced me" (Nabokov 1955: 132). Even what has become known as the "lap scene" in the original novel comes about in Pera's rendition through Lolita's contrivance. She approaches Humbert with "lips … almost impeccably painted" carrying a "red apple" with the intent of "hypnosis" since "no man can resist a woman who has an apple in her hand" (1999: 101). She gets his attention by sitting on the couch and tossing the apple until he grabs it from her, and they scuffle. As she begins to "feel that trunk of his swelling, bigger and bigger," she lets him inspect a bruise "so he can touch me right at the edge of my underpants" (102), knowing that he concocts this excuse to arouse himself. Notably here, it is not only Humbert who "tries to act normal so I can't tell how excited he is," but also Lolita who must "pretend nothing's happening," despite being "all hot inside" and wanting to "hug and kiss him without all these pretenses" (103). Lolita even seems to share in the climactic moment saying,

> I fling my head back, and for a second feel his mouth on my throat. I press against him, until he holds me still, interrupts the nursery rhyme, and, all trembling, forgets to keep up his pretense. I feel weird, too, I melt, and something goes by without my really seeing it, a whir of swift wings, it disappears in an instant and we sit there looking at each other, all blushing, not knowing what to do. (103)

Lolita's erotic experience followed by a post-climactic stillness transforms her from what Humbert in the original *Lolita* imagined as being a "safely solipsized" (Nabokov 1955: 60) child into an active orchestrator and participant in the sexual act.

Still, even Pera acknowledges Lolita's victimization. After their first episode of intercourse in *Lo's Diary*, Humbert becomes "all perked up and wants to do it again and again and again, and in the end it hurts" (1999: 132). And after Lolita learns that "the hen is dead" (135), she regrets her actions, thinking, "If he'd told me right away ... I wouldn't have gone in for that wild screwing. I would have taken it more slowly, much more slowly. Today all day it's been hurting, because this morning he made me do it three times in a row" (136). Her status as the "poor little orphan" who is "lonely" and "scared of the dark" pushes her into his arms where he "starts with caresses" and "comes back in and he doesn't give a god damn that I don't want him to, that he's hurting me" (138). From this point, Humbert is depicted more overtly as a violator, which directly contests her fear that "he'll tell the hen I raped him" (132). Instead, as she describes, "He pins my hands down and he says, See, you're all wet, you want it; and he holds me still and I don't have the strength to kick. I don't care about anything anymore, nothing in the world." She now feels that she "stink[s] of incest" (138) and is "the sex slave of a French creep" (140). Despite their initial sexual encounter during which she was the actor upon his unresponsive body, the realization of her mother's death (and the accompanying fact that she is now legally, bodily, and psychologically at Humbert's mercy) depicts her more clearly as a victim.

Undermining Nabokov's "Aesthetic Bliss"

These writers underscore Lolita's victimization to combat Nabokov's aesthetic bliss, seeming to subscribe to the theory that such "bliss" comes at the expense of the girl. At one point in *Roger Fishbite*, Lucky realizes that "another person's pain was like a picture on the wall to him, an object you could take off and put in the closet if it got in your way." Here, Lucky questions the ethics of not only Fishbite's bliss, but also the ethical stance of a reader or watcher who can enjoy another's "pain ... like a picture on the wall" (1999: 92). Morrissey's poems, too, suggest a protest against aesthetic bliss by aligning the reader with Quilty and Humbert. The title of the book, of course, suggests that these poems are specifically addressed to the "men who dream of Lolita." Not only are Quilty and Humbert these very men, but this evocation also includes Nabokov and all male readers who derive aesthetic bliss from the story of Lolita. It is as if Morrissey has taken up the issue that Kauffman objects to in *Lolita*'s lap scene: "the father's body is the site and the source of not only aesthetic bliss but literal orgasm; both come at the same time—if, that is, the reader is male" ([1989]1992: 135). Kauffman's accusation that male readers derive both aesthetic bliss and physical orgasm at the expense of the victimized Lolita echoes with Morrissey's lines from "Parlour Tricks" when Lolita says,

> you long for this dream-child, forgetting
> the stale smell of her fear
>
> you want a lover you can love without sex (1992: 39)

The reader longs for this "dream" girl without culpability. To "want a lover you can love without sex" perhaps is to be aroused by *Lolita* without feeling complicit in the formation of the girl's pain. But Morrissey's Lolita suggests that aesthetic bliss comes not only at the expense of the imagined girl, but also of real girls. She accuses Quilty of wresting his "plays" from the "girl who cries" (1992: 39) and being only self-interested, as she says, "for you there is only the sex … only your pleasure" (34). Still, Morrissey's opening untitled poem suggests the warning that the "private" "Book of Dolores B. Haze" comes "with a curse" (3). She suggests,

> put me back in my box
> and be happy (3)

Here, Morrissey seems to link the girl's story to opening Pandora's Box, an invitation to misery for both the girl writer/Lolita as well as the male reader.

In *Roger Fishbite*, Prager mimics the direct address of *Lolita*, also seemingly to disrupt aesthetic bliss. The construct of her novel is that Lucky has become famous, empowering her to bring her salacious story to the mainstream, while advocating on behalf of girls. Lucky says, "Dear Readers and Watchers of tabloid TV and press, I want you to know the truth" (1999: 6). Some might criticize the heavy-handedness of Prager's irony here, but what she does is constantly remind us, as readers, of the "tabloid" sensationalism of the story and our complicity in its enjoyment. The first time that Lucky allows Fishbite to perform oral sex on her, she interrupts the story by saying, "Dear Readers and Watchers, I must stop here lest I join the illustrious company of titillators and muddy my intent" (93), much like Humbert interrupts *Lolita* with exclamations, notably shifting to "gentlewomen of the jury" (1955: 135) from "gentlemen" (1955: 125) as he describes the night they became "technically lovers" (132). In *Roger Fishbite*, Lucky states that she is "not so interested in the pornography of the affair as in chronicling the sort of man who initiates it" (1999: 93). Of course, we are left to wonder if perhaps not only Humbert but Nabokov, too, is meant to be part of this "illustrious company of titillators" (93). Lucky never mentions Nabokov, but she offers the "example" of Lewis Carroll "who may or may not have interfered with his Alice," although Lucky believes this to be so "from the sad look on her face in the photogravures" (12). Lucky asks, "You think great literature comes out of nothing? Nothing can come out of nothing." And then she contemplates, "Is the innocence of one girl child so important next to *Alice in Wonderland*? Does it matter if it wasn't quite soooo wonderful for her? A hundred years of beautifully bound editions? Can anyone honestly say that they would save the child and lose the book?" (13). Here, Lucky picks up an unspoken question in Ray's foreword to *Lolita* when he suggests that if Humbert had received psychological help "there would have been no disaster; but then, neither would there have been this book" (Nabokov 1955: 5). What would we truly give up in exchange for aesthetic bliss? Is the girl more valuable than art? Or, in other words, is an ethical narrative more important than aesthetic bliss?

What is ultimately at issue is not only the lack of ethics of the writer, but also of the reader. In addition to reading "you" as both Quilty and the reader, Morrissey more directly addresses the complicity of the audience. Her poem "Parlour tricks" begins thus: "You push pins through my flesh at a party" (1992: 33). Here, Lolita accuses "everyone" of enjoying a trick that involves "pressing silver through skin" despite her pain.

> everyone knows
>
> with tricks,
> the pleasure is all in the audience
> all in the stillness and the pain
> no one mentions (33)

The audience derives "all" the pleasure here, again at the expense of the girl's unspoken stillness and pain. So later, when she writes,

> this is not erotic
> and you are obscene
> as you sit, fully clothed
> saying no (42)

we might imagine the un-erotic scene of the reader of *Lolita* who denies complicity with a tale in which a young girl is abused. In this way, Lolita's accusation,

> ... a girl is a girl
> is a girl (43)

and her wake-up call

> I want to slap you   to force you
> to listen I want to say: No
>
> My name is Dolores
> write that *love* (43)

is as much for Quilty as it is for any author or reader who "dreams" of Lolita. The interchangeability of "girl" is a trap for writers and readers who generalize the girl and fail to confront the real child victim.

The Ethics of Girls' Victimization

Perhaps ironically, contemporary critical re-interpretations of *Lolita* suggest that the novel's aesthetic bliss is not at the expense of the imagined or real girl, but in support of her. In short, they advance a so-called moral message of the novel, despite Nabokov's warning that there is no such moral. Susan Quayle notes, "It is through Humbert's awareness of the 'real' Lolita that Nabokov advances his "moral message on pedophilia" (2009: n.p.), while Nicolas Estournel suggests that the "incuriosity" (2013: 3) of Humbert leads the novel to be "ethical" in the way it "lead[s] the reader to consider morality by questioning the narrators' points of view" (7). Christine Grogan notes how "Nabokov anticipated that the pendulum tracking the book's reputation would swing. Confident in the immortality of his masterpiece, he predicted the day when some critic would cry that *Lolita* shows that he was really a moralist at heart" (2014: 53). Grogan notes that although originally feminists "criticized Nabokov for portraying the sexual exploitation of a pubescent girl as a joke, or, worse, a romance," more recent critics "have gone so far as to argue in favor of Nabokov's feminist sympathies and claim *Lolita* as a proto-feminist narrative" (2015: 53). These scholars find the moments of Lolita's lack of interest and her "revulsion and reluctance with regard to engaging in sexual activities" (Quayle 2009; n.p.) as proof of even Humbert's acknowledgement of abuse. Rather than Lolita's having been successfully "solipsized" (Nabokov 1955: 60) as Humbert suggests and earlier scholars feared, recent scholars contend that her lack of consent comes through her "weeping and her stony silences" which "even Humbert cannot control," and her narrative or linguistic "disruptions" (Shelton 1999: 289), and Lolita's ultimate escape from and rejection of Humbert. Scholars have noted that Lolita's words in the original novel, such as "the word is incest" (Nabokov 1955: 119) or "the hotel where you raped me" (202), clearly highlight her nonconsent, emphasizing "the fact that Humbert is holding her against her will" (Grogan 2014: 202), so that "Humbert inadvertently makes available to readers a mechanism ... through which they can attend to Dolly's story" (Shelton 1999: 289). In our current moment, to read *Lolita* ethically is to understand it as a tale of victimization—and to argue otherwise would place one in untenable critical terrain.

In consideration of the ironic multiplicity of apparent authorial intent (Humbert's, Ray's, Nabokov's), it seems hard not to find a critical shift from aesthetics to ethics, or from an enjoyment of the novel's aesthetic bliss to interpretations of the novel as a feminist fable, rather ironic. In Ray's foreword, he asserts that "in this poignant personal study there lurks a general lesson; the wayward child, the egotistic mother, the panting maniac," which "warn us of dangerous trends; they point out potent evils" (1955: 5). Such hazards require protective action; he suggests that "*Lolita* should make all of us—parents, social workers, educators—apply ourselves with still greater vigilance and vision to the task of bringing up a better generation in a safer world" (6). Ray partially sees the object of disciplinary action as the "wayward child" (5) who must be subjected to greater parental and pedagogical influence, observation, and control.

What might it mean that mainstream critical reception now finds itself more aligned with Ray than not? Ray's warning sounds strangely similar to the *Report of the Task Force on The Sexualization of Girls*, in which the authors note that it developed in response to "journalists, child advocacy organizations, parents, and psychologists [who] have become alarmed, arguing that the sexualization of girls is a broad and increasing problem and is harmful to girls" (Zurbriggen et al. 2007: 1). In effect, Lolita is the quintessential "sexualized girl" as Simone de Beauvoir first articulated in her 1959 *Esquire* essay, coining the term "Lolita Syndrome" and arguing, as McCracken puts it, that "Lolitas" are not "sexual young girls but rather ... young girls being sexualized by men" (2001: 130). Lolita's narrative, in fact, fits at least two of the four sexualization criteria developed by the Task Force: "the imbuing of adult sexuality upon a child" and "being sexually objectified" (Zurbriggen et al. 2007: 2).

Yet, the question that continues to resound with girlhood studies scholars is how to read girls' sexual desire and agency amidst the realities of sexualization. Scholars often declare the need to hear from girls themselves to unravel these complexities. Deborah Tolman et al. note that "there is a dearth of qualitative psychological research on how girls navigate sexualization that can capture the contradictions, nuances, complexities and various venues in which girls engage with sexualizing processes. The voices of girls themselves are disturbingly absent in the US psychological literature to date" (2015: 79). However, if we allow girls like Lolita to speak, do we believe them?

What we do choose to believe may have more to do with adults' perception than that of girls, and it directly connects to how we "read" girls—aesthetically and ethically. Kathryn Bond Stockton considers the alternating "dialectic of harm and agency" (2009: 140) for Lolita and inspires us to understand the matter of Lolita's consent as a matter of aesthetics. She notes how Adrian Lyne's 1997 film adaptation of *Lolita* was nearly banned "due to its depictions of a sexual child" (33), while Angelica Houston's 1996 film adaptation of *Bastard out of Carolina*, which includes the young girl Bone being "raped on-screen at agonizing length" was not (33). Stockton argues that what makes *Bastard* more acceptable is, in fact, Bone's lack of consent. A raped child confirms "the child's need for protection and her weakness in these moments confirms the child's innocence" whereas a desiring, consenting child suggests an "erotic pleasure" (33) on the girl's part, which clearly makes audiences uncomfortable. In other words, the representation of a girl's rape can be "art" (and thus ethical aesthetic bliss), while a girl's sexual desire and agency must be pornography (often perceived as bliss lacking aesthetics or ethics). Stockton argues that "Lolita can be sexual on her own terms only if, definitely, and also finally, we can't accuse ourselves of perversion" (151). As readers or viewers, we may be reluctant to imbue Lolita with sexual agency because we view her agency, and our own pleasure in it, as perverse. This reluctance may have much to do with what Allison Pease notes as a shift from early twentieth-century "dominant aesthetic practice … to validate as fine arts only those that invoke disinterested contemplation rather than a sensuous interest on the part of a reader or viewer" to a new "aesthetic project: to bring the body and its senses more overtly into relation with the ethical and social realm" (2000: 165–166). With the "body, and a bodily response" as a "necessary constituent of the modern reading practice," the only way to "avoid a purely pornographic reading" is for "the body … to be attached to a greater ethical project" (191). In other words, today it might be seen as ethical to derive intellectual pleasure from *Lolita*'s literary prowess and style, but it would likely be seen as unethical to derive sexual pleasure from the novel's depiction of a young girl and an older father figure. In our contemporary American cultural understanding of childhood, pornography, and sexual abuse, the ethics of consent preclude this as ethical aesthetic bliss.

The Puzzle of Lolita's Sexual Agency

Today, it might be equally urgent to acknowledge Lolita's sexual desire as her victimization. M. Gigi Durham acknowledges how "Nabokov's Lolita is a nuanced character whose sexuality is complex—like many preadolescent girls, she is sexually curious—but she has no control over her relationship with Humbert, which is abusive and manipulative" (2008: 25). Although Durham's interpretation clearly labels Lolita a victim, she also recognizes the girl's sexual curiosity. What *Lolita* and its iterations offer us are representations of the complexity of a girl's desire and sexual agency amidst her oppression. Here, we might recall Judith Butler's theories of subjectivity; she argues that "the subject might yet be thought as deriving its agency from precisely the power it opposes, as awkward and embarrassing as such a formulation might be" (1997: 17). It is perhaps for this reason that all the revisionary texts of *Lolita* attempt to demonstrate the girl's sexual desire and agency, despite her victimization.

Prager's novel, in particular, demonstrates the choices Lucky makes as a subjugated girl with a lecherous father figure. Unlike Humbert and Lolita, Fishbite and Lucky never have intercourse. In their first sexual encounter, Lucky pushes his hand away, saying, "Okay, okay … You can give me oral sex" and despite his initial confusion manifesting in "an odd look on his face as if presented with a dilemma he simply could not solve," he "did as I asked" (1999: 92). When he finishes, he "dully" asks her, "And will you do me?" to which she responds, "No" with "irritation" telling him "Yucchy. Never. No, I will never touch you. Why would I want to?" (93). At another time when Fishbite proposes intercourse, begging, "Please can't we make love?" she responds:

> 'Officer!' I would shout as loud as I could, and he would cringe. 'Lose my virginity to you? What are you, nuts? What's in it for me?'
>
> Then he would list the presents and clothing and trips we would take if only I would give in. (103)

She refuses intercourse despite these bribes, but her allowing him to perform oral sex on her convolutes the lines of consent and nonconsent of their interactions since she says, "So I enjoyed it while I was forced to, and enjoyed forcing Fishbite to, and it amused me that we were both being forced to do it, and it was pretty confusing" (128). Throughout the novel, Lucky envisions herself both as prey and predator—as a rabbit being chased and as a "rabid ferret girl" (174). Even when Lucky alludes to her victimization, she refuses to accept it simplistically. When Lucky replies to her "Dear Readers and Watchers" who want to know "Do they rape here?" in reference to her residential facility, her response creates a consent puzzle. "And the answer is, they rape—some do—like anywhere. Even at Chutney, some did. Did they rape me? Not without my consent they didn't" (69). For Lucky then, rape means something other than simply nonconsensual sex, although exactly what it does mean is unclear. Thus, the novel resists a straightforward ethics of consent in which there is a clear perpetrator and victim—at least from the point of view of the girl.

Even Morrissey addresses the confusion often inherent in a girl's sexual consent. In her poem, "Saturday Matinee, June 3," Lolita experiences a more palatable feast for the senses with her peer Kenny Knight,

> tasting the butter-salt corn
> the clean warmth of boy skin
> the hot breath (1992: 8)

that belies her reaction to his advances. We read that he

> put his hand on my knee
> I said no and stared at the screen (8)

Here, Lolita's no does not mean no. She says,

> I said no, meaning do
> what you like, Kenny Knight
>
> but don't ask (8)

This confusion seems to be explicitly tied to a cultural presumption that coercion exists within seduction. While girls are often seen as the gatekeepers of sexual behavior, boys and men are often depicted as the drivers of the seduction, attempting to persuade the girl to engage in some activity (Bay-Cheng: 2015). Although they do not state it explicitly, many of the *Lolita* iterations seem to ask the question of how we might find the ethical line between persuasion and coercion for the girl.

Conclusion: The Ambiguity of *Lolita*'s Ethics

Consciously or not, these writers have written girls' sexual subjectivity into the text of *Lolita*. If these novels espouse a moral it might be that to maintain Lolita's sexual desire is not to deny her victimization, and to acknowledge her victimization is not to deny her sexual subjectivity and agency. Michael Wood ponders "the moral question" (2003: 191) in *Lolita*; he says, "At the risk of sounding like a chastened John Ray, Jr., I would suggest that one of the most important things Nabokov's novel does is help us understand better just what an offense against a child is and understand this morally, not merely technically. But it does this only by getting everything slightly wrong and leaving the rest to us" (193). Wood draws on the concept of consent to demonstrate his point, suggesting that when Lolita goes to Humbert in despair after she has learned of her mother's death, "a double confusion reigns in this scene, in Humbert and Lolita, and that it centers on the unnamed notion of consent. This confusion is precisely Nabokov's point." He argues, "Neither of them knows anything about consent. Humbert doesn't know that Lolita can't have consented, even when she seemed to, even when she came sobbing in the room. She doesn't know that the very chance of her consent has been destroyed for good" (194). I would agree that "confusion [seems to be] precisely Nabokov's point" here, although I would not reach the conclusion that "neither of them knows anything about consent." Rather, I would argue that the novel suggests how consent can be distressingly unclear, remaining in this novel, as in its many iterations, a puzzle, even, as Guy Hocquenghem has called it, a "trap" (1988: 285). We may design laws that protect girls from statutory rape but the lines we draw remain unstable (demonstrated in, among other ways, the constantly shifting age of legal consent). *Lolita*'s moral may be simply to point out how flawed our over-simplified dichotomies of lust and love, seduction and rape, child and adult, child and girl are. *Lolita* does not merely show us "just what an offense against a child is" as Michael Wood says, but shows us that "Humbert is not an ordinary pedophile, and Nabokov's Lolita is not a Lolita. But are there ordinary pedophiles? Isn't this a dangerous notion in itself, and doesn't Humbert, in spite of himself, do us a bit of good by giving the notion such a hard time?" (2003: 189). The *Lolita* narratives force us to rethink the boundaries we draw for the girl for her own good and to wrestle with the complex nature of consent, and the vastness of the gray area between the black-and-white cases. The ethical and aesthetic puzzles of consent, in fact, persist in *Lolita*'s reiterations because they are part of what makes the narrative so endlessly fascinating, disturbing, and perplexing.

MICHELE MEEK is an Assistant Professor in the Communication Studies department at Bridgewater State University in Massachusetts. Most recently, she edited the compilation *Independent Female Filmmakers: A Chronicle Through Interviews, Profiles, and Manifestos* (2019) and presented her talk, "Why We're Confused About Consent—Rewriting Our Stories of Seduction," at TEDx Providence. Her essay, "'It Ain't For Children': 'Shame-Interest' in the Adaptations *Precious* and *Bastard Out of Carolina*" was published in *Literature/Film Quarterly* in 2017. She has also published in the *Journal of Popular Film and Television*.

References

Bay-Cheng. 2015. "The Agency Line: A Neoliberal Metric for Appraising Young Women's Sexuality." *Sex Roles* 73: 279–291.

Butler, Judith. 1997. *The Psychic Life of Power: Theories in Subjection*. Stanford: Stanford University Press.

Durham, M. Gigi. 2008. *The Lolita Effect: The Media Sexualization of Young Girls and What We Can Do About It*. Woodstock, NY: Overlook Press.

Estournel, Nicolas. 2013. "The Relevance of Voice for Understanding Ethical Concerns Raised by Nabokov's *Lolita* and Burgess's *A Clockwork Orange*." *Opticon 1826* 15 (11): 1–8. http://dx.doi.org/10.5334/opt.bi.

Gill, Alexandra. 1999. "Little Lo Lost in a Literary Feud." *Toronto Globe*, 16 October.

Grogan, Christine. 2014. "*Lolita* Revisited: Reading Azar Nafisi's *Reading Lolita in Tehran*: a Memoir in Books." *Women's Studies* 43 (1): 52–72. http://dx.doi.org/10.1080/00497878.2014.852422.

Hocquenghem, Guy, Michel Foucault, and Jean Danet. 1988. "Sexual Morality and the Law." In *Politics, Philosophy, Culture: Interviews and Other Writings, 1977-1984*, ed. Lawrence D. Kritzman, 271–285. New York: Routledge.

Kauffman, Linda. 1992. *Epistolary Modes in Modern Fiction*. Chicago: Chicago University Press.

McCracken, Timothy. 2001. "Lolita Talks Back: Giving Voice to the Object." In *He Said, She Says: An RSVP to the Male Text*, ed. Mica Howe and Sarah Appleton Aguiar, 128–142. Madison: Fairleigh Dickinson University Press.

Morrissey, Kim. 1992. *Poems for Men Who Dream of Lolita*. Regina, SK: Coteau.

Nabokov, Vladimir. [1955] 1991. *Lolita*. New York: First Vintage Books.

Paglia, Camille. 1994. *Vamps & Tramps*. New York: Random House.

Patnoe, Elizabeth. 1995. "Lolita Misrepresented, Lolita Reclaimed: Disclosing the Doubles." *College Literature* 22 (2): 81–104.

Pease, Allison. 2000. *Modernism, Mass Culture, and the Aesthetics of Obscenity*. Cambridge: Cambridge University Press.

Pera, Pia. 1999. *Lo's Diary*. Trans. Ann Goldstein. New York: Foxrock.
Pifer, Ellen. 2005. "The Lolita Phenomenon from Paris to Tehran." In *The Cambridge Companion to Nabokov*, ed. Julian W. Connolly, 185–199. Cambridge: Cambridge University Press.
Prager, Emily. 1999. *Roger Fishbite*. New York: Random House.
Quayle, Susan. 2009. "Lolita *is* Dolores Haze: The 'Real' Child and the 'Real' Body in *Lolita*." *Nabokov Online Journal* 3. http://www.nabokovonline.com/uploads/2/3/7/7/23779748/v3_07_quayle.pdf (accessed 14 December 2015).
Shelton, Jen. 1999. "'The Word is Incest': Sexual and Linguistic Coercion in *Lolita*." *Textual Practice* 13 (2): 273–295. http://dx.doi.org/10.1080/09502369908582341.
Stockton, Kathryn Bond. 2009. *The Queer Child, or Growing Sideways in the Twentieth Century*. Durham, NC: Duke University Press.
Tolman, Deborah L., Christin P. Bowman, and Jennifer F. Chmielewski. 2015. "Anchoring Sexualization: Contextualizing and Explicating the Contribution of Psychological Research on the Sexualization of Girls in the US and Beyond." In *Children, Sexuality and Sexualization*, ed. Emma Renold, Jessica Ringrose and R. Danielle Egan, 71–88. New York: Palgrave Macmillan.
Vaingurt, Julia. 2011. "Unfair Use: Parody, Plagiarism, and Other Suspicious Practices in and Around *Lolita*." *Nabokov Online Journal* 5. http://www.nabokovonline.com/toc-5.html (accessed 13 January 2016).
Wolf, Naomi. 1997. *Promiscuities: The Secret Struggle for Womanhood*. New York: Random House.
Wood, Michael. 2003. "Revisiting *Lolita*." In *Vladimir Nabokov's Lolita: A Casebook*, ed. Ellen Pifer, 181–194. Oxford: Oxford University Press.
Zurbriggen, Eileen L., Rebecca L. Collins, Sharon Lamb, Tomi-Ann Roberts, Deborah L.Tolman, L. Monique Ward, and Jeanne Blake. 2007. *Report of the American Psychological Association Task Force on the Sexualization of Girls*. Report to the American Psychological Association, Washington, D.C.

CHAPTER 11
Hope Chest
Demythologizing Girlhood in Kate Bernheimer's Trilogy

Catriona McAra

> I have been amazed more than once by a description a woman gave me of a world all her own which she had been secretly haunting since early childhood. (Cixous 1976: 876)

In the last two decades, the American writer Kate Bernheimer has emerged as an important custodian and curator of the fairy tale genre. This is evident from her numerous edited collections of short stories, a journal, and trio of fairy tale novels: *The Complete Tales of Ketzia Gold* (2001), *The Complete Tales of Merry Gold* (2006a) and *The Complete Tales of Lucy Gold* (2011), hereafter *Ketzia*, *Merry*, and *Lucy*. The trilogy, hereafter called "The Complete Tales" for convenience, constitutes a decade-long investigation into the significance of girlhood by way of embodiment in and through the text. Much of the project is based on Bernheimer's own transition from childhood to adulthood; she grew up on the east coast of the US during the historical moment of the late 1960s and early 1970s with its radical politics and sexual liberation. Each novel, all laden with coded references to Bernheimer's biography, focuses on the life of one of the three fictional Gold sisters.[1]

Notes for this section can be found on page 187.

Illustration 11.1: Joseph Cornell, Untitled (Pink Palace), ca. 1950. Wooden box containing photostat with ink wash, wood, mirror, plant material, and artificial snow; 8 5/8 x 14 1/4 x 4 3/8 in. (21.91 x 36.2 x 11.11 cm) San Francisco Museum of Modern Art, Purchase through gifts of Mr. and Mrs. William M. Roth and William L. Gerstle © The Joseph and Robert Cornell Memorial Foundation / Licensed by VAGA, NY/DACS, London 2017. Photograph: Katherine Du Tiel.

The Complete Tales trilogy is slippery in terms of its narrative and non-chronological structure; each novel moves between first and third person narration and among scenes from girlhood, adolescence, and the professional adult career of the relevant sister. Arranged episodically, the seemingly tangled narratives deliberately confound the teleological beginning, middle, and end of conventional fairy tales. Bernheimer has explained that each novel was carefully patterned with the others in mind with a plot structure of repetition both in and across the volumes that enables recurrent readings of the same episode told from each sister's perspective.[2] In a sense, each character serves as the unreliable narrator of her own memory; as an author of fiction, Bernheimer grants herself creative license to do this. As fictional characters, the Gold sisters are obliged to be neither reliable nor objective; they are the curators of their own narratives. Another literary device used by Bernheimer is the re-contextualization of existing fairy tales. This lends the trilogy an intertextual dimension or what Mieke Bal (1999) might term an exercise in quotation in that Bernheimer's girl characters live the very fairy tales (Yiddish, German, Russian) they are reading as a critically self-conscious practice. As Bernheimer herself explains, "Reading fairy tales—or writing about them—is, I can assure you, one of the few ways adults can recreate that delicious somatic childhood chill" (2007: 11). The self-reflexive gesture of the sisters' reading of fairy tales is also a form of *mise-en-abyme* or nested narratives (Harries 2001; Stewart [1984]1993) evoking Scheherazade, the female narrator of tales from the *Arabian Nights* cycle (Warner 2011) who tells her husband a story and then begins a new one immediately after finishing the previous one for 1001 nights in order to evade her own death; her husband's curiosity keeps her alive. One nested theme that unites the three Gold sisters, and their slippery spectrum of narrative growth, is that of the hope chest.[3] It serves as a recurrent motif throughout the trilogy as both a memory vessel and a prophetic device, a trap or a cage, as well as a symbol of comfort and security.

Keepsake: A Short History of Hope Chests

I suggest that the hope chest is an unruly metaphor for the transition from childhood into adulthood, one of the primary themes of Bernheimer's trilogy. The cultural history of the hope chest is revealing for the study of girlhood, particularly in terms of what this tradition discloses about young American women historically, and how their values and ideological beliefs are instilled, and their future fantasies directed. Before I explore further Bernheimer's literary uses of the hope chest, it is worth dwelling on its meaning and position as an exulted piece of furniture and social shrine to maturation beyond girlhood. One of the best illustrations occurs in Miranda July's film *Me and You and Everyone We Know* (2005), when Sylvie, crucially on the verge of adolescence, explains that her "hope chest or trousseau in French" represents her "dowry" to her future husband and daughter, of whose social and biological certainty she has no doubt. Sylvie's hope chest contains domestic gadgets and towel-sets, commodities that she has purchased from her local mall with her pocket money. Lon Schleining expands on this peculiar social tradition. "Since late medieval times at least, it has been customary in many Western countries for a woman to gather her trousseau—clothing, linens, plates, and other household goods—in anticipation of marriage" (2001: 43), and explains that the chest was often woodworked and handcrafted by a significant male presence in the bride's life, usually her father or husband-to-be, adding that its true significance was to hold "her hopes and dreams for the future" (45). Gaston Bachelard reminds us of the heirloom-like qualities of the hope chest.

> The casket contains the things that are *unforgettable*, unforgettable for us, but also unforgettable for those to whom we are going to give our treasures. Here the past, the present and a future are condensed. Thus the casket is memory of what is immemorial. ([1958]1994: 84, emphasis in original)

Transatlantic exchanges and the nineteenth century mores of Victorianism are responsible, in part, for the cultural heritage of such literary boxing or nesting. As Celeste Olalquiaga points out,

> Victorian interiors, apparently merely ornamental had a practical purpose to cover the emptiness left behind by the absence of tradition. Material proliferation was legitimised by the pretended usefulness of things that contained other things—albums, armoires, boxes, glass cases—often protecting them from this era's arch-enemy dust. (1998: 89)

The menace of dust or physical traces of the proprietor's own bodily matter inevitably raises the spectre of the abject which must be eliminated or kept out. As Mary Douglas claims, "Dirt is a by-product of systematic ordering and classification of matter, in so far as ordering involves rejecting inappropriate elements" ([1996] 2000: 36). Often the box functions as the *sine qua non* of the abject, each reliant on the other for its separate comprehension. This is true, too, of the relationship between the transitional, pubescent child-woman and her sanitary habits—just as unwanted matter such as menstrual blood and body hair are rarely dealt with directly, the boxing of the imagination offers a metaphor of psychic compartmentalization for their being purged from consciousness. Julia Kristeva's (1982) notion of abjection, as the infant's distancing itself from the maternal body in order to form psychically into a separate, autonomous subject, is significant here—the hope chest becomes an alternative womb, pregnant with future promises which are not necessarily ever going to be delivered. As we will see, it is a device coveted by hysteria. The hope chest is also a tomb, both containing and repelling death by storing precious heirlooms for future generations as a narcissistic form of self-memorialization; the hopes of the capitalist, female subject are nurtured on such materialistic fantasies.

There exist a few cultural rebellions to these narratives.[4] Curiously, in July's film, Sylvie's hope chest is located beneath a poster of an erupting volcano—a prelude to her adolescent angst or dormant aspirations. One trusts that the girl in this particular text will ultimately burst out of the social confines of her domestic hope chest. July pokes fun at the polite suburban cushioning around Sylvie that will soon struggle to contain her erotic desires and sexual maturing, hinted at through her peeping at other characters. The memory box in Dorothea Tanning's surrealist novel *Chasm: A Weekend*

(2004)[5] offers another example of a socially abnormal or dangerous casket, this time one in which the contents have transformed into wet specimens and dead matter. Belonging to the doll-like, seven-year-old Destina Meridian (born in 1958, and thus a prime candidate for a hope chest), Tanning's literary memory box is painted on the outside with deceptively innocent cherubim. However, the contents surprise the reader since they include rotting eyeballs and the skins of reptiles, gifts from the prey of Destina's imaginary friend, a lion. Once the little girl is reunited with her great-grandmother, the alternative heirlooms disintegrate and the lion symbolically disappears. Bernheimer's three novels similarly extend and complicate repressed cultural narratives of the hope chest as a representation of girlhood, offering more inspiring, albeit ambiguous, models for reading the girl in the text.

There are many literary theories of memory boxes, but two in particular can be used to excavate, unlock, and demythologize[6] Bernheimer's box imagery, both from a psychoanalytic perspective: Laura Mulvey's feminist essay "Pandora's Box" (1996); and Sigmund Freud's "Dora: An Analysis of a Case Study of Hysteria" (1905). Both revolve around the metaphor of the box, jar, or locket—with the dovetailing themes of the irresistible container and transgressive curiosity. In the myth of Pandora, the female figure cannot resist the temptation to open a box or, in the original, to break the seal on a pottery jar. Sent by Zeus to punish humankind for having been given fire by Prometheus, her opening of the box unleashes havoc. Like that of the biblical Eve who bites into the forbidden fruit, the myth of Pandora has been deployed traditionally to warn of the dangers of feminine curiosity. However, Mulvey rewrites this narrative in order to review Pandora's deed as an active form of feminist curiosity that champions the desire for knowledge and the psychic necessity to unlock meaning. Freudian psychoanalysis provides a touchstone for Mulvey; Freud's Dora is cited in Mulvey's essay. Dora (Ida Bauer) was a young, bourgeois, Jewish-Viennese woman who underwent Freudian analysis and was diagnosed with hysteria after receiving unwanted sexual attention from Herr K, an adult male friend of her parents. This case study reads as a romance or "modern novel" (Marcus 1985: 64), and box imagery appears several times, linked by Freud to Dora's unconscious frustrations and desires. She dreams of her neurotic mother's *Schmuckkästen* (jewel-box) that her father prevents from being rescued in a household fire. She is given a box by Herr K, and on another occasion, during analysis, sports a fashionable box-shaped purse which she plays with throughout her therapy session. Freud suggests that her "automatic" fiddling with this receptacle is a representation of Dora's unconscious fantasies of masturbation involving her vagina, and later ponders rhetorically, "Is 'jewel-box' not a common image for the unstained, intact female genitalia?" (2013: 77). Bernheimer read this essay at college in 1982 and understood Freud to be a feminist writer.[7] As Peter Brooks reminds us, "If we turn toward Freud, it is not in the attempt to psychoanalyze authors or readers or characters in narrative, but rather to suggest that by attempting to superimpose psychic functioning, we may discover something about how textual dynamics work and something about their equivalences" (1984: 90). A case study such as that about Dora (as a canonical fairy tale itself) provides a useful reference point for reading Bernheimer's novels as well as a symbolic language that has been re-appropriated for a feminist project (Cixous and Clément 1996).

Freud's essay "The Theme of the Three Caskets" (1913) provides further ways of accessing Bernheimer's material, particularly as Freud demonstrates the capacity of psychoanalytic methodologies for unlocking the meaning of fairy tale objects and numbers, in this case the number three and the curious choice between three sisters, daughters, or boxes, with Freud querying the "concealed motives" (1997: 109) for the peculiar outcomes, ultimately declaring, according to Peter Brooks (1984), that the act of choosing enables the selector to triumph over death. Again, the hope chest offers both redemption and self-preservation. Following Freud, D. W. Winnicott's notion of the "transitional object" could also be key to accessing Bernheimer's hope chest, "the first 'not-me' possession" ([1971] 2005: 2) which, like Kristeva's notion of abjection, assists the infant in transitioning between subjective and objective worlds. The transitional object is usually a comforter "between the thumb and the teddy bear" (2). While Bernheimer (2006b) explores the life spectrum of the sisters and the possessions of their infancy—Merry's stuffed monkey, Ketzia's plush seal, and Lucy's book-doll, all objects of affection and dread—it is the transitioning away from such childhood comforts that concerns us here. I wonder if the hope chest, as both an object and a collecting practice, operates transitionally at a later stage of psycho-sexual development between girlhood and womanhood as a solidification of the psyche? It is certainly a durable container that can accommodate softer, nostalgic forms, and future projections. For me, Bernheimer's box imagery toys with Freud but ultimately offers an expanded vision of the transitional, transgressive, and curious child-woman of Mulvey's creation.

I read *Lucy* through the theme of the significance of lead, *Ketzia* as a rewriting of "Bluebeard," and *Merry* as a demythologized Pandora.

Lead: The Third Sister

The Complete Tales of Lucy Gold is a study of bliss. In this episodic series of non-chronological short chapters, typical of the rest of the trilogy, we learn of Lucy's happy childhood, the untimely loss of her boyfriend, her career as a high-flying animator then solitary doll-maker, and many ecstatic deaths. In some ways she serves as a synthesis or conceptual foil to the two older sisters who represent thesis and antithesis. The number three is significant in the fairy tale genre, particularly in terms of the choice between three sisters. Drawing on Shakespeare's symbolism of the box in *The Merchant of Venice* (1605), Freud reminds us that the successful suitor must select the most virtuous of the three boxes in order to marry fair Portia: one box is made of gold (sun), one is of silver (moon), and one is of lead (stars). The lead box is the unlikely winner, poorest in material wealth yet richest in poetic association. This allegory reminds us that the best choice may not necessarily be the most attractive or obvious. In his subsequent examples, Freud switches the sex of the selector. The theme is revealed to be mythological, reminiscent of Paris's choice between the three beautiful goddesses. Freud cites Charles Perrault's "Cinderella" (1697), another example of a tale in which the main character is the youngest and ultimately the most successful compared to her ugly stepsisters. He puzzles over the meaning of the recurrent selection of the third sister, deducing that it must be on account of her "concealment and dumbness" ([1913] 1997: 112). Although Lucy can speak, she is put in the classroom for slow children at school and is described as "airy-fairy" (2011: 6), which some might consider dumb in the colloquial sense of the word. Moreover, her eccentric behavior and delirious contentment with the mundanity of life reinforces the third sister predicament. She is believed unanimously to be the favored child. The suggestion that each sister can also be represented by her hope chest as a metaphorical, analytical trope, is also worthy of further consideration: meanness, gold, sun, Merry, sadness, silver, moon, Ketzia, and happiness, lead, stars, Lucy.

As the most orderly of the three sisters, Lucy's character is predisposed towards an everlasting *mise-en-abyme*. Her tale begins with a rewriting of Grimms's "The Golden Key" (1819). In Bernheimer's version of the tale, the protagonist discovers the titular object in the snow and then imagines a chain of events in which "a locked iron box" full of "glittering treasures" (2011: 1) is excavated. However, the protagonist has no desire to look in the box, and leaves the reader's curiosity unrequited. Later, "The Golden Key" source text is reprised. This time a boy digs up the box, but the story ends before he turns the lock, once again failing to satisfy the reader's curiosity. Both tales question the notion of possession and suggest that the treasure chest is far from the goal of a character's narrative drive. Like the psychoanalytic layering of the mind, the archaeological process of searching is given more emphasis than any prize in this fairy tale. Bernheimer mines Brooks's reading of narrative desire which "comes into being as a perpetual want for (of) a satisfaction that cannot be offered in reality" (1984: 55). Desire itself is queried recurrently throughout the trilogy, with curiosity or "epistemophilia" or "the desire to know" (Mulvey 1996: 96) often substituting for sexual desire.

Lucy's need to cherish things borders on obsessive compulsion. "From a young age, Lucy liked to keep things tidy in boxes or shoes or in nutshells or pockets—like many children, she found it pleasant for things to fit into this or that place" (2011: 26). Bernheimer explores Lucy's psychology further, revealing that Lucy's favorite toy is also a container, a fake book housing a doll, known as *A Doll's Book*: "a doll in a book that wasn't even a book! Tiny things inside tiny things, so very appealing!" (27). Infatuated with the miniature, Lucy approximates Bernheimer's (2006b) own coveting of surrealist box-maker Joseph Cornell's *Pink Palace* (c.1950)—another representation of a hope chest as a soothing fantasy device and physical fairy tale. Susan Stewart designates Cornell's miniature as "uncontaminated" (1993: 68) mirroring Lucy's domestic habits and career. Lucy grows up to become first an animator, then a doll-maker. Despite her admission that "a love of dolls is neurotic" (2011: 30), Lucy becomes the doll inside her own text. She must carve doll faces, a violent activity that the author advises "children should never see" (31). Indeed, in Bernheimer's literary imagination, boxes and dolls always exhibit malicious leanings and are imbued with ominous intent. The unpacking of Lucy's ascetic tendencies directly implicates the imaginative grounds of the hope chest.

> In a metal trunk at the foot of her bed—the very same trunk Mrs Gold had taken to camp when she was young, which either was or was not a camp where you might have been killed—Lucy kept her favorite belongings. This trunk that resembled the treasure chest of a pirate, and also evoked danger: Lucy did not want to add to its collection ... Among the items in there: a sewing kit, a plastic doll, a knitted shirt. (11–12)

Here the evocation of concentration camps and pirates endows the box with peril. The limited contents include specific objects that epitomize Lucy's two disturbed sisters, both of whom self-harm. Moreover, when Lucy believes she is becoming engaged to her high school sweetheart, she kicks the chest playfully.

> 'Oh treasure chest, hope chest, my dearest friend,' I said. 'Sam Han loves me.' Oddly, the chest sounded hollow. I opened the trunk and brightness shot at me. For a moment I had no sight. When I'd regained my vision, I discovered all of my treasures were gone. The next morning I learned that Sam Han had died, taken by his own hand. (23)

Here the hope chest is closely associated with the momentary blindness of the young woman. As her vision returns, the chest is revealed to be an empty vessel or coffin, offering a condensed metaphor for a false promise. The dumbness of symbolic lead returns. The extinguishing of her treasures and future hopes correlates symbolically with her fiancé's suicide. It is a cruel life lesson for a material girl who commits suicide on many occasions, whether choking on a beloved stone or vanishing like her treasures.

Transgressive Curiosity

Ketzia Gold (2001) is a discourse on melancholia and masochism. The protagonist wanders the desert after her quiet career as a transcriptionist. We learn that her husband selected her over her two sisters, returning to the magic number in Freud's "Theme of the Three Caskets" ([1913] 1997) because of the way Ketzia ate her cheese; when it came to the rind "[she] didn't take off too much and [she] didn't take off too little" (2001: 125), However, in terms of its forbidden boxes, Ketzia's narrative is surely more closely related to variations of Charles Perrault's "Bluebeard" ([1697] 2008) in terms of secret spaces and insatiable curiosity. In this French folktale a newly-wed king gives his young wife a key and forbids her from opening his secret chamber while he is away. Curiosity supersedes and she unlocks the door to find his former wives' remains. Mulvey revises Perrault's tale in critical terms, with emphasis on the protagonist's curiosity. While Mulvey's text centers on demythologizing the figure of Pandora, she also makes reference to "Bluebeard" which emphasizes curiosity as a feminine trait. The hope chest is a cipher for this narrative drive, a symbol for the acquisition of knowledge, wherever the emotional compass might point. Components of "Bluebeard" are recurrent in *Ketzia*, particularly the theme of the husband's hiding treasures, locked up in cupboards or in caskets buried deep beneath the ground, from his wife.

> One day ... I discovered a cigar box full of jewelry... I felt my stomach drop with intuition. 'Whose are these,' I said holding up feather earrings. 'And these,' holding up three silver rings. 'I wasn't hiding it from you,' Adam said when he got home.

'I just wanted it where we'd never touch it.' He stroked my ears and put it back in the ground. (2001: 110)

Ketzia's embodiment is made palpable through the dread in the pit of her stomach and in her estranged husband Adam's stroking of her ears as if she were being disciplined like an obedient dog or caressed like a good little girl. Forbidden touching suggests something masturbatory, as in Freud's ([1905] 2013) observation of Dora's unconscious fingering of her purse which, as mentioned earlier, she does neurotically during therapy. Furthermore, in Dora's analytic universe, her mother's jewel-box functions as a significant object (or representation of her female genitalia) which must be rescued from a household fire, symbolic of Dora's concern for her own virginity and dislike of anything wet or anomalous as Hannah Decker (1991) and Douglas ([1996] 2000) remind us. This is made manifest in the mention of the contents—her mother's pearl-drop earrings function as symbols of wetness. In *Ketzia*, the jewelry indexes the intimate parts of an absent significant other—a rival female body is evoked through these ornaments alone. By way of rebellion, Ketzia trades the whereabouts of her guilty husband's booty for boxes of candy doled out by the neighborhood boys. The name of her husband, Adam, becomes significant in biblical terms with the sweets akin to Eve's being tempted by the serpent, thus positioning Ketzia as the guilt-ridden bearer of original sin. Hope for sweetness, denoting innocence, pervades her tale but Ketzia is often revealed to be the hopeless, willing victim. Through this characterization I suggest that Bernheimer provides insight into the awkwardness and paradoxes of femininity.

A later episode confirms Adam as the tyrant Bluebeard figure when Ketzia says, "On our first anniversary Adam gave me a huge string of keys. 'These are the keys to all the rooms of my house,' he said. 'But do not open the tiny closet at the end of this hallway, okay?'" (135). The fact that Ketzia does not even remember seeing this cupboard in her own house suggests a latent desire that becomes manifest upon the voicing of its realization. Components from the fairy tale "Bluebeard" come to the fore, and enable intertextual empathy with the inevitability of Ketzia's subsequent actions. She says, "Obviously, I couldn't stop myself" (136). After the fateful act of viewing the contents of Adam's secret closet, Ketzia applies a mud-mask in order to conceal her guilt, or, more precisely, herself, consistent with Mulvey's view of Pandora as a cosmetic surface that "dissembles" (1996: 55) but ultimately "defetishizes" (59) by prioritizing the active pursuit of knowledge acquisition over disavowal or "a refusal to see" (64).

Pandora: Dangerous Women and 'Flushed Secrets'

Merry Gold (2006a) concerns the ice-queen. Merry is a talented pattern-cutter but alcoholism leads to her downfall. Merry is the coldest and meanest of the three sisters, even transforming into a small ice-cube at one point. Tellingly, she transgresses containment throughout her narrative—a Pandora or bad omen. However, her dark memories and discovery of pornographic collections offer emancipatory ways of interpreting Merry through the metaphor of the hope chest.

Merry is fascinated by boxes of pornography, particularly 1970s *Hustler* and *Playboy* magazines that feature fairy tale fantasies. Bernheimer has commented on the trendy literature her parents read in the background of her own childhood, from the soft porn of Judith Krantz's *Princess Daisy* (1980) to the illustrated guide *The Joy of Streaking* (1974), both real publications which appear as cameos in the trilogy, demonstrating Bernheimer's purloining of popular culture of liberal minded families of the period.[8] However, there are also odious reimaginings at play in *Merry Gold*, which may or may not be consistent with Bernheimer's biographical facts. Brooks points out that "in the manner of so many fairy tales, the realization of desire comes in sinister forms, destructive of the self" (1984: 50). Bernheimer tells us that her grandfather was connected mysteriously to Warner Brothers or The Walt Disney Company, screening feature-length animations for his grandchildren in his basement (2006b). As Cristina Bacchilega writes, "The Disney-like uniformity reproduces and sells itself internationally by turning the fairy tale into a standard value-and-dreams package" (1999: 143). This "value-and-dreams package" is appropriated by Bernheimer into her personal mythology and fairy tale trilogy. In her fictional world of the Gold sisters, the grandfather is a malevolent absentee, represented by his extensive collection of pornography. Such pornographic hoards loom large in all three novels, located in the "pink suitcases" (2006a: 99) of the attic where the children play. Tableaus featuring "Little Red Riding Hood" and "Snow White" are enthralling to the Gold sisters. Yet Merry harbors concern that the women in these scenarios are "without hope" (100), suggesting that she aspires to something more empowering than the exhibits of her grandfather's secret stash. Often the sisters, especially Merry, choose to encounter this bounty naked, eager to learn about sexuality through performing these scenes in the safe company of siblinghood and within the privacy of their domestic surroundings. Writing about Dora's guilty interest in pornographic literature, Freud tell us that "children never read forbidden material in an encyclopedia calmly. They are tense with alarm as they do so, looking anxiously around to see whether anyone is coming" ([1905] 2013: 85). Bernheimer similarly confesses her childhood reading of fairy tales as "flushed secrets" (2006b: 69). Merry and Ketzia are competitive in their sexual research, particularly through their games of "The Punish," that overlaps in all three novels. In *Merry* we read,

> Down the basement stairs crept Merry, while her sister sat underneath them, waiting for punishment. Today it would be extreme. Though the exact origins of The Punish remained unclear, the game was of Merry's design and was based on at least three precise sources: a magazine she had seen at her grandfather's house ... films from Temple Shalom of girls' heads getting shaved; and a dramatic exercise she and her best friend invented. ... These were combined into The Punish by Merry who played Sir. (2006: 73)

This game affects both sisters psychologically. They remember their encounters slightly differently. Helen Pilinovsky notes the dissymmetry between Merry's and Ketzia's respective accounts of "The Punish" scene:

> Throughout Ketzia's tale, traditional oppositional construction has contributed to the demonization of Merry; if Ketzia is a victim then by nature Merry must be a villain: however, *The Complete Tales of Merry Gold* indicated that reflexive subjectivity can be a false mistress. (2009: 145)

Such lapses in memory evoke trauma. In this trilogy, themes of child abuse and pedophilia provide a subliminal undercurrent, represented by the unspeakable blanks in *Lucy Gold* when her unhinged sisters confess the root causes of their unruly natures. "'I'm going to tell you something,' she started. But I can't tell you what she next said. Fill it in, with the worst thing you could imagine: _____." (2011: 76). Bernheimer has confided that when it came to writing this part of the trilogy, she "couldn't actually say it so it was the only way [she] could do it."[9] The blanks in the text offer unspoken truths, akin to long forgotten trunks of storage material or the empty box of hope. Throughout the trilogy, Ketzia and Merry appear to be the most somatically damaged by their childhood encounters, but Lucy's blissful ignorance and multiple suicides imply that she has been the most profoundly imprinted. Their collective, fragmented memories suggest a hidden meaning, and thus an undoing of the cozy family album. "The Complete Tales" prove, paradoxically, to be incomplete.

Conclusion: Hope in the Expanded Field

The hope chest reveals itself to be a quiet, ambivalent, yet persistent motif in Kate Bernheimer's trilogy, mimicking the narrative structures of the novels in terms of memory and prophecy. Like the contemporaneous hope chests of Dorothea Tanning (2004) and Miranda July (2005), Bernheimer's use of this symbolism challenges and expands conventional views about the place of girlhood in society, and about projections of the self. The theoretical boxes of Lucy, Ketzia, and Merry not only demand something more than the happily-ever-after of the bourgeois ritual of marriage but also reveal the complexities of feminist engagements with the figure of the child-woman and what she might do to disrupt expectations. Like the fairy tale, the hope chest can be wicked, lonely, and damaging to self-identity yet also consoling, rewarding, and aspiring—a place to put things, emotional or otherwise. The hope chest functions as a variation of Winnicott's transitional object, though for an adolescent rather than an infant. It is a vehicle for desires that may go unrequited. Although it tends to serve a conservative function, Bernheimer demonstrates that the hope chest can be reread as a transgressive, empowering accoutrement with which to augment the tensions of girlhood and manage the achievements and disappointments encountered in growing up. For Bernheimer, the hope chest operates much like a fairy tale text.

At the end of each of her novels, Bernheimer collages herself and her real-life family into the narrative—photographs of the three Gold sisters in their Halloween costumes are actually the Bernheimer sisters in fancy dress, while the photograph of the "lovely half-dressed girl" (2001: 97) found in the overnight bag of Ketzia's husband is, in reality, a staged photograph of Bernheimer herself imitating the pose of a *Playboy* model, a biographical fragment chanced upon in the fictional space of her hope chest novel. The girl in the text becomes a secret that is revealed. (The heading of my conclusion departs from but is inspired by Rosalind Krauss.)

Illustration 11.2: Kate Bernheimer, A Lovely Naked Girl, 2001. Reproduced with kind permission of Kate Bernheimer.*

Acknowledgments

I would like to thank Kate Bernheimer, Elspeth Mitchell, Ann Smith, and the anonymous reviewers for helping shape this chapter.

CATRIONA MCARA is University Curator at Leeds Arts University. She has published extensively on the art and literature of Dorothea Tanning and Leonora Carrington with a particular focus on feminist aesthetics and surrealist legacies in contemporary practice. She is author of *A Surrealist Stratigraphy of Dorothea Tanning's Chasm* (2017), co-editor with Jonathan P. Eburne of *Leonora Carrington and the International Avant-Garde* (2017), and editor of *In Fairyland: The World of Tessa Farmer* (2016). Catriona is currently researching the novels and curatorial work of Chloe Aridjis, Kate Bernheimer, and Heidi Sopinka.

Notes

* The quality of this photo is intentional and how it appears in the original source.

1. I encountered these novels in the summer of 2011 when I was finishing my doctoral research on Dorothea Tanning; I was interested in her contemporary relevance. I then interviewed Bernheimer in Arizona the following summer while I was conducting research on Tanning's time in Sedona.
2. Interview with Kate Bernheimer, 2012.
3. I have opted for the American term hope chest because of the nationality of Kate Bernheimer and her own explicit use of this term in *The Complete Tales of Lucy Gold*. Such memory boxes are known by regional variants, such as, for example Italian *cassone*, Australian glory boxes, and Indian *damchiya*. Bernheimer told me that she owns a hope chest from childhood—a red metal trunk.
4. Written in the early twenty-first century, Bernheimer's novels appear at the same moment as does a second generation of feminist re-visionary literary criticism, another medium channelled immediately by Bernheimer.
5. Artworks by Dorothea Tanning were used on the covers of two of Bernheimer's novels in this trilogy.
6. The writing of Angela Carter provided another literary touchstone for both Bernheimer and Mulvey (1996: 60). Carter's "demythologizing" approach, discussed in her feminist statement "Notes from the Front Line" ([1983]1997: 38), seeks to dismantle perpetual mythmaking, especially as it relates to and obstructs the feminist project. Bernheimer (2006b) acknowledges that much of her practice has been molded by Carter's critical legacy.
7. Personal communication with Kate Bernheimer, 2017.
8. Interview with Kate Bernheimer, 2012.
9. Interview with Kate Bernheimer, 2012.

References

Bacchilega, Cristina. 1999. *Postmodern Fairy Tales: Gender and Narrative Strategies*. Philadelphia, PA: University of Pennsylvania Press.
Bachelard, Gaston. [1958] 1994. *The Poetics of Space*, ed. John R. Stilgoe. Trans. Maria Jolas. Boston, MA: Beacon Press.
Bal, Mieke. 1999. *Quoting Caravaggio: Contemporary Art, Preposterous History*. Chicago: University of Chicago Press.
Bernheimer, Kate. 2001. *The Complete Tales of Ketzia Gold*. Tallahassee, FL: FC2.
Bernheimer, Kate. 2006a. *The Complete Tales of Merry Gold*. Tuscaloosa, AL: FC2.
Bernheimer, Kate. 2006b. "This Rapturous Form." *Marvels and Tales: A Journal of Fairy Tale Studies* 20 (1): 67–83. doi: 10.1353/mat.2006.0003
Bernheimer, Kate. 2007. "Introduction." In *Brothers and Beasts: An Anthology of Men on Fairy Tales*, ed. Kate Bernheimer, 1–12. Detroit, MI: Wayne State University Press.
Bernheimer, Kate. 2011. *The Complete Tales of Lucy Gold*. Tuscaloosa, AL: FC2.
Brooks, Peter. 1984. *Reading for the Plot: Design and Intention in Narrative*. Cambridge, MA: Harvard University Press.
Carter, Angela. [1983] 1997. "Notes from the Front Line." In *Shaking a Leg: Collected Journalism and Writings*, ed. Jenny Uglow, 36–43. London: Penguin Books.
Cixous, Hélène. 1976. "The Laugh of the Medusa." *Signs* 1 (4): 875–893.
Cixous, Hélène and Catherine Clément. [1975] 1996. *The Newly Born Woman*. Trans. Betsy Wing. London: I.B. Tauris Publishers.
Decker, Hannah. 1991. *Freud, Dora and Vienna 1900*. New York: Macmillan, The Free Press.
Douglas, Mary. [1966] 2000. *Purity and Danger: An Analysis of the Concept of Pollution and Taboo*. London: Routledge.
Freud, Sigmund. [1905] 2013. *A Case Study of Hysteria (Dora)*. Trans. Anthea Bell. Oxford: Oxford University Press.
Freud, Sigmund. [1913] 1997. "The Theme of the Three Caskets." In *Writings on Art and Literature*, ed. Neil Hertz, 109–121. Stanford, CA: Stanford University Press.
Harries, Elizabeth Wanning. 2001. *Twice Upon a Time: Women Writers and the History of the Fairy Tale*. Jersey, NJ: Princeton University Press.
Kristeva, Julia. 1982. *Powers of Horror: An Essay on Abjection*. New York: Columbia University Press.
Marcus, Stephen. 1985. "Freud and Dora: Story, History, Case History." In *In Dora's Case: Freud, Hysteria, Feminism*, ed. Charles Bernheimer and Claire Kahane, 56–91. London: Virago.
Mulvey, Laura. 1996. "Pandora's Box: Topographies of Curiosity." In *Fetishism and Curiosity*, 53–64. Bloomington: Indiana University Press.

Olalquiaga, Céleste. 1998. *The Artificial Kingdom: A Treasury of the Kitsch Experience*. New York: Pantheon Books.
Perrault, Charles. [1697] 2008. "Bluebeard." In *The Fairy Tales of Charles Perrault*, ed. Jack Zipes. Trans. Angela Carter, 5–10. London: Penguin.
Pilinovsky, Helen. 2009. "The *Complete Tales* of Kate Bernheimer: Postmodern Fairytales in a Dystopian World." In *Fairy Tales Reimagined: Essays on New Retellings*, ed. Susan Redington Bobby, 137–152. Jefferson, NC: McFarland.
Schleining, Lon. 2001. *Treasure Chests: The Legacy of Extraordinary Boxes*. Newtown, CT: The Taunton Press.
Stewart, Susan. [1984] 1993. *On Longing: Narratives of the Miniature, the Gigantic, the Souvenir, the Collection*. Durham, NC: Duke University Press.
Tanning, Dorothea. 2004. *Chasm: A Weekend*. London: Virago.
Warner, Marina. 2011. *Stranger Magic: Charmed States and the Arabian Nights*. Cambridge MA: Harvard University Press.
Winnicott, D. W. [1971] 2005. *Playing and Reality*. London: Routledge.

Filmography

July, Miranda. 2005. *You and Me and Everyone We Know*. USA.

CHAPTER 12

The Girl in the GIF
Reading the Self into Girlfriendship

Akane Kanai

Reading Girlhood in Digital Spaces

I approach the question of how individuals recognize themselves in discourses of girlhood by foregrounding the interaction between readers and texts. Focusing on the production of identity in digital spaces, I suggest that participating in digital girlhood can be interrogated, not only by examining girls' blogging, chatting, and profile construction, but by considering the discursive circulation of girlhood via texts and the reading they invite. I examine these dynamics through a set of blogs hosted on the platform, Tumblr, authored by young women and comprised of a highly popular original blog named WhatShouldWeCallMe (WSWCM), together with five spinoff blogs that do their own adapted versions of the founder. Following the terminology of Limor Shifman (2014), these will be referred to respectively as the founder blog and follower blogs. I show how the blogs, their circulation, and readership form a digital public premised on knowledges of the discourses and affects of youthful femininity. As such, reading is positioned in this analysis as not simply a process of reception, but a creative, affective (Wetherell 2012) and social act.

Notes for this section can be found on page 203.

In the public based on WSWCM and its follower blogs, each blog expresses self-representative experience through a reaction-GIF format: in each post, a GIF, an image capturing about three seconds of movement from diverse media material ranging from television and film to internet videos, is combined with a caption describing an emotive reaction to a situation. Reading and relating to the experiences in these highly affective posts draws on a gendered social imaginary structuring the way in which commonality and connection with other girl participants in the public may be felt. Drawing on the work of Louise Rosenblatt (1978, 1995) and Michael Warner (2002), I propose the term spectatorial girlfriendship to explain how the self is positioned in the imaginary of the public amongst other, unknown girlfriends, through the process of reading. Thus, rather than drawing a line between discourses of girlhood and actual girls, in this article I aim to theorize the mechanisms through which the self is actively implicated within such discourses via participation in online texts.

Understanding Digital Girlhoods

To begin this discussion, I will address the question of why I am discussing girlhood when it has been made clear that the blogs are authored by young women. When I use the term girlhood, I refer to a discourse that does not necessarily correspond to a biological development of youthful bodies (Projansky 2007) but, rather, encompasses a set of cultural, gendered constraints, regulatory requirements, and incitements girling certain bodies of varying ages. Such cultures, in the West, are often described as postfeminist (Gill 2007; Projansky 2007), requiring both the performance of feminine capacity and empowerment but under narrow, intertwined conditions of beauty, heterosexuality, and neoliberal success in education and employment (McRobbie 2009).

Much contemporary work on digital girlhood has focused on how girls, through digital spaces, negotiate such postfeminist regulatory requirements. Notably, Angela McRobbie (2009) argues that the postfeminist sexual contract requires active participation in the public sphere, but such participation must be marked by a girlish non-threatening demeanor. Accordingly, scholars have shown that blogging and social network activity, in particular, are mechanisms through which girls negotiate or manage normative standards of appearance, popularity, and sexuality (Brandes and Levin 2013; Dean and Laidler 2013; Elm 2009; Holmes 2016; Marwick 2015; Mazzarella

2008; Shade 2008; Stokes 2010; Vickery 2010). This girls' studies scholarship explores the possibilities of digital media in helping to transcend those restrictions on femininity that aim to render girls docile and passive (see, for example, Keller 2015). Other discussions have focused explicitly on girls' online negotiations of sexual double standards. Jessica Ringrose's work (2010) illustrates how girls' use of digital media on social networks corresponds to the negotiation of postfeminist discourses of sexuality in which girls must appear confident, sexually attractive, and knowledgeable, yet are still confronted by gendered double standards that limit their capacity to act of their own accord. Similarly, Amy Dobson's research (2011) demonstrates central preoccupations with what she terms heterosexiness in the production of young women's profiles on MySpace.

Dobson's and Ringrose's research suggests how girls' self-production in digital spaces is regulated by postfeminist discourses that instate certain parameters of legibility and recognizability as girls. Banet-Weiser's work on girls' YouTube videos shows how girls shape themselves into "detached saleable images" (2011: 285) within similar postfeminist parameters, amenable to digital viewing, audience engagement, and circulation. Relatedly, I suggest that these discursive regulatory cultures and their negotiation inflect knowledges of how to do girlhood in digital spaces in ways that invite a felt sense of commonality with unknown audiences (Kanai 2017). As such, certain discourses and associated affects such as the connection between confidence and slim, conventionally heterosexy bodies (Dobson 2011), shape the terms on which certain girlhood experiences may be considered intelligible or common. As I explore here, these intertwined affects and discourses have an important part to play in the social imaginary invoked by these blogs that readers are assumed to share, presented as knowledges that can catalyze a sense of belonging and social recognition. Given that these blog posts convey feelings associated with particular situations that readers are expected to recognize and decode, here I adopt Margaret Wetherell's (2012) affective-discursive approach in understanding affect as a loose, socially-based form of emotion that cannot be productively disentangled from discursive context.

Responding to Sonia Livingstone's (2008) call to revive the text-reader approach in research on digital culture, I operationalize reading as a central way through which bodies may attach to affective and discursive circulations of girlhood in the formation of digital publics, rather than furthering the well-researched terrain of girls' negotiation of gendered standards via blogging and online profile construction. While the importance of reading for girls has certainly been explored in offline contexts (Singer 2015; Willis 2009), reading as a primary form of participation in digital girlhood requires further scholarly attention. This focus on reading is important given the way that many social media platforms reconfigure reading as an active, curatorial practice, not simply that of receiving information but a central way of engaging and participating in the sociality of a platform. Reading is integral to social media actions such as liking, sharing, retweeting, or, in the case of Tumblr, reblogging. Somewhat similar to the sharing function on Facebook, reblogging is a function on Tumblr that re-circulates blog posts authored by another user, while simultaneously pinning that blog post to one's own blog; approximately 95 percent of all posts on Tumblr at any given time are reblogged posts (Strle 2013). Accordingly, reblogging is a central, active means through which readers can acknowledge posts with which they feel connections, and through which attachments to social identities such as girlhood may be articulated.

Spectatorial Girfriendship: Connecting Discourses, Texts, and Publics

To introduce the idea of reading the self into affective-discursive circulations of girlhood it is important to understand how the blogs, as the central texts I discuss, are premised on a particular form of address to readers. Begun in 2012, the popular anonymous founder blog, WSWCM, was created by two young women, who saw themselves as best friends, in law schools on opposite coasts of the United States, as a means of keeping in touch with each other (Casserly 2012). However, the blog soon became more than a simple means of dyadic correspondence. Drawing up to 1.5 million views per day shortly after its inception (Duncan 2012), WSWCM also inspired the creation of dozens of follower blogs by other anonymous young women, adapting its format to articulate their own experiences. The posts in these blogs follow a similar structure to the founder blog; they combine a GIF with a caption to express experiences associated with youthful femininity. These feelings and situations often pertain to the difficulty of meeting standards of beauty, (hetero)sexuality, and pressures to succeed, echoing McRobbie's observations of the pressures on what she terms "top girls" (2009:56). Examples range from the shame associated with weight gain, dejection with the difficulties of university, or the contempt felt when espying a rival girl flirting with one's ex-boyfriend featured below. All these types of moments are expressed, like Illustration 12.1, in the present tense, and as a generic, potentially recurring moment, with little other contextual detail.

Illustration 12.1: Ex-boyfriend problems

Viewed online, this post shows a looping movement, with the young woman centrally featured in the GIF straightening up, focusing her gaze on the young woman whose back we see, as the words "bitch mode activated" flash repeatedly. The post articulates feelings of frustration and contempt boiling to the surface in relation to an undeserving sexual rival. Certain girl knowledges and dispositions based on discourses of girlhood are assumed: first, beauty or being hot, as stated above, is translated automatically as a normative feminine trait, following the postfeminist emphasis on personal appearance (McRobbie 2009). Accordingly, the figure of the less hot girl is an easy target; she is less deserving of the opportunity to flirt with the ex. The ex is a significant figure here, summoning affects of possessiveness as a reaction structured by a monogamous and heterosexist world, in which a girl's "erotic capital" (Winch 2013: 21) depends on the attachment of a boyfriend. Evidently, the stern young woman who is straightening up stands in for the author of this blog post. Yet, she also stands in for a number of indefinite others: in the moment of reading, the post invites the reader to imagine the self amongst other likeminded girls who channel their pain from their experience with their ex onto the new girl who seeks the ex's attention. The reader is offered the opportunity to belong by imagining the self amongst other girlfriends who may admit or share such ugly feelings in confidence.

Recognition of being situated amongst a group of likeminded others is enacted through this blog post on a number of levels. The anonymous nature of the post and the highly general way such feelings are described structure the feeling as a common one felt by girls, and as such, is amenable to being shared in digital forms of circulation. In some ways, posts like this may be read as an inside joke between the two best friends who had begun the founder blog. Yet, as noted above, others read their way into the joke. The popularity of this funny blog spoke to a shared imaginary of a sizeable (feminine) audience, attracting media coverage by *Forbes* (Casserly 2012) as part of its *Forbes Woman* section, and *Allure* (O'Neill 2012), an American women's magazine, amongst others, for its ability to connect to a "collective popular subconscious of young women" (Casserly 2012: n.p.).

I reframe this "collective popular subconscious" (Casserly 2012: n.p.) as a public, following Warner, who argues that a public is a social space and set of relations that come into being through the circulation of discourse addressed to strangers or "indefinite others" (2002: 59). Strangers are vital for the formation of publics: indeed, "a nation, market, or public in which everyone could be known personally would be no nation, market, or public at all" (57). Hosted on Tumblr, a platform that operates on norms of anonymity and where the majority of content is publicly available (Cho 2011), these blogs operate on the basis that the experiences and feelings articulated in the posts are shared by strangers, rather than known acquaintances. A digital public is formed here, on the basis of the attention of numerous young women, unknown to each other, who stumbled across this set of digital texts, and through which they were addressed as participants—indeed, as subjects in girlhood discourses. Notably, a public is made up not simply of its physical participants, but the social imaginary that they bring to the texts: it is both "notional" and "empirical" (Warner 2002: 53). The social imaginary readers bring to the texts constructs a shared world through the texts, and at a second level, conceives of the strangers, the other readers who inhabit this world, as having a similar shared disposition towards the world outside the public. This public is formed on the basis of reading the self into a common social imaginary shared with strangers, a social imaginary that draws on a constellation of discourses and affects of girlhood articulated through the founder and follower blogs and circulated through their liking, reblogging, and adaptation on Tumblr.

I use the term spectatorial girlfriendship to describe the operation of the social imaginary at play here in the circulation of the blogs that invites the reader to understand forms of girlhood as representative of both the blogger and reader as girlfriends who have certain experiences and knowledges in common. This readerly invitation is a key mechanism through which the self is placed in a common position with others in the discourses of girlhood that underpin the blog posts. The notion of spectatorial girlfriendship draws on Amy Dobson's notion of relational premise (2010), as well as Alison Winch's (2013) concept of girlfriendship. Relational premise, like Nancy Thumim's (2012) articulation of genre, is a way of conceptualizing the expectations that structure the ways in which individuals participate in mediated worlds like social media; girlfriendship speaks to assumptions of the commonality of young women based on and in their attachments to a normative girlness. This commonality as girlfriends does not necessarily connote friendship but an assumption of common knowledges and reference points within parameters of normative femininity including a shared understanding of affects linked to girlhood discourses, such as the rivalry and contempt for the figure of the less hot girl mentioned above. Spectatorial girlfriendship, then, cannot be understood within oppositions of artifice and reality: it is a relation to others offering particular forms of belonging, structured through a social imaginary underpinned by discourses of girlhood.

What becomes evident is that being able to read the above blog post does not rely on a simple decoding of the words and the movement of the central girl. Rather, it shows how reading this post draws on and recreates an imaginative re-living of a social moment through spectatorial girlfriendship. The reader understands that what is articulated is a feeling experienced by someone else, while also recognising that this feeling is intended as a description of a generic experience of girlhood that encompasses the reader. For example, in the above post and in others like it, articulating the rivalry when a girl is flirting with one's ex, the post's open address purports to document self-representative experience that also coincides with general experience. The post operationalizes an open-ended social imaginary speaking to an audience as girls; the brief, openly worded caption is expected to invoke girlfriend norms of heterosexual rivalry, contempt for the other girl mentioned in the post, as well as possessiveness of the erotic capital represented by the ex. Given the lack of context and detail in the post, such feelings of judgment towards this other girl are expected to be commonsensical—the standard reaction that the reader is assumed to understand, and to which the reader is expected to relate. In this address to girlfriends, the text mobilizes the implicit assumption that other, unknown girls are competitors rather than colleagues, in line with notions of feminine governmentality discussed by McRobbie (2009) and by Winch (2013). Through spectatorial girlfriendship, the physical reader is positioned in relation to other unknown readers, together with the author of the text, where all can be imagined as possessing a commonality as girls or girlfriends, addressed and regulated by girlhood discourses.

This call to spectatorial girlfriendship may be observed in the way in which the texts are keyed, partnering a sense of authorial self-representation with a textual openness that invites the reader to reflect upon the commonality of their own experience. The general way the posts are penned invites an active self-referentiality on the part of the reader. The reader's skills of interpreting and organizing meaning in the discourses that circulate in the texts are made central in parsing and attributing a meaningful structure of common girlfriendship to the process of engaging with these digital texts.

Reading the Self into Girlfriendship

I suggest that the practice of reading should be seen as the primary means through which the "empirical" participant in the public, and the "notional" (Warner 2002: 53) social imaginary of the public are bridged, using the reader's literacy, knowledge, and experiences to enter into a relationship of spectatorial girlfriendship. According to Jessica Laureltree Willis (2009), reading is an affective practice that produces a (real) social imaginary of possibilities for girls, and, I suggest, in addition, a practice that configures a relational identity, positioning the self as part of a broader public. Further, reading ought to be understood as the process through which concrete audiences not only engage with knowledges of girlhood circulating in this public, but also produce them. Reading might be seen as the final act, the receiving end of the public address of discourse. However, I use reading as a way of thinking through the connection between the circulation of these digital texts, the formation of the public, and participation in girlhood discourses.

In making this argument, I draw on Rosenblatt's (1978, 1995) theory of the textual transaction, which, misleadingly, has little to do with exchange and more to do with a commingling of both reader and text in the production of meaning. Developed when she was an educator, Rosenblatt's work in reader response remains significant in its impact on scholarship of literature, pedagogy, and education (Karolides 1991; Pantaleo 2013) as well as in creating intersections with the study of New Literacies (Hammer 2007; Sanders 2012).

If we draw on Rosenblatt's germinal text, *The Reader, the Text, the Poem* (1978) the act of reading can be understood simultaneously as a mode of social membership and thus an active part of the public-making here, rather than an activity that constructs readers, authors, and texts as separate things.

Rosenblatt observes that the reader's relationship to a text is summed up in the common phrasing, "The reader finds meaning in the text" (1978: 14). However, she contends that this suggests an overly linear relation. Reading, rather, is a "situation, an event at a particular time and place in which each element conditions the other" (16), which Rosenblatt calls "the transaction" (17). It is the reader's organization and animation of the text, otherwise symbols and lines on a page that constitute the act of reading, that becomes an act of simultaneous creation and fusion. The reader, in response to a set of cues, marshals her or his repertoire of knowledge and experience in constructing the text. The text itself is thus not separable from the reader as Rosenblatt illustrates through quoting from the poem, "The House was Quiet and the World was Calm" (1954) by Wallace Stevens.

> The house was quiet and the world was calm.
> The reader became the book; and summer night
> Was like the conscious being of the book.
> The house was quiet and the world was calm.
> The words were spoken as if there was no book,
> Except that the reader leaned above the page.

For Rosenblatt, the reader, thus fully absorbed and evoking the world of the book, enters into a "coming-together, a co-penetration, of a reader and a text" (1978: 12).

Not each transaction requires this intense absorption, evidently. Although the reader must always call upon her or his imaginary in order for the reading to occur, the experience may be quite different depending on the form of transaction. Rosenblatt proposes two ends of a spectrum on which an act of reading might be located. The first is a non-aesthetic or efferent reading that focuses on the residue that remains following reading. Thus, efferent reading focuses on the information that one remembers from the reading and the actions to be carried out. This is the form of transaction in which summarizing a text is possible; one summarizes, in order to be able to instrumentalize the text. The residue of the text becomes more important than the experience of reading itself. However, in what Rosenblatt terms aesthetic reading at the other end of the transactional spectrum, what happens during the reading event is privileged: the "associations, feelings, attitudes and ideas that these words and referents arouse" (25). Rosenblatt calls this form of transaction "the poem" (12).

Drawing on these insights, the social imaginary of this public may be understood as being built through such transactional poems in the many GIF-based moments in which text and reader become productively entangled. Based on the structure of readers' encounters with these digital texts, I argue that these transactions involve aesthetic reading through which this girlhood-based public comes into being. The GIF, in its looping action, is particularly conducive to this form of experiential reading, requiring the making of the text during the few seconds it takes for the GIF's movement to be completed. The GIF invites the reader to immerse the self in the moment of the post, to waste time, to spend time consuming a humorous, generic moment that invites the sense of belonging in that moment as the reader waits for the GIF's looping movement to finish in order to get the joke contained in the post. As James Ash (2015) and Alexander Cho (2015) argue, the repetitive structure of the GIF can work to amplify the intensity of affect, enhancing the feelings of immersion and resonance that users experience with Tumblr. Jason Eppink notes that in contemporary visual culture, the author of the GIF is de-emphasized and is, rather, shared as part of a "cinema of affiliation" (2014: 1) with imagined others.

Rosenblatt's idea of the transactional poem produces a sense of the complex experiential work that goes into constructing meaning. Aesthetic reading, which focuses on the experience of reading rather than using the reading residue for a purpose, encapsulates the form of social reading that grounds this public. The reader is playfully invited to fill in the gaps of the "mesh" (Rosenblatt 1978: 76) of the text by squaring the incongruous, bright, moving GIF and the situational-but-generic caption, being rewarded with getting the joke and a consequent sense of relating to the moment. Indeed, it is the sociality of reading these posts, rather than an instructive purpose, that stands as the primary reason for engaging with these texts. The act of reading these texts requires personal involvement. In an interview with a follower blogger, who had adapted the founder blog format for her own blog, I discussed the pleasures of reading reaction-GIF posts and the difficulty in explaining them to others. The blogger, Amelia, concurred with me. She said: "You *cannot* explain posts to people; you just have to show them the post."[1]

As Rosenblatt observes, one cannot summarize the reading of a poem. With these affective GIF-based texts, readers must engage personally in the visual transactional moment themselves; it is ineffectively explained or paraphrased by someone else. The GIF, together with the caption, constitutes the aesthetic poem, the momentary puzzle that the reader must interpret, experience, and (re)make.

In the public I discuss here, the reader, in transacting with the GIF and caption, engages in an act of stranger sociability that Warner (2002) describes. The reader recognizes or deciphers the post while understanding that many indefinite others who are part of this public also participate in recognizing themselves in the affects and discourses of girlhood. While each post describes a moment that its author may have experienced, its sparse, open, and generic description invites the unknown reader to fill the self personally into a common situation through spectatorial girlfriendship into an imaginary that is both personal and social. Here, reading, as a social practice, produces the self as part of a larger public tethered to a common position in affects and discourses of femininity. Consider the post below: "When I'm shoveling food in my face and someone cute walks by."

Illustration 12.2: Struggling to act cool

WHEN I'M SHOVELING FOOD IN MY FACE AND SOMEONE CUTE WALKS BY

Although the experience of the post is ostensibly the author's own, it has been pared down, and details that might otherwise overly personalize the experience have been removed. The main figure in the post, as stated above, is "someone cute," rather than a named, specific participant in the author's life. It is a call to spectatorial girlfriendship through its non-specific articulation of the experience of routinely meeting expectations of grace and girlish demeanour, particularly in heterosexualized interactions, an area of life that is heavily surveilled and regulated for girls. Though the GIF technically depicts a situation that might *prima facie* appear somewhat removed from the situation articulated in the caption, it is the imaginary brought by the reader that does the work of synthesis, transforming the GIF and caption into a social moment. When viewing the repetitive movement of the GIF online, the reader is able to see the squirrel, representing the author, suddenly dropping the nut being held to its mouth, but the image, in and of itself, is far from straightforwardly representative of the scenario. The reader must square the act of the animal with her own experience and knowledge of norms of gendered conduct implied in this potentially romantic scenario to bring to life the author's (and reader's) awe at the attractiveness of the person passing, resulting in the dropping of the food. The reader must draw on personal and social knowledge and imagination to transform the squirrel's actions into the far from elegant demeanor catalyzed by a love interest's arrival *en scène*. Drawing on shared codes of feminine poise and postfeminist sexual discernment made normative in top girl discourses (McRobbie 2009), the post pokes fun at girls' occasional inability to act cool in the heat of such an encounter.

Engaging in this process projects a social world and, in a double movement, asks readers to project themselves into it, as girlfriends, amongst similar, indefinite others, through the address of the text. I note, however, that simply because these texts are addressed to indefinite others who may see themselves in this general situation, it is not necessarily an inclusive public, available for all to enter. Rather, the possibility of entering into spectatorial girlfriendship depends on both the textual invitation and what is imaginable from the reader's social location (Kanai 2016). The requirement of commonality in order to belong in this public provides a sense of connection. However, it also secures that connection to sameness of experience, necessarily producing insiders and outsiders based on the reader's own location in relation to the discourses of femininity that circulate in the blogs. And indeed, assumptions of sameness and universality may be derived from a perspective linked to dominant classed and raced social locations (Kanai 2017).

The public, despite its open address, is thus never simply out there waiting for any participant to gain entry; it is a product of working with and recreating existing social worlds and positions in discourses of girlhood. This poetic worldmaking is why, according to Warner (2002), publics should not be understood as simply based on rational-critical discourse where entry is *prima facie* transparent and the terms of entry are equally available. The apparent openness of the call in the text, found as it is online and accessible without any privacy restrictions, obscures the way in which the text itself forms a gatekeeping transaction. A public's boundaries are maintained through the borders of the social imaginary it depends on. Thus, in this public, feelings of commonality cannot be considered as simply co-terminous with feminist solidarity. Accessing this public is not a simple matter of clicking a link or finding the actual page on Tumblr; it is a matter of a personal reading of the self into the spectatorial girlfriendship catalyzed through the circulation of these digital texts.

Conclusion: Feeling Like the Girl in the Text

In arguing for aesthetic reading as an active way of being in the world, Rosenblatt claims that the aesthetic transaction between reader and text is a "poem... an event in time" created through the "coming-together" (1978: 12) of reader and text. As readers, while we generate this poem, we produce feelings, attitudes, and ideas that shape who we are. Thus, in thinking through reading as an active process through which ideas are not simply relayed but co-produced, Rosenblatt's work is key to understanding how the girl in the text cannot be neatly separated from the social world, nor the reader from the text. The spectatorial girlfriendship here is experienced through texts. At the same time, it shapes and is shaped by lived girlhood experience, providing a scaffolding through which attachments, loyalties, and commonalities with others may be felt. Indeed, through the entanglement of readers and texts, digital cultures of circulation create collectivities—imagined and concrete publics based on girlhood's associated affects and discourses. Rosenblatt's transactional theory suggests how patterns of interpretation and imagination come to matter.

In this chapter, I have positioned reading as a means of participating in girlhood in digital space, and spectatorial girlfriendship as a mechanism through which the self may be positioned in a common social imaginary with other, unknown girls. The narrow frames of experience articulated through texts require readerly cooperation to be legible. Neither simply representation nor construction, spectatorial girlfriendship enables those who are already addressed by girlhood discourses and affects to imagine the self, through the process of reading, in connection with others. Thus, reading, even the type of reading that tends to be erased by terms such as scrolling or browsing in digital spaces, has been foregrounded in this account as a means of participating in girlhood as an affective and discursive circulation. In the case of the humorous, digital texts I have explored, the invitation to spectatorial girlfriendship, for some readers, enables pleasures of recognizing and producing the self within a shared social imaginary, one girl amongst others.

Acknowledgments

My thanks go to the bloggers who permitted me to reproduce their posts. I would also like to thank the Faculty of Arts at Monash University for their generous support during my PhD candidature, and my supervisors, Professor JaneMaree Maher and Dr Amy Dobson, without whom this work could not have been accomplished.

AKANE KANAI is a lecturer in the School of Media, Film, and Journalism at Monash University, Australia. Her research on shifts in femininity, affect, and media culture has been published in the *Journal of Communication, Social Media + Society*, the *Journal of Gender Studies, Celebrity Studies,* and *Feminist Media Studies*. Her book, *Gender and Relatability in Digital Culture: Managing Affect, Intimacy and Value*, was published in 2019. She is currently researching the relations between feminism, identity, and affect across digital and media culture more broadly.

Note

1. Personal communication, 28 April 2014.

References

Ash, James. 2015. "Sensation, Networks and the GIF: Toward an Allotropic Account of Affect." In *Networked Affect*, ed. Ken Hillis, Susanna Paasonen and Michael Petit, 119–133. Cambridge, MA: MIT Press.

Banet-Weiser, Sarah. 2011. "Branding the Post-Feminist Self: Girls' Video Production and YouTube." In *Mediated Girlhoods: New Explorations of Girls' Media Culture*, ed. Mary Celeste Kearney, 277–294. New York: Peter Lang.

Brandes, Sigal Barak, and David Levin. 2013. "'Like My Status'." *Feminist Media Studies* 14 (5): 743–758. doi: 10.1080/14680777.2013.833533.

Casserly, Meghan. 2012. "#WhatShouldWeCallMe Revealed: The 24-Year Old Law Students Behind the New Tumblr Darling." *Forbes*, 29 March. http://www.forbes.com/sites/meghancasserly/2012/03/29/whatshouldwe callme-revealed-24-year-old-law-students-tumblr-darling/ (accessed 24 March 2013).

Cho, Alexander. 2011. "Queer Tumblrs, Networked Counterpublics." Paper presented at the 61st Annual International Communication Association Conference, Boston, 26–30 May.

Cho, Alexander. 2015. "Queer Reverb: Tumblr, Affect, Time." In *Networked Affect*, ed. Ken Hillis, Susanna Paasonen and Michael Petit, 43–58. Cambridge, MA: MIT Press.

Dean, Marissa, and Karen Laidler. 2013. "A New Girl in Town: Exploring Girlhood Identities through Facebook." *First Monday* 18 (2). http://journals.uic.edu/ojs/index.php/fm/article/view/4230 (accessed 5 September 2015).

Dobson, Amy Shields. 2010. "Bitches, Bunnies and BFFs (Best Friends Forever): A Feminist Analysis of Young Women's Performance of Contemporary Popular Femininities on MySpace." PhD diss., Monash University.

Dobson, Amy Shields. 2011. "Hetero-sexy Representation by Young Women on MySpace: The Politics of Performing an 'Objectified' Self." *Outskirts: Feminisms Along the Edge* 25. http://www.outskirts.arts.uwa.edu.au/volumes/volume-25/amy-shields-dobson (accessed 12 March 2013).

Duncan, Fiona. 2012. "Across the Tumblrverse: The Creators of 'WhatShouldWeCallMe' Speak." http://bullettmedia.com/article/across-the-tumblrverse-the-creators-of-what-should-we-call-me-speak/ (accessed 28 January 2014).

Elm, Malin Sveningsson. 2009. "Exploring and Negotiating Femininity: Young Women's Creation of Style in a Swedish Internet Community." *Young* 17 (3): 241–264. doi: 10.1177/110330880901700302.

Eppink, Jason. 2014. "A Brief History of the GIF (so far)." *Journal of Visual Culture* 13 (3): 298–306. doi: 10.1177/1470412914553365.

Gill, Rosalind. 2007. *Gender and the Media*. Cambridge: Polity Press.

Hammer, Jessica. (2007) "Agency and Authority in Role-playing 'Texts'." In *A New Literacies Sampler*, ed. Michelle Knobel and Colin Lankshear, 67–94. New York: Peter Lang.

Holmes, Su. 2016. "'My Anorexia Story': Girls Constructing Narratives of Identity on YouTube." *Cultural Studies* 31 (1): 1–23. doi: 10.1080/09502386.2016.1138978.

Karolides, Nicholas J. 1991. *Reader Response in the Classroom: Evoking and Interpreting Meaning in Literature*. New York: Longman.

Kanai, Akane. 2016. "Sociality and Classification: Reading Gender, Race and Class in a Humorous Meme." *Social Media + Society* 2 (4): 1–12. doi: 10.1177/2056305116672884.

Kanai, Akane. 2017. "Girlfriendship and Sameness: Affective Belonging in a Digital Intimate Public." *Journal of Gender Studies*, 26 (3): 293–306 . doi: 10.1080/09589236.2017.1281108.

Keller, Jessalynn Marie. 2015. "Girl Power's Last Chance? Tavi Gevinson, Feminism, and Popular Media Culture." *Continuum* 29 (2): 274–285. doi: 10.1080/10304312.2015.1022947.

Livingstone, Sonia. 2008. "Engaging With Media—A Matter of Literacy?" *Communication, Culture & Critique* 1 (1): 51–62. doi: 10.1111/j.1753-9137.2007.00006.x.

Marwick, Alice E. 2015. "Instafame: Luxury Selfies in the Attention Economy." *Public Culture* 27 (75): 137–160. doi: 10.1215/08992363-2798379.

Mazzarella, Sharon. 2008. "Introduction: It's a Girl Wide Web." In *Girl Wide Web: Girls, the Internet and the Negotiation of Identity*, ed. Sharon Mazzarella, 1–12. New York: Peter Lang.

McRobbie, Angela. 2009. *The Aftermath of Feminism: Gender, Culture and Social Change*. London: Sage.

Pantaleo, Sylvia. 2013. "Revisiting Rosenblatt's Aesthetic Response through *The Arrival*." *Australian Journal of Language and Literacy* 36: 125–134.

Projansky, Sarah. 2007. "Mass Magazine Cover Girls: Some Reflections on Postfeminist Girls and Postfeminism's Daughters." In *Interrogating Postfeminism: Gender and the Politics of Popular Culture*, ed. Yvonne Tasker and Diane Negra, 40–72. Durham: Duke University Press.

Ringrose, Jessica. 2010. "Sluts, Whores, Fat Slags and Playboy Bunnies: Teen Girls' Negotiation of 'Sexy' on Social Networking Sites and at School." In *Girls and Education 3–16: Continuing Concerns, New Agendas*, ed. Carolyn Jackson, Emma Carrie, and Emma Renold, 170–182. Maidenhead: Open University Press.

Rosenblatt, Louise M. 1978. *The Reader, the Text, the Poem*. London: Southern Illinois University Press.

Rosenblatt, Louise M. 1995. *Literature as Exploration*. New York: The Modern Language Association of America.

Sanders, April. 2012. "Rosenblatt's Presence in the New Literacies Research." *Talking Points* 24 (1): 2–6.

Shade, Leslie Regan. 2008. "Internet Social Networking in Young Women's Everyday Lives: Some Insights from Focus Groups." *Our Schools/Our Selves*: 65–73.

Shifman, Limor. 2014. *Memes in Digital Culture*. Cambridge, MA: The MIT Press.

Singer, Amy. 2015. "Little Girls on the Prairie and the Possibility of Subversive Reading." *Girlhood Studies: An Interdisciplinary Journal* 8 (2): 4–20. doi: 10.3167/ghs.2015.080202.

Stokes, Carla E. 2010. "'Get on My Level': How Black American Adolescent Girls Construct, Identify and Negotiate Sexuality on the Internet." In *Girl Wide Web 2.0: Revisiting Girls, the Internet and the Negotiation of Identity*, ed. Sharon Mazzarella, 45–67. New York: Peter Lang.

Strle, Danielle. 2013. "In Conversation with Danielle Strle of Tumblr." *Social Data Week*, 20 September. http://library.fora.tv/2013/09/20/In_Conversation_with_Danielle_Strle_of_Tumblr (accessed 12 November 2013).

Thumim, Nancy. 2012. *Self-Representation and Digital Culture*. Basingstoke: Palgrave Macmillan.

Vickery, Jacqueline Ryan. 2010. "Blogrings as Virtual Communities for Adolescent Girls." In *Girl Wide Web 2.0: Revisiting Girls, the Internet and the Negotiation of Identity*, ed. Sharon Mazzarella, 183–200. New York: Peter Lang.

Warner, Michael. 2002. "Publics and Counterpublics." *Public Culture* 14 (1): 49–90. doi: 10.1215/08992363-14-1-49.

Wetherell, Margaret. 2012. *Affect and Emotion: A New Social Science Understanding*. London: Sage.

Willis, Jessica Laureltree. 2009. "Girls Reconstructing Gender: Agency, Hybridity and Transformations of 'Femininity'." *Girlhood Studies: An Interdisciplinary Journal* 2 (2): 96–118. doi: 10.3167/ghs.2009.020207.

Winch, Alison. 2013. *Girlfriends and Postfeminist Sisterhood*. Basingstoke: Palgrave Macmillan.

CHAPTER 13

Girls' Perspectives on (Mis)Representations of Girlhood in Hegemonic Media Texts

Paula MacDowell

Who or what represents girlhood and girl culture in the global, digital age? How are girls' identities marketed, distributed, and consumed by popular media texts that are persistently communicating gender messages with attitudes, interpretations, and conclusions already built in? Rebecca Hains (2012) reminds us that making sense of media as texts that construct and relay meanings is a habitual and often unconscious practice that girls carry out as they respond to images, ideas, and sounds while engaging with diverse media forms (for example, watching television, playing video games, listening to music, and interacting online). While it is no secret that today's girls are simultaneously inhabited by, immersed in, dependent upon, and often indifferent to the media messages with which they are bombarded and acculturated by every day, the challenge is educating them to understand how the media's rhetoric influences their notions of girlhood and girl culture, and hence the ways in which they see themselves in these texts and how others see them (Hobbs 2010; Long and Wall 2012).

Notes for this section can be found on page 221.

In her influential work, *Girls Make Media*, Mary Celeste Kearney (2006) finds that girls with agentive experiences as media producers are less vulnerable to manipulation by commercialized media artifacts and texts, and more informed about the effects of the media on the re/production of knowledge and the re/formation of gender roles. Educational research by Hedy Bach (1998) and Ricki Goldman-Segall (1998) further documents how youth involved with the process of creating their own media works are more likely to expose and question the ways in which they are positioned by the dominant storylines, values, and norms embedded in media culture. Hence, I presented a team of 10 girls with the creative challenge of producing a PSA with three enabling constraints: it had to be written, directed, and edited by girls; produced for a specific audience of females their age; and themed around the portrayal of tween-aged girls in the media and what is at stake given these (mis)representations.

PSAs are a vital part of media culture and a significant format for this study since, as Renee Hobbs (2010) and Paul Long and Tim Wall (2012) point out, they are texts used to raise awareness (locally and globally) about an issue and persuade the audience to do (or not do) something. For example, a well-known PSA created to raise and change public consciousness is the iconic *This Is Your Brain on Drugs*, produced in 1987 by the Partnership for a Drug-Free America (PDFA). In this PSA, a male actor puts an egg (representing the brain) into a sizzling frying pan (representing drugs) to illustrate the dangers of drug abuse; he warns, "This is your brain. This is drugs. This is your brain on drugs. Any questions?" Building on the 1987 campaign, the PDFA launched a second anti-drug PSA in 1997 starring the female actor Rachel Leigh Cook who slams the frying pan down onto the egg and then destroys the whole kitchen with it. Twenty years later, on 4/20[1] the PDFA (now The Partnership for Drug-Free Kids) released a third PSA on the same topic that also starred Rachel Leigh Cook, but this PSA includes scenes of teens asking questions.

Although PSAs are often part of a larger media campaign with a strategic vision, the PSA reported on in this article was a one-time opportunity for an all-girl team to explore new identities as social activists advocating on girls' issues and as media producers deconstructing the role of the media in their lives.[2] In my analysis, I examine how the coresearchers reflected on their transformative learning experiences of identity construction, meaning making, and knowledge production as they scripted, directed, and produced their own PSA at 101 Technology Fun. While the findings are not intended to be representative of everyone who identifies as a girl, they do reveal some of the ways in which contemporary media texts are appropriated, negotiated, rejected, and remade by female youth through their media production processes. I believe that if we want to learn more about girls we need to listen to their stories. Additionally, if we want girls to transform gender stereotypes in popular media we need to educate and empower them to create their own texts as counter-narratives to media texts that marginalize, manipulate, and misrepresent them.

Research Setting and Coresearchers

The research setting for this article was an equity-oriented initiative called 101 Technology Fun, an annual summer camp for girls with learning labs in animation, game design, movie production, robotics programming, and web development. The goal of 101 Technology Fun was to provide a respectful, inclusive, and non-stigmatizing learning environment for anyone in grades six or seven genuinely interested in engaging in an all-girl technology camp on the University of British Columbia campus. Our project team had an inclusive view of the word girl and we welcomed trans, genderqueer, and non-binary youth. During the summer of 2012, I worked closely with the How We Learn lab to develop and supervise two one-week camps that included 30 girls (aged between 10 and 13) from diverse racial and socio-economic backgrounds. These girls were recruited from three culturally diverse elementary schools located in a densely populated and transient area of the west side of Vancouver, Canada. Everyone who submitted a camp application and parental consent form was accepted into the summer camp. Although the girls created artifacts using a variety of media forms (such as media diary, documentary, game, interview, photograph, PSA, survey, video, and website), the specific dataset selected for this article focuses on one PSA titled *The Media?*

Foundational to this article, following Bach (1998) and Kearney (2006), is the perspective that respects girls as legitimate and knowledgeable experts in how they learn about and come to understand the media texts in their daily lives and worlds as real and meaningful. Hence, on the first day of camp, I established the participants as coresearchers, presenting each with a personalized name badge and a professional portfolio in which to store their fieldwork and design works. The participatory and girl-centered research setting was innovative and somewhat unconventional since all the coresearchers were involved in designing the camp infrastructure and curriculum. They also had genuine opportunities to contribute their ideas and perspectives to the development of the research design, including data collection, data selection, data analysis, and the assembly of shared research findings. For example, the coresearchers were asked to prepare (at home) for a team meeting by creating a list of their questions concerning media studies and girlhood. We worked together to create the 101 Technology Fun interview guides based on their research questions, including these:

> Who or what did the popular girl look like when you were our age?
>
> Why is it that girls are kind of treated like a toy or object these days, like when posing inappropriately in an ad?
>
> Why are woman always draped over men in advertisements?
>
> What do you think society values more: beauty, brains, or body?
>
> Do more or less than 50 percent of all the girls in Vancouver care more about their grades than their looks?

Questioning was fun at summer camp and conducting interviews was a popular activity. As my coresearcher Aslin[3] reported, "It's fun being with a bunch of girls and having talks about the media, and learning how girls are being affected by what they put in ads." I facilitated all the large group interviews and the girls interviewed each other in pairs using hand-held video cameras. I believe that girls benefit from making a video reflecting on their media creation processes and productions since this generates another layer of analysis while creating rich artifacts evidencing their learning. Further, providing girls with alternatives to written summaries helps to improve their oral communication skills and provoke introspection. As Salina observed, "The questions and stuff we talked about [was valuable because] normally we don't [do so] at home or with our friends or at school."

Drawing on participatory research practices that seek to shift marginalization and give voice and visibility to a variety of girlhoods (Keller et al. 2015), the 101 Technology Fun research setting was designed to provoke scholarly reflection about girls' rights and roles concerning the knowledge made about, for, by, with, and against them. Claudia Mitchell discusses various challenges and limitations of participatory research with girls, and asks us to consider "whether this type of work can really shift the boundaries of knowledge, or whether such a shift is only something that is part of the hope of do-good researchers" (2015: 153). These were my questions:

> To what extent can girls identify, analyze, and communicate their lived experiences and expressions of media culture?
>
> Who will listen to girls' evocative stories and media scripts that deconstruct gender stereotypes?

How will our research at 101 Technology Fun be valued and interpreted?

Will our research generate more equitable and progressive possibilities for girls to examine their media relationships with a critical eye towards empowered transformation beyond preconceived notions of girls as apolitical, conformists, or consumers?

Method

To ground my approach to studying with child participants as coresearchers, I developed the Tween Empowerment & Advocacy Methodology (TEAM) approach (see MacDowell 2015). TEAM serves to give voice and visibility to female youth who are often studied in social-science research but seldom privileged as authorities on issues concerning their lives and learning circumstances. Characterized by tween fieldwork, design works, and Doris Allhutter's (2012) work on mind scripting, TEAM encouraged and supported the coresearchers to find their voice and make it heard as a counter-narrative to hegemonic media texts and discourses. Using mind scripting I worked to foster complex understandings and analytical thinking. For example, I challenged the girls to identify and question how they are positioned (by themselves and others) in media and technology cultures. I also provoked my team to analyze media literacy questions. How is a media text constructed? What techniques are used to shape the messages in the text? Whose point of view is represented? Why might people take different meanings from the text?

The specific design problem presented to the coresearchers was to produce a PSA depicting how girls are portrayed in the media and then present their work to a live audience. Importantly, we had group sessions involving both technical demonstrations and intellectual support including discussions on the ways in which media makes meaning, unconscious gender biases, and how to achieve a critical distance from various media forms. The girls had two eight-hour days to brainstorm, research, storyboard, script, rehearse, shoot, direct, and edit. These different stages were achieved by iteration and intuition not as a linear or required sequence of steps. My team had exclusive girls-only access to three learning labs in the UBC Education Building. The materials they chose to use from the labs included the Smart Board for brainstorming, large sheets of recycled paper for storyboarding, high definition video cameras for filming, iMovie software for editing, and an assortment of used magazines including *Adbusters, chickaDEE, Cosmo Girl, National Geographic Kids, People Weekly, Seventeen, Shape, TIME, Today's Parent, Vogue,* and *Wired* for research purposes.[4]

The coresearchers arrived at camp with much to say in big and bold ways. My role was to set up a media-rich and girl-centered learning environment in which they could work, and then to stay out of their way and let them lead. Although I expressed my genuine interest in their creative and intellectual ideas, I did not interfere with my team's content choices, production techniques, or creative decisions. I was ever present, however, following them to document the making of their media works. My intent was to discern their perspectives and points of view, appearing inconspicuous yet always trying to capture their stories about girlhood in relation to pervasive media texts. In total, four PSAs were produced at 101 Technology Fun. During one of our team meetings, *The Media?* was selected by the coresearchers for further analysis. Our approach to data selection and analysis was guided by John Seidel's inductive method of qualitative data analysis, "a process of noticing, collecting, and thinking about interesting things" (1998: 1) while repeatedly engaging and re-engaging with the dataset.

Although this chapter focuses on a detailed analysis of one PSA, it is important to acknowledge that the girls were individually challenged to make a personal *ME Documentary* about the meaning of media and technology in their lives. The topic-focused PSA broadcast and open-ended *ME Documentary* presented two different opportunities for the coresearchers to engage with the technical tools and creative practices to express their ideas, concerns, talents, and volition both during and beyond the domain of the summer camp program. Parents, guardians, and UBC Teacher Candidates were invited to a premiere screening of the *ME Documentaries* and PSAs, thereby building the community's media literacy, as well as reinforcing the importance of educating girls in media studies.

Data Collection and Creation

As Kearney (2006) advocates, we need many diverse and detailed accounts of how contemporary media shapes our notions of girlhood and girl culture to test the largely theoretical or survey-based research that dominates the literature. Further, girls' perspectives need to be respected and given influence in the research concerning the knowledge created about their lives, health, and well-being. This serves as an emancipatory practice that supports them to resist stereotypical notions of girlhood and to transgress their doubly insubordinate status in the media sphere. Both gender and generational dynamics have historically marginalized girls' involvement (Mitchell 2015;

Wajcman 1998). Hence, in this section I offer the complete transcript of *The Media?* PSA followed by my analysis in conversation with the girls' analysis and interpretation of their media production.

FADE IN. INTERIOR: UNIVERSITY LIBRARY
A serious-looking 13-year old girl is standing in a brightly lit library with a large shelf of books behind her. She is speaking directly into the camera.

Jayden: The world is filled with many problems. A big problem is the media. Girls everywhere have low self-esteem because of this. They look in a magazine for three minutes and feel bad about themselves. This commercial shows how everything is being affected. How girls are mistreated and how the media is bad.

The camera turns to a 12-year old girl who is sitting on a chair in front of several aisles of library textbooks. She is articulate as she reads from a script.

Salina: Welcome to Mother Earth. The land of waving flags, flying bullets, and unsettling noise. Green valleys, soybean crops, mountain peaks, desert storms, inaugurations, declarations, and starving children. The land of crime, poverty, oppression, racism, and the unequal distribution of wealth. A land of pig-headed, over-confident, self-assured, ego-centric, self-righteous people who are blind and insensitive to the weak and the poor. Blinded by their determination and their compulsive behavior and the daily struggle for non-essential commodities.

The camera slowly zooms in to focus on the facial expressions of five different girls as they take turns speaking.

Jayden: Is…
Kim: This…
Aslin: What…
Jordan: You…
Salina: Want?

A girl is standing beside the sign pointing directions to the washrooms. Her left hand is covering up the female figure, leaving only the male figure visible.

Kim: Girls' rights are slowly disappearing. After all the hard work that we did to almost be equal. And now that we have the right to vote … would you want that to happen?

The camera quickly zooms in to focus individually on a collection of pink sticky notes. Each note is stuck on a different aisle of books. The notes read: "0.5 billion," "1 billion," "1.5 billion," "2 billion," "2.5 billion," and "3 billion." Jayden is standing beside and pointing at the last note.

Jayden: Three billion people don't look like the people we see in magazines and only… (the camera follows her as she runs to the end of the book aisle and picks up a pink sticky note which she holds up to the camera and reads) a couple people do.

Two girls are standing in front of the library stacks. They are both covering up their faces with a large cutout head of a supermodel from a magazine.

Aslin: Do I look like this?
Jordan: Does anyone look like this?
Aslin: (exclaiming) There are three billion people in the world who don't look like this!

Jordan: Seven out of eight people in magazines are photoshopped.

The camera zooms through a gap between the textbooks on the shelf to focus on the face of a 13-year-old girl who reports with great concern in her voice.

Kim: These days a banana is not just a banana. Wake up in the mindscape of North America. Where twelve billion display ads, three million radio commercials, and two thousand million television commercials are dumped into the collective subconscious daily. You are the test subject in the largest psychological experiment ever carried out on the human race. But this experiment is unusual in one fundamental way: no one is keeping track of the results.

The screen fades to black and then a question appears: "What is a media girl supposed to do?" Following this, the camera zooms in, one at a time, on seven words cut out from the subversive Canadian magazine *Adbusters*: consume, acquire, eat, dress, drive, drink, and fuck. Next, the camera slowly zooms in on the heads of nineteen models, one at a time, that the girls cut out from magazine advertisements. While the camera is panning the heads, in a clockwise circle, we hear (but do not see) Aslin.

Aslin: All of these people are photoshopped!

The screen fades to black and then the camera zooms in, to highlight the big smiles (not the entire faces) of the girls one at a time. They take turns speaking in positive and encouraging tones.

Jayden: (smiling) Be yourself!
Salina: (smiling) Be yourself!
Kim: (smiling) Be yourself!
Aslin: (smiling) Be yourself!
Jordan: (smiling) Be yourself!

The girls' bright smiles dissolve into a black screen, and the following message appears: "Be yourself, because everyone else is taken."

FADE OUT

Data Analysis: Part One

As I analyze *The Media?* I hear my team speaking with agency and without hesitation. They are mocking pervasive media culture and oppressive stereotypes with their assertive voices, creativity, and intelligence. I am proud to see girls soaring on the power of their words and watching their PSA come to life. Their girl-produced media production challenges the dominant identities and dubious ideals that, as Sarah Banet-Weiser (2011) notes, they feel pressured by mainstream media to believe in and become. Young girls are not typically portrayed as powerful or influential change makers in media culture and, as Leslie Farmer (2008) reports, most young females do not yet know how powerful they are. Developmentally, they are at an emotionally intense stage of negotiating their sense of self-esteem and self-worth (Callero 2003). As they explore their identities, girls are trying to distinguish who they are, both to themselves and others. They are navigating complex tensions as they establish their identities in relation to the popular media texts about girlhood with which they are growing up and that they are being acculturated to believe (Banet-Weiser 2011; Hains 2012). For example, the coresearchers criticize how the media narrowly portrays and trivializes females by emphasizing the traits of exterior beauty and sexuality as being more important than character, intellect, or talent.

What is a media girl supposed to do? This troubling question, raised by the coresearchers, provokes me to pause. Instead of making them fit into limiting stereotypes, how might we empower young females to experience and effect their own agency, influence, and power by contributing their stories to recreate and shape media culture (see Stuart and Mitchell 2013)? As content creators, my team lists some of the entrenched inequalities and limiting labels about girlhood. For example, *The Media?* reveals the internal and external pressures that many young females feel to conform to the perfect media ideal, someone they perceive as a homogenous photoshopped person who is limited to doing seven basic things: "consume, acquire, eat, dress, drive, drink, fuck." *The Media?* evidences the coresearchers' awareness of how contemporary media shapes their developing sense of self, yet they are still struggling with the lack of agency and confidence to be themselves.

Three mounting issues for my team include pressures to conform to traditional gender roles, unrealistic standards of beauty, and normalized expectations to be perfect super-girls. These media constructions and cultural fictions tell compelling tales about girls' abilities, attitudes, and behaviours, and girls have cultural antennae and sensitive receptors that absorb these media-generated texts, roles, and storylines (Callero 2003; Hobbs 2010; Long and Wall 2012). Many conform to and perform these roles but this is not necessarily who girls are or how they want to be. For Jordan, "the media is everywhere all around us. It's not just on your laptop, and it has a very good and bad influence on girls."

As producers of their own PSAs, the coresearchers draw on the themes, plots, values, and characters contained in other cultural tales that have also been remade and retold. For example, to summarize their PSA in a powerful way, the girls used a quote they found in a magazine while researching and writing their script: "be yourself, because everyone else is already taken." We had a productive conversation about how this quotation is a widespread meme that is routinely and perhaps mistakenly attributed to Oscar Wilde.

I believe that my team's ability to understand, question, and integrate popular media texts alongside their understanding of girlhood demonstrates a sense of agency that William Sewell defines as an "actor's capacity to reinterpret and mobilize an array of resources" (1992: 19). By producing their own PSA and analyzing the media works of other girls, the coresearchers demonstrated agency in negotiating and expanding the mainstream media texts that circulate in and around their lives. Deeply engaged in a community of practice in which they can see the positive impact of their insights and technical skill, they exerted their autonomy and influence when they challenged the oppressive gender stereotypes that undermine female roles in local and global media culture and politics. I am wary, however, of overvaluing the transformative potential of their production work given that these girls are growing up within the constraints of a limiting cultural framework in which their unique ideas, opinions, and concerns are not always respected and valued. Girls do not develop outside of cultural frames in which their voices have long been ignored, silenced, or unheard, both collectively and individually (Mitchell 2015; Wajcman 1998).

Data Analysis: Part Two

After screening *The Media?* the coresearchers and I had a mind scripting session that involved productive rethinking about their PSA. In addition to giving each other feedback and positive affirmation, the coresearchers were very interested in engaging in another layer of analysis about the pitfalls of media stereotyping. The following dialogue is a partial transcript from our mind scripting meeting. This analysis is framed as a girl-led conversation, rather than the usual researcher and participant one in which the power to ask questions usually belongs to the researcher to whom the interviewee responds. The 10 coresearchers and I were sitting around a large round table in a sunlit area of the library. We each had a research journal for collecting fieldnotes and oversized pencils that were three feet long. Halina was holding the voice recorder:

> 'A girl in my class said that she once saw a mannequin in a store that was size –1 or 000. The clothes were cinched tightly at her back to fit her,' Halina reported with concern. She reached into her research journal and held up a print version of a graphic that she created during a camp storyboarding session. We could all see a modified photo of Halina eating a piece of paper that said, 'You don't have to be size 0 or –1 to look good.'
>
> Chani took the voice recorder from Halina and responded,

'Girls try to impress people. If they look more like girls in magazines, then they will be more accepted.'

'When they pick the girls to wear the clothes on the commercials, they only pick the beautiful girls. Even though you are not similar to her,' commented Salina.

'Lots of time they will use people who have been photoshopped and stuff and they will alter them and then you think, if I use this, then I will look like them,' Jordan criticized.

Jayden exclaimed, 'No, you don't have to look like those people. Like, just stop and think. Just looking at a magazine can change your perspective of who you are. Media tests your self-confidence. Ads target children because they are the most emotionally vulnerable. Don't fall for it!'

Nodding her head in agreement, Raywin continued, 'Yeah, I ordered the magazine *Kids* by *National Geographic* and they had before and after. Before they took a random girl with nice hair but not nice skin. After they used Photoshop to take away all her measles and acne, so she looked perfect and fake like a Barbie doll. I think it's really upsetting that they photoshop everyone. There can't be one model that is normal looking to advertising something.'

'The thing I find upsetting is when you go to Safeway or whatever grocery store you go to, there are ten thousand magazines right before the checkout with pretty girls and women who have their zippers all the way down or low cut shirts or clothing that is really inappropriate and then you go: What's that? And so I hide myself in a cooking magazine cuz I don't want to look at them, and I'm not kidding. But they are everywhere and it's really hard to avoid cuz they are all always catching your eyes. And you are always taking a second look. Why do they put them there in the first place? To make you want to open the magazine and then to make you want to buy it and the stuff advertised inside. Well that's my pet peeve. It's like insane,' Meledy reflected with annoyance.

'I find this so offensive! These girls are losing their dignity. Most women don't dress like this. I wish this would stop,' protested Chani.

Kim motioned that she wanted a turn to speak. 'Girls and boys in clothing stores are always in a kissing pose and all lovey-dovey with each other. It's like they are advertising love or something, not clothes. Another thing is that TV people are all photoshopped but when you go to the store and actually look at the products, they are not as good.'

Jordan advised, 'Yes, but we have the responsibility to change this! We won't ever be able to truly change how the media controls us, but we can change how the media portrays us.'

'Yeah, like we can believe in ourselves and ignore the media,' replied Salina.

Aslin added, 'We can pride ourselves on not being photoshopped!'

'It's not just the media. People expect us to be beautiful. Men expect us to be beautiful,' Raywin countered.

Jordan questioned, 'Who says girls aren't beautiful? And why can't we be smart?'

Kim nodded her head and agreed, 'A girl doesn't want to be the only one who doesn't care about what she looks like.'

Chani criticized, 'Girls are worried about fitting in and being popular. Am I fitting in or being down casted by the popular people? It's not enough to just be yourself these days.'

'It's hard to be yourself when so many other girls who are completely not themselves. Like they are also having difficulties trying to figure out who they are,' Meledy complained into the voice recorder.

'We should all just live in computers,' joked Jill.

A round of laughter is shared, serving to lighten up the heaviness of our conversation.

As the coresearchers responded to each other's analyses and interpretations, they seemed to shift confidently from one viewpoint to another, positioning themselves in diverse and complicated ways. Their reflections and questions evidence awareness of how contemporary media texts shape their developing sense of self yet their conversations are marked by the desire to overcome insecurities, channel rage toward positive ends, and just feel good about themselves. My team articulated how and why agency emerged as a salient theme quite early on during our interactions and investigations at 101 Technology Fun. They examined media texts about make-up, beauty, body diversity, and Photoshop. Their analysis is made up of artifacts, signs, and messages as much as the models in the magazines the girls used are made up of the same. Meledy's story is touching as she recalls grocery shopping with her mother where she sees all those magazines that are prescriptive texts telling her how to be and picks up a cooking magazine that acts as a mask or screen to hide behind. By sharing her viewpoints, Meledy finds strength. She uses her voice. By co-producing a PSA to deconstruct the portrayal of females in the media, she has some agency to break down gender barriers, debunk stereotypes about girlhood, and inspire other girls to see that they can create change too.

As I analyze my team's analysis of their experiences as media producers, what strikes me most profoundly is the juxtaposition of the girls' intelligence with their internalized anxiety concerning the effects of the media in and around them. For example, Halina expressed concern about the unrealistic standards of beauty that are normalized when "all the girls in the ads are edited to look picture perfect." Although she feels controlled and manipulated by popular media culture, Halina has also learned how "fun and effective making a PSA can be to tell other girls what we think about the media." Aslin was empowered by her new role as a media producer: she said, "I'm really interested to make videos about how girls are being affected by what they put on ads and the Internet." Jayden was knowledgeable about the ways media undermines girls' self-confidence. "Just looking at a magazine can change your perspective of who you are."

Jill's criticism of the media is not what I typically hear tween-aged girls talking about: "You have to be anorexic and skinny and dress like a slutty child. Make sure your eyes are as big as fuck too." Her internal tensions and external concerns do not fit into the dominant and stereotypical discourses of femininity that tend to be confining and that induce passivity in girls. As I contemplate what Jill's biting words reveal, I wonder about other fears that she may be concealing. What else does she (along with the other girls in this study) truly think and feel about growing up in today's media culture, but dare not say? (see MacDowell 2015).

Conclusion: From Appropriating to Remaking Girl in Media Stereotypes

This chapter examines, elaborates on, deconstructs (and, in some cases, reconstructs) representations of girlhood in mainstream media, print, screen-based, and digital texts through the experiences of 10 young girls producing a PSA. Alongside my team, in the context and locale of 101 Technology Fun, I explore how girls can engage in knowledge production as media creators (not merely passive consumers) by analyzing media texts that are part of their lives and writing scripts for texts that tell their own stories. The coresearchers, engaged in their own learning processes, were supported and challenged to evaluate their roles as both viewers and producers in constructing meaning about girlhood in interaction with media texts that, as I have already discussed, and as Jean Stuart and Claudia Mitchell (2013) have made clear, have perspectives, explanations, and inferences already built into them. The coresearchers' voices resonate throughout this chapter as powerful ones that resist and reconfigure (rather than simply receive and reproduce) the already-interpreted and oppressive cultural scripts written about girls that serve, as Banet-Weiser (2011) reminds us, to justify, produce, and perpetuate gender marginalization, bias, and inequity.

"Youth voice is far too often absent from important discussions and decision-making processes about issues that impact them" (CYCC Network 2013: 20), so capturing girls' perspectives and learning from them cannot happen often enough or too soon in girls' studies and media education research. Unequivocally, today's girls are considerably disadvantaged and disempowered if they do not understand how digital media and popular culture are new types of texts that construct meanings about girlhood which need to be evaluated for presuppositions, biases, and limitations. When I analyzed my team's multilayered analysis about their experiences creating and interpreting their own media scripts, I was bothered by what remained unspoken. Why, for instance, didn't the coresearchers talk about being too creative, intelligent, skilled, or talented? Instead, my team members expressed their insecurities and self-doubts concerning the intense cultural pressures put on girls to conform to destructive expectations of heteronormative, cis-gendered female perfection.

I have demonstrated here that presenting girls with meaningful experiences to engage with the tools and creative practices for making media (on their own terms and in their own ways) supports the development of a new generation of female youth who have the capability to question, remake, and deconstruct gender stereotypes in contemporary media culture rather than simply receiving and reproducing male-dominated traditions and hierarchies. It is difficult, however, for girls to feel agentive and powerful unless we listen to them and value their work (MacDowell 2015; Mitchell 2011). Girls also need to know that their questions, answers, stories, and perspectives are valued for these are primary sources from which their identities are formed (Bach 1998; Callero 2003). As look back at the coresearchers' highly personal interviews and challenging questions, it is clear to me that we (parents, teachers, and researchers) need to provide more opportunities for girls to ask their questions, and we need to demonstrate that we are genuinely interested in listening to them and talking in an open, respectful, and contemplative manner so that positive, feminist, and pro-social energy may flow freely. Asking questions and encouraging media inquiry will help girls and young women develop the kind of lifelong learning capabilities and self-initiative that are necessary for them to reject, remake, and rethink the (mis)representation of girls and girlhood in hegemonic media texts.

Acknowledgments

I gratefully acknowledge Ann Smith, Claudia Mitchell, and the two peer reviewers for their constructive feedback on drafts of this article. Special thanks to my coresearchers: may you continue to ask difficult questions, challenge media stereotypes, and expand horizons for girls everywhere.

PAULA MACDOWELL is a Lecturer in the Faculty of Education at Simon Fraser University, British Columbia, Canada, working on research and advocacy initiatives to empower girls through education and technology. Motivated by a social justice orientation to education and firmly committed to ethical practice, diversity, and equity, Paula studies the design of constructionist learning environments and works closely with teachers to integrate technology in the classroom for meaningful learning. She uses design-based research methods to create and analyze tools that support youth innovation in addressing humanity's challenges and opportunities to achieve sustainable change with and for communities.

Notes

1. In cannabis culture, April 20 is known as the day on which people worldwide smoke marijuana at the same time. Hence, it was a significant for the PDFA to release their anti-drug PSA on this day in 2017.
2. The coresearchers' PSA is also part of my doctoral research study (see MacDowell 2015).
3. The coresearchers' names have been changed to ensure confidentiality.
4. The magazines were donated by the coresearchers and UBC Teacher Candidates.

References

Allhutter, Doris. 2012. "Mind Scripting: A Method for Deconstructive Design." *Science, Technology & Human Values* 37: 684–707.
Bach, Hedy. 1998. *A Visual Narrative Concerning Curriculum, Girls, Photography, etc.* Edmonton, AB: Qual Institute Press.
Banet-Weiser, Sarah. 2011. "Branding the Post-Feminist Self: Girls' Video Production and YouTube." In *Mediated Girlhoods: New Explorations of Girls' Media Culture*, ed. Mary Celeste Kearney, 277–294. New York: Peter Lang.
Callero, Peter. 2003. "The Sociology of the Self." *Annual Review of Sociology* 29: 115–133.
CYCC Network. 2013. *Youth Engagement: Empowering Youth Voices to Improve Services, Programs, and Policy*. http://cyccnetwork.org/en/engagement (accessed 22 December 2016).
Farmer, Leslie. 2008. *Teen Girls and Technology: What's the Problem? What's the Solution?* New York: Teachers College Press.
Goldman-Segall, Ricki. 1998. *Points of Viewing Children's Thinking: A Digital Ethnographer's Journey*. Mahwah, NJ: Lawrence Erlbaum.
Hains, Rebecca. 2012. *Growing Up with Girl Power: Girlhood on Screen and in Everyday Life*. New York: Peter Lang.

Hobbs, Renee. 2010. *Digital and Media Literacy: A Plan of Action*. Washington, DC: Aspen Institute.

Kearney, Mary Celeste. 2006. *Girls Make Media*. New York: Routledge.

Keller, Jessalynn, Morgan Blue, Mary Celeste Kearney, Kirsten Pike, and Sarah Projansky. 2015. "Mapping New Methodological Approaches to Girls' Media Studies: Reflections from the Field." *Journal of Children and Media* 9 (4): 528–535.

Long, Paul, and Tim Wall. 2012. *Media Studies: Texts, Production, Context*. New York: Routledge.

MacDowell, Paula. 2015. "Empowering Girls as Change Makers in Maker Culture: Stories from a Summer Camp for Girls in Design, Media, and Technology." PhD diss., The University of British Columbia.

Mitchell, Claudia. 2011. *Doing Visual Research*. New York: Sage Publications.

Mitchell, Claudia. 2015. "Girls' Texts, Visual Culture and Shifting the Boundaries of Knowledge in Social Justice Research." In *Girls, Cultures, Texts*, ed. Clare Bradford and Mavis Reimer, 139–160. Waterloo, ON: Wilfred Laurier University Press.

Seidel, John. 1998. "Appendix E: Qualitative Data Analysis." *The Ethnograph* 4: 1–15.

Sewell, William. 1992. "A Theory of Structure: Duality, Agency, and Transformation." *The American Journal of Sociology* 98 (1): 1–29.

Stuart, Jean, and Claudia Mitchell. 2013. "Media and Social Change: Working Within a 'Youth as Knowledge Producers' Framework." In *Routledge Handbook on Children, Adolescents, and Media Studies*, ed. Dafna Lemish, 359–365. New York: Routledge.

Wajcman, Judy. 1998. *Feminism Confronts Technology*. University Park, PA: Pennsylvania State University Press.

CHAPTER 14

Using Fiction, Autoethnography, and Girls' Lived Experience in Preparation for Playwriting

Genna Gardini

> When you had a crack, you saw things more clearly. (Kohler 1999: 26)

At the beginning of 2013, I began to reread Sheila Kohler's novel *Cracks* (1999), an exploration of South African girlhood[1] conducted within the confined context of a girls' boarding school in the 1960s. I had first encountered *Cracks* as a schoolgirl at St Mary's Diocesan School for Girls, understood to be an all-girls[2] boarding school in KwaZulu-Natal, in 2004. A decade into South Africa's democracy, this institution should not have been so similar to the anglicized, racist, and patriarchal school in Kohler's book, created very much within the British colonial model, with a student body that was still predominantly white and with rules that enforced stifling notions of gender normativity. When I revisited the novel as an adult, I had just started my MA in Theatre-Making at the University of Cape Town (UCT) and intended to use the duration of the two-year course to write a play about local queer histories. However, *Cracks* made me consider the importance of revisiting and problematizing the context from which I came—one of privilege and unacknowledged societal toxicity. Rereading

---
Notes for this section can be found on page 237.

and thinking about the novel made me reassess my education and doing so cracked things open for me theoretically, creatively, and politically. I also felt that it was important to recognize that South African queer histories are mostly the stories of LGBTQIAP+[3] people of color and I understood that my telling these stories as a white ciswoman[4] writer would be to appropriate them. I felt that my political and creative responsibility was to discuss and dissect the world I came from by looking at how prescriptive ideas of girlhood had been enforced in that context.

After considering feminist theatre scholar Sue-Ellen Case's assertion that feminist and queer "scholarship or writing, and activism are caught up in a complex, interactive paradigm of production" (2009: 102), I decided to attempt to write a play assessing what girlhood might mean for some people in South African schools similar to the one depicted in *Cracks*. I chose to use the novel, and what I regard as the theory underpinning it, as a way into doing this, particularly in the research stage of writing the play, *Handsome Devil*. I tried to construct an autoethnographic approach to the research by using writing to prompt responses about my own experience and understanding of girlhood. I then decided to broaden the scope of the project and invite a group of young women to use the same process to explore their own responses to the idea of girlhood.

The members of this group (hereafter referred to as the cast), and I functioned as co-researchers, although the hierarchal nature of our relationship had been established by virtue of my positioning as the playwright and theirs as the cast. The process of generating our research findings involved discussions, creative writing, correspondence, and performance about our understandings and experiences of girlhood. We then set about collating our findings in journals and a performative exhibition for my first MA project which I used to influence the mood as opposed to the content of *Handsome Devil*. In other words, I used the research process and the exhibition to produce an emotional response in myself that I tried to channel into the writing of the play.

As the research process developed, I began to understand how exploring girlhood could also provide a way for us to dismantle and investigate various social norms surrounding gender identity in South Africa, albeit from the perspectives of a group of ciswomen. As art historians Catherine Grant and Lori Waxman argue in *Girls! Girls! Girls! In Contemporary Art*, "A focus on girls can expand the discourse on gender. Rather than simply replaying stereotypes of femininity, the figure of the girl has been used by many contemporary artists to question the stability of sexual and gendered identity"

(2011:1). I found that questioning the validity of the figure of the girl from the perspectives of five young women, myself included, served to both undo and reinforce it as a fixed point from which to make creative work. Grant and Waxman reference Freud's psychoanalytic view of the girl as a way of expanding the discussion of girlhood as an open structure instead of a transitional biological state. Freud felt that girlhood was a training phase in which importance was placed on what it moved from and towards rather than on itself: for Freud, in a sense, "the little girl does not exist, with femininity being learned in the passage towards womanhood. The figure of the girl, then, stands in for an identity that is defined as being "in progress, not quite one thing or another" (2).

Cracking

Before conceptualizing the play and beginning the research process to develop it, I attempted to grapple first with my interpretation of the theories regarding girlhood written into the narrative of *Cracks*. In the novel, Kohler writes that people who identify or are identified as girls can "see things more clearly" (1999: 26) by using their feelings about a potential future, manifested in the figure of an older woman, as a means of navigating their way out of girlhood. Kohler later implies that this process can be reversed by describing women who revisit memories of their girlhood by returning to both the geographical and psychological sites associated with them. This ties into the writing of Grant and Waxman (2011) who argue that some contemporary women artists use their work to reclaim their personal experiences of girlhood and also to secure it as an allegorical state that can be revisited and repurposed. For these scholars, the psychological meaning packed into the way girlhood is both a spoken and a written text allows it to transcend the limitations of the presumed biological, becoming instead an open structure that can be returned to through art. This creative journey back to girlhood is not framed as an inability to move forward but, rather, as a trip to pay homage to the significance of that stage. Grant and Waxman argue that by using the figure of the girl in their work, contemporary women creatives are reclaiming a sense of nostalgia about girlhood as a significant moment of brevity and flux while simultaneously setting it up as a state that can be revisited in order to better understand their experiences of it. This is a response to cultural critic Anita Harris's 2004 assertion that "girlhood is not a fixed period of time but is subject to historical and social specificities" (quoted in Grant and Waxman 2011: 3). These scholars go on to say that looking at adolescence "as a structure points to its possibility as not only a particular biological moment but as a space that can be returned to at any point in life" (4) specifically through creative investigations and depictions of girlhood.

Kohler establishes that the main characters in *Cracks*, a group of schoolgirls, use their swimming teacher Miss G to see past what is positioned as the membrane of their ordinary and tightly structured life at their school, into more fluid and sublime versions of it: "Miss G was our crack" (1999: 26). The ability to escape from and return to their reality, with its repressive rules and regulations, lies with the group of girls but is facilitated through their relationship with the crack that functions as both porthole and conduit. Kohler associates this relationship with being submerged in water. If, in the book, the girls' crack is their swimming teacher, then their ability to "see things more clearly" (26) because of and through her involves being submerged in an emotional atmosphere, likened here to water, which is outside of everyday logic and verbal communication. As discussed earlier, cracking is initially intimated to be the process through which events and people are closely scanned and reinterpreted. By placing Miss G in front of the structures of their lives, the girls see what they understand to be a truth behind these structures, and, importantly, routes out of them. Much of this work is done in the teacher's unofficial classroom—the school's swimming pool. Miss G's job, in both her official capacity as a swimming teacher and her informal occupation as a crack, is to introduce the swimming team to an environment markedly different from that of the rest of the school and, supposedly, to instruct them in how to negotiate it. Water can be understood to be immersive, atmospheric, and, arguably, outside of spoken and written language. The rules for the girls' survival within this aquatic environment are different from those that determine whether or not they can pass their mathematics or poetry examinations, a distinction that is reinforced by Miss G. "She told us, 'What is important in learning to swim well . . . is *desire*'" (33, emphasis in original).

In the first half of the novel, the narrators refer only to Miss G as their crack in their younger incarnations. When the older versions of most of the swimming team revisit the school, the geographical site of their girlhood, they do not use this term again. Instead, in the tellingly titled chapter, "We Remember," these women appear to return instinctively to the process of cracking by revisiting their girlhood memories. It could be argued that an irreparable rift was created during their time at the school which later facilitates a kind of re-cracking process. As adults, they do not need an outside figure to function as a crack but seem to use themselves instead as the tools through which to view their past, a reviewing that allows them greater clarity. By simultaneously functioning as both crack and cracker, it is implied that they take on both the role of girl and woman. The women in *Cracks* employ the process of re-cracking to clarify what occurred during their girlhood. It is through this reviewing that they can finally recall that which caused the rift in their relationships with each other as well as with their teacher—their physical abuse, rape, and murder of one of their peers. This re-cracking process facilitates, for the first time in over thirty years, a moment in which the people involved in the horrific incident are able to admit to and, in some way, address it. "Lit up, our small world widens" (1999: 163).

Journaling

Drawing on my interpretation of *Cracks* and the theories of cracking and re-cracking, I established a process of autoethnographic research for myself and the participants that I hoped would influence the tone and mood, as opposed to the content, of *Handsome Devil*. This distinction was important because I did not want to base the play on any of the personal stories shared through writing or discussion during this research process but, rather, wanted to allow the feelings that they provoked in me to inform my writing. I invited four Drama students at UCT, all of whom were between the ages of 19 and 22 and who understood themselves to have once identified and been identified as girls,[7] to work on the project. Despite originating from and occupying different socio-political contexts, almost all of us had, at one time, attended a so-called all-girls school. I wanted to try to invoke personal responses to the ideas of girlhood from the cast and myself through a specifically designed research process. We set up strict parameters for this work with the understanding that the cast would share only the responses they felt comfortably willing to offer, each individual monitoring how specific or general her reactions were. As Daisy Pillay et al. point out, "In autoethnography the central research participant is the researcher herself" (2016: 8). Within this process, the cast and I would, on our own terms, revisit our individual experiences of girlhood. Before my official playwriting began, our findings had to be reflected on, archived, and presented in some way in order to position them as research and us as co-researchers. This was important, I felt, in order to make sure that the cast's work in generating research that influenced my writing was acknowledged. I decided to return to methods of exploring and then documenting personal responses that I had used during my own girlhood—discussion with peers first, and then journaling.

When the cast and I began to rehearse, most of our time together was dedicated to discussing understandings of girlhood from our own perspectives and what we considered to be our respective societal ones. This meant that we discussed what we thought about girlhood now as adults and how we felt we had been taught about girlhood in school, at home, and through the media to which we were exposed as children. By dealing initially with various topics verbally, as opposed to doing so in writing, to which we later progressed as a form of archiving, I felt that we allowed our thoughts about our own sense of girlhood to form an emotional environment out of which I was able to write the play.

I set up a series of autoethnographic tasks and exercises for the cast and myself that were geared towards slicing open my usual solitary writing process and inserting a new step between finding reference material and writing a draft, a step that hinged on the participation of the cast. I had asked each person attending the first meeting to bring a piece of music, a text, and an image that resonated with her personally as a way of introducing ourselves to each other. At the end of that session, I began a routine of giving the cast a material pack, which at that time included a collection of images, writings, songs, and videos that had influenced my initial conceptualization of *Handsome Devil*. I also presented each member with a journal in which she could record any reactions to the material and meetings that she felt able and willing to share. After they submitted their journals to me, I began to write content that was influenced by my own emotional reactions to the cast's responses to these prompts. This eventually led to my sketching out characters that were not necessarily based on the cast members themselves but, rather, on the feelings and notions that we had discovered while discussing and experimenting with our separate understandings of girlhood. The importance of the journals as a way of documenting these personal and collaborative findings resonates with Alexandra Sutherland's argument that journaling functions as a tool of both "self-reflexivity and self-confrontation" (2007: 111) in the studying of Drama. She discusses the use of journals in relation to Carol Witherell and Nel Noddings's (1991) argument in Stories Lives Tell: Narrative and Dialogue in Education "that narrative can be an epistemological tool that can open ways of knowing ourselves and other knowers" (2007: 111). In this research phase, we were attempting to do just that—know and share our own ideas of girlhood in order to create space for characters and a theatrical narrative to emerge. This is related to a technique that Kathleen Pithouse-Morgan and colleagues refer specifically to as "poetic inquiry" (2014: 149), a collective means of generating creative responses to specific subjects. We used different kinds of creative writing, including poetry, in our journals as a way of documenting and expanding on topics brought up in our discussions as individuals and as a collective. In line with the point made by these authors, this proved an effective way to "enhance and nuance our meaning making as a research team" (4).

Handsome Devil is a narrative that straddles the space between autobiography and fiction, an intersection from which the cast and I were operating in our attempt to move beyond our personal experiences of girlhood. Journaling the progression of this journey allowed us to fictionalize the process of revisiting the feeling of that time. We were performing the process of diarizing with the understanding that our discussions and the journals were a space in which to explore and share ideas that would assist in my creating new nuanced characters for the play. In turn, there was an agreement that these characters were not based on any of us but were, rather, a complicated and varied amalgamation of our responses to my research prompts first in the rehearsal space and then in the journals. Sutherland writes that "the journal writing process opens possibilities for negotiating uncertainty, difference, self and other, as well as providing an important space to understand and learn from the immediacy and ephemerality of the performance act in a world characterized by instability" (2007: 111). For her, as for us, the use of journals allows the student to document as opposed to capture experiences in the transient space of play, a space that can be revisited through memory and responses to those memories.

Mining for Narrative

Through researching with the cast and then writing *Handsome Devil*, a text that acknowledges and then seeks to destroy parameters around our understanding of girlhood, I tried to create Kohler's symbolic cracking and re-cracking processes to clear a route between adulthood back to girlhood. In this extract from *Handsome Devil*, schoolgirl Rebecca is reflecting on her past relationship with the teacher who was meant to educate her, and her own new understanding of what exists beneath those rules.

> MISS: *(to Rebecca)* You have clearly learnt nothing from me.
>
> REBECCA: Maybe not, Miss. But I learnt something about you.
>
> MISS: Unless it is about interrogative adverbs, I have no interest in hearing it.
>
> REBECCA: Not everything is about interrogation, Miss. Some things you find out from what people don't write on the board.

The research process leading to the play was, in many ways, a response to Hélène Cixous's (1981) call for women to write themselves into existence. It used the collaborative nature of our discussions and journaling to create these characters who were not based on but were, in many ways, based *in* us, to be written into existence. By consulting the journals as records of the feeling of our time together, I was able to establish both the characters and the greater arc of the play. As for Sutherland, "my reading of the journals became a reading of a narrative, in which theme, plot, characters, metaphor, action, setting and outcome formed a structure" (2007: 111–112).

In order to develop these characters and their respective narratives, I wanted to explore whether the members of the research group, myself included, accessed this cracking or re-cracking process through reinvestigating our experiences and understandings of girlhood. I attempted to work safely with the group members, always at their own pace and, as mentioned above, with the understanding that they did not have to share anything they did not feel comfortable disclosing, to explore our disparate reactions to, thoughts about, and, importantly, embodied knowledge of girlhood, by which I mean information and codes relating to girlhood that we felt were taught to us through implication and suggestion. I was interested in what theatrical possibilities this embodied knowledge might offer because of Case's assertion that it "is positioned differently, though centrally, in the institutional practices of both feminism and theatre" (2009: 101). This kind of reflection, using the self as material, functioned as self-study, a way of analyzing our own actions and reactions.

The Girls

In creating the characters of *Handsome Devil*, I considered how *Cracks* and other texts had influenced my understanding of what kind of girl could be both referenced and rejected in the play. Most of the girl-centered literature that I had been introduced to as a child seemed to overtly, covertly, or inadvertently erase experiences outside of white and middle-class social structures. In reaction to this, I had purposefully chosen to work with young women of varying racial, class, cultural, and sexual identities as a way of combating the assumed heteronormativity and whiteness of canonical writing about girlhood that I had encountered as a younger person. This was, in particular, a direct response to the world of *Cracks* in which all the main characters are white, with little acknowledgement and inclusion of the people of color who existed within that space, and where the only character to show interest in someone of the same gender is a pedophile. My desire to engage with a diverse cast stemmed from my hope that I could work towards routes of acknowledging experiences of girlhood that were different from my own. I also wanted to problematize how whiteness in girlhood is so often set up as normative. Alude Mahali writes that "the assumption has been made that a white girl's experience of girlhood is the same as that of a black girl and as a result this has led to the under-representation or misrepresentation of black girlhood" (2009: 9). It became clear to me that choosing to situate my research in an understanding of girlhood that foregrounded only the experiences of white people was tantamount to complicity in participating in this erasure, one that is very much a part of the world of *Cracks*. While I understand that I cannot ever accurately represent a girlhood outside of my own positioning, I am also aware that it is important to acknowledge (as opposed to claim) experiences that might be more familiar to the majority of girls in South Africa. By working with young women of color, I hoped to speak respectfully to this dearth of representation.

The characters in *Handsome Devil* were created with a vague understanding that they bore some similarities to a few of the girls in *Cracks*. Kohler's introduction of her characters is theatrical: a cast list separates the "Thirteen Girls on the Swimming Team" (1999: i) from a roll call of the staff. These stereotypical characters shift somewhat in their particular contexts, though. For example, in the novel, Ann is framed as the most academic in her group. "[She] came first for maths, Latin, English, French, history" (1999: 20). In *Handsome Devil*, Sarah does well in her studies but struggles to understand the jokes and references made by her friends. She says, "I've won the Intraschool Memory Competition for three years in a row. I did, don't laugh!" Pamela, "who later took a First at sex" (Kohler 1999: 20) is not unlike Hannah in the play, who is understood to be the most sexually active of the girls. In *Handsome Devil*, Rebecca, rebellious and feared, is the leader of the group, much like Di Radfield in the novel. In *Cracks*, Fiamma is assaulted and dies at the climax of the novel. *Handsome Devil*'s Eve, in turn, disappears, her absence forming the great and unresolved mystery of the play. I decided that the cause of her absence should remain unresolved in the play for two reasons. First, as a playwright, I was interested in exploring an uncertainty about experiences in a failed attempt at cracking through an experience to discover its meaning. This led me to write a new character, Lilly, to be played by the same actor who portrays Eve at the start of the play. Lilly appears suddenly and without notice, proving to be a crack herself. Through her ability to recall a scholastic experience elsewhere, she allows the other girls to understand more about the underlying horrors of their world than they were able to see before. My second reason for refusing to impose a tidy solution to Eve's disappearance was personal—the loss of coresearcher and performer Rosa Carlyle-Mitchell, for whom the character of Eve was created. A month after the performative exhibition of our research findings, Rosa died. Rereading a letter she had written to me, I came across her reaction to a monologue that I wrote for Eve, a response that I think speaks to both the potential and to the limitations of remembering and investigating girlhood. She wrote, "I praise the perceptive nature of youth. And there is more irony here. What child tires of the world? It is so self-aware. It is like an aspect of myself that I have always known." In many ways, this excerpt from her letter surprisingly and devastatingly encapsulated what was being explored through our research process: a girl, who is meant to view the world innocently, manages, instead, to understand an underlying, unspoken truth about her context.

The Teacher

I found that the research process set up a particular hierarchical, almost scholastic relationship between the *Handsome Devil* cast members and myself. This dynamic referenced, at least in structure as opposed to intention, the connection between students and teacher in *Cracks*. Although the journaling conducted in these research sessions was not framed as academic, an educational association between myself and the cast, all of whom I had taught during my postgraduate studies, had already been established. Now, I had to trouble (if not seek to dismantle altogether) the intricacies of that relationship while still maintaining the basic configuration. I needed to function as the facilitator of the process even though I was also participating as a co-researcher and we were generating an atmosphere together. Despite this, it would have been impossible to establish a completely equal relationship between myself and the cast since, ultimately, this was my project and the application of the research findings were dependent on how our time together had made me feel. Nevertheless, the stakes in this top-down relationship had shifted. As a teacher, I could not function like Miss G in *Cracks* nor like Miss in *Handsome Devil*—educators whose focus is very much on systemic rules that mask a troubled subtext about girlhood. Instead, I had to establish a methodology that did the opposite in trying to extract and mine our subtext—a personalized understanding of girlhood—in order to explore and discover the structures that had enforced it in both our formal and informal education.

During this process, I provided broad thematic prompts and then encouraged individual creative responses to those prompts. In establishing this set-up, I tried to prioritize personal and unedited response to these themes in which control was maintained by the participant. Once I was allowed access to that information, with the co-researcher's permission, my job as the playwright was to determine how to construct a separate narrative influenced by those responses. An important aspect of doing this was to avoid initially dismissing any of the cast's reactions, no matter how irrelevant I felt they might be to the greater story of the play. In ignoring their reactions I felt that I would risk alienating the cast from freely participating in the generation of the material. After I wrote texts for the cast to perform in rehearsal, the group completed more exercises in their journals related to their monologues, allowing them to explore the possibilities in the writing but also to air any uncertainties they were experiencing. Katya Mendelson, for example, felt that the first piece of writing with which I provided her did not encapsulate her character as much as did a poem of mine, completed when I was about the same age that she was during the workshops, that she had read some weeks before. After hearing her very well thought-out rationale, I had to agree that she was right and began to accept that the next phase of the writing might have to include the cast as an editorial board of sorts. Suriamurthee Maistry discusses the importance of a supervisor or teacher investigating and questioning his or her own response as an educator in order to encourage self-reflection from students. Reflecting on his former pedagogical approach, he writes that "much of this positioning was done in an attempt to assert myself and gain the student's confidence in my ability, thereby exhibiting my own need for recognition and acknowledgement." Although we operate in different realms as educators, I identify with Maistry's attempt to amend and reflect on his responses to the work of his

233

students, actively participating in an exercise of both relating to and guiding them. Like him, "in my current practice, I do far more careful and attentive listening and constant self-reminding of how the construction of my feedback might be received and interpreted by my students" (2015: 96).

The School

After six weeks of working together, the cast and I were faced with the task of having to decide how to showcase all the collected and generated material that we felt comfortable sharing for my first MA course task, *Handsome Devil: Minor*. I had framed this mini-project as a performative installation in which we did not display the entire set of journals themselves but, rather, curated a display of our findings from them. Through the performers, each character claimed a specific area of Room 313, a rehearsal space in the UCT Drama Department's Rosedale building, as her own and began to decorate it with selected information from her journals associated with, and generated in response to, her character. Some members of the group secreted objects and pictures in hidden cubbies or laid them out for all to view, some wrote their monologues across walls in tiny pencil shorthand for the audience to attempt to decipher, and others memorized their lines. I chose this particular room because I think it looks like a stereotypical classroom. The project exhibited all the material produced, reacted to, rethought, reworked, and collected in the journals during the six weeks over which we had conducted our research. The group, including me, formed part of the installation, as much its material as the various media in the room, and read a selection of the writing that I had produced or recycled as a result of the process.

After the performative exhibition, the cast and I decided to undertake one more collaborative research exercise. We were all about to leave for various parts of the country for the better part of two months and wanted to ensure that our conversations about girlhood and these characters would continue. So, I began to write them letters. Each week, I would send them a page outlining what had happened to me over the preceding days but also asking them two questions, one of which they could answer as themselves and the other as their character in the time period before the action of the play takes place. In these letters, we continued our conversation about our own experiences, with the cast answering the questions above and beyond the cursory platitudes that I had expected, speaking openly and honestly about what it was to be a young woman. In our correspondence, they also told me about their ideas regarding the characters as girls and what their girlhoods might have been like along with the finer details of who they imagine those people were before the time period the play would cover. These letters provided intriguing writing challenges for me at times. When I asked what the last thing each character had done that she was ashamed of, I received this enigmatic answer from Qondiswa James's character, Rebecca: "I do a lot of things."

The Change

> We do not walk back the way we came.
> We take another path and go slowly across
> the flat veld beneath the darkling sky. (Kohler 1999: 165)

A few months after the initial phase of research and the performative exhibition of our findings were completed, I was accepted into the Royal Court Theatre's New Writing program. This program paired young South African writers with British playwrights who assisted in developing the former's original play over a year and a half. I was assigned London-based writer Winsome Pinnock as my mentor. The play she encouraged me to work on with her was *Handsome Devil* despite my pitching two other ideas given that I was feeling uncertain about this work after the loss of Rosa. This meant that over the following eighteen months I would no longer be the teacher: I had to adopt the role of student again. During this time I experienced a process similar to Kohler's cracking in that Pinnock was now positioned as the porthole and conduit allowing me to access deeper meanings below the words that I could neither reach nor facilitate a route to on my own. During this process of surrendering power, I revisited and also questioned both my own girlhood in the dynamic but also the discoveries and grief I now associated with the research project itself. That was a period when the cast and I had worked together towards a creative outcome before being interrupted by that traumatic loss that changed the way we saw the atmosphere and relationships created during that time. This perhaps connects to Maistry's thinking about re-approaching teaching (for him, specifically supervision) "with a view to disrupting and deconstructing hegemonic practices in which [he has] become complicit" (2015: 89). The roles of teacher and student had to be reversed for the systems of learning I was attempting to critique in *Handsome Devil* to be fully realized. By maintaining my own journal and consulting those of my co-researchers, I was allowed a space in which to reflect on this journey of understanding the implications of girlhood by both engaging with myself but also with the cast. As Sutherland points out, "The journal writing process opens possibilities for negotiating uncertainty, difference, self and other" (2007: 111).

Conclusion

The process of using Kohler's novel *Cracks* as a starting point in constructing ethnographic research methods to influence the writing of my play *Handsome Devil* involved the revisiting, problematizing, expanding on, and eventually fictionalizing various responses to girlhood. Working with a group of Drama students who had all identified and/or been identified as girls at some point instead of relying solely on my own responses was an attempt to achieve a varied, as opposed to strictly autobiographical, reflection on girlhood. By positioning all of us as co-researchers, I set up a dynamic of co-flexivity, defined as "collective reflexivity" (Pillay et al. 2016: 4) and generated by the co-composing of creative writing. Through this process, we could reflect on what we had generated together instead of reflecting only on the individual. I then had to investigate what it meant to work with the personal responses of the cast (which was always done with their consent) and how those reactions, along with the template provided by *Cracks*, could function as an influence rather than as storylines for *Handsome Devil*. Reflecting back on this process of self- and group-study as a means of informing the writing of this play, it is clear to me that autoethnographic approaches proved useful in the creation of plot and character because they encouraged "innovation for the sake of enhancing and nuancing interplay between inner and outer dialogues" (8). By engaging in this research project, we had participated in a process of cracking through to a deeper sense of girlhood, one that could eventually be theatricalized in the text of a play.

I recall that as I attempted to bring the research stage of this project to a close, moving towards the actual writing of *Handsome Devil*, I kept hearing Rosa's voice asking, "What's next, Gen?" before I gave out the next writing prompt for the group to respond to in their journals and letters. At the time, the only answer that I could possibly give her was to keep cracking at the surface of things and see what appeared beneath.

GENNA GARDINI is a writer, editor, and theatre-maker based in Cape Town. She holds an MA in Theatre-making from UCT and is currently a PhD candidate at Queen Mary University of London. She and Gary Hartley co-founded the queer theatre company Horses' Heads Productions in 2013. Her debut collection of poems, *Matric Rage*, was published by uHlanga Press in 2015. Gardini has won multiple awards for her work as a writer and theatre-maker, including Standard Bank Ovation Awards and the DALRO New Coin Poetry Prize. She works as a Drama lecturer at CityVarsity and is the Poetry Editor for *Prufrock*.

Notes

1. I acknowledge that this is a very specific experience of girlhood, operating from the perspectives of cisgender, white, and mostly middle-class young women.
2. I qualify it as such because many transmen and non-binary individuals who were assigned female at birth are enrolled in such schools as children.
3. This term refers to Lesbian, Gay, Bisexual, Transgender, Queer, Intersex, Asexual, Pansexual, and more.
4. The term ciswoman refers to a woman who identifies with the gender assigned to her at birth.
5. This play has not yet been published.
6. See, too, Taru Elfving's chapter in this volume, "Haunted: Writing with the Girl."
7. This group of co-researchers initially included Ameera Conrad, Qondiswa James, Katya Mendelson, and Rosa Carlyle-Mitchell. They all have me permission to use their real names in this chapter.

References

Case, Sue-Ellen. 2009. *Feminist and Queer Performance: Critical Strategies*. New York: Palgrave Macmillan.
Cixous, Hélène. 1981. "The Laugh of the Medusa." In *New French Feminisms*, ed. Isabelle de Courtivron and Elaine Marks, 245–265. Brighton: Harvester Press.
Elfving, Taru. 2011. "Haunted: Writing with the Girl." In *Girls! Girls! Girls! In Contemporary Art*, ed. Catherine Grant and Lori Waxman, 107–124. Chicago: The University of Chicago Press.
Grant, Catherine, and Lori Waxman. 2011. "Introduction: The Girl in Contemporary Art." In *Girls! Girls! Girls! In Contemporary Art*, ed. Catherine Grant and Lori Waxman, 1–16. Chicago: The University of Chicago Press.
Kohler, Sheila. 1999. *Cracks*. Cambridge, MA: Zoland Books.

Mahali, Alude. 2009. "Piecing Together a Girlhood: (Re)visiting Memories of Site Using Nostalgia as a Catalyst for Coping with Atopia." MA diss., University of Cape Town.

Maistry, Suriamurthee. 2015. "Towards a Humanising Pedagogy: An Autoethnographic Reflection of My Emerging Postgraduate Research Supervision Practice." *Journal of Education* 32 (2): 85–102.

Pillay, Daisy, Inbanathan Naicker, and Kathleen Pithouse-Morgan. 2016. *Academic Autoethnographies: Inside Teaching in Higher Education*. Rotterdam: Sense Publishers.

Pithouse-Morgan, Kathleen, Inbanathan Naicker, Chikoko Vitallis, Daisy Pillay, Porholo Morojele, and Toboho Hlau. 2014. "Entering an Ambiguous Space: Invoking Polyvocality in Educational Research through Collective Poetic Inquiry." *Perspectives in Education* 32 (4): 149–170.

Sutherland, Alexandra. 2007. "Writing and Performing Change: The Use of Writing Journals to Promote Reflexivity in a Drama Studies Curriculum." *South African Theatre Journal* 21 (1): 109–122.

INDEX

A

activism
    educational, 7, 37, 100
    feminist, 224
    of girls, 96
    queer, 224
adolescence, 3, 95, 175–6, 186, 226
    angst, 177
    eating disorder, 3
    femininity, 67
    girls, 32, 140
    information practices, 73
    preadolescent girls, 169
    readers, 73, 140
    representations in novels, 144, 151–5
    sexuality, 63, 81, 169
    young women, 33
affect, 115, 190, 192
    affective blog posts, 191
    affective-discursive, 192–3
    of femininity, 200
    of GIFs, 199
    of girlhood, 195–6, 200, 202
    of possessiveness, 194
    reading as affective practice, 197
    of youthful femininity, 190
agency, 7, 25, 31, 36, 58, 61, 63–64, 123, 130, 152
    artist, 10, 119, 122
    children, 151
    Indigenous, 5
    LGBTQ youth, 98
    neoliberal narratives, 40
    political, 41
    readers, 154
    sexual, 4, 6, 61, 66, 69, 158, 162, 167–9, 171
    young females, 214–6, 218
Aladdin, 104
Alice in Wonderland, 5, 127, 165
Allhutter, Doris, 211
Alter, Joseph S., 104
American Girls, 4, 61, 65
Arnett, Dugan, 64
art, 114, 131, 159, 165, 176, 225
    and agency, 123
    and subjectivity, 5, 112
    art grants, 123
    art historian, 224
    art project, 122
    cover art, 18
    restorative value, 119
    role of art, 122
    visual arts, 123
Ash, James, 199
Asher, Jay, 45, 50, 54, 56
Ashmore, Ruth, 81
A Stranger at Home, 127–8, 131, 134, 136–8
Auteri, Stephanie, 70

B

Bacchilega, Cristina, 184
Bach, Hedy, 208–9
Bachelard, Gaston, 176
Bakhtin, Mikhail, 14, 17
Bal, Mieke, 175
Banet-Weiser, Sarah, 192, 214, 219
Battiste, Marie, 139–40
Baumgardner, Jennifer, 63
Before I Die, 48
Before I Fall, 51, 56
Bent, Emily, 40
Bernheimer, Kate, 6, 8, 10, 174–6, 178–81, 183–6
bias, 61, 122–3
    cultural, 120
    gender, 120, 211, 219
bigotry, 118
Blyton, Enid, 14, 18, 24
Boston Evening Globe, 87
Boston marriage, 79, 81, 88
Brooks, Peter, 179, 181, 184
bullying, 9, 47, 54, 115–6, 119, 122
    bullycide, 56–57
    bystander, 113, 118, 120–1
    contexts, 113
    culture, 4, 118
    ethnic-based, 112–3, 117, 120
    gender-based, 46, 113
    girl-bullying, 5, 51, 111–2, 120
    relational, 60
    representations in novels, 5
    research, 112–3
    victim, 10, 51
    victimization, 50
Burka Avenger, 5, 94–100, 103, 105–7
Butler, Judith, 15, 17, 169

C

Caamaño, Beatriz, 151
Campbell, Joseph, 95
Campbell, Nicola, 129
Capdevila-Argüelles, Nuria, 153
cartoon, 9, 95
Case, Sue-Ellen, 224, 230
censorship, 58, 89, 144, 149–51, 155
Chasm: A Weekend, 177
Cheater, Christine, 130, 139
child-woman, 6, 8, 177, 179, 186
Cho, Alexander, 199
Cincinnati Enquirer, 86
Cixous, Hélène, 174, 230
comics, 94, 96, 101–2, 106
Cox, Suzy, 50
Cracks, 6, 223–7, 230–3, 236
Craig, Ian, 150
crush, 77–82, 88

D

Dangarembga, Tsitsi, 1, 3, 8–10
    Nervous Conditions, 1, 8
Davies, Bronwyn, 15, 46
Davis, Katharine Bement, 82–83, 85–86, 89
death, 2, 46–57, 88, 95, 145, 154, 163, 171, 176–7, 179–80
de Beauvoir, Simone, 167
de Certeau, Michel, 96, 104, 106
Decker, Hannah, 183
decolonization, 127, 129, 131, 133, 140
desire, 2, 16, 21, 57, 65, 161, 181, 186, 226
    agency of, 61
    and empowerment, 63–64
    awareness, 61, 63, 184
    desirable dead, 9
    desired object, 4–5, 60–61, 63–64, 67, 72
    desiring subject, 61, 63
    ethics, 8
    female desire, 89
    for independence, 151
    for knowledge, 112, 133, 178
    for revenge, 10, 119
    latent desire, 183
    male desire, 63, 66, 103
    romantic, 55, 83
    same-sex desire, 79, 89
    sexual, 6, 10, 49, 67, 78–82, 85, 158, 167–70, 177, 181
    young women's narratives, 64

INDEX

development, 30
    international development, 32–33
    international development policy, 30
    Western development discourses, 31
dialogue, 112–4, 119, 121, 148–9, 236
    about identity, 31
    first person, 148
    professional dialogue, 16
    scripting, 216
    style, 155
    with texts, 14
diaspora,
    Puerto Rican, 5, 124
    writers, 114
Díaz-Plaja, Ana, 151
discourse, 16, 30
    about veiling in Islam, 97
    authoritarian, 9
    colonial, 36
    competing, 25
    cultural, 46
    development, 31
    dominant, 15–16, 31–3, 39, 211, 219
    femininity, 190, 201, 219
    gender, 224
    girlhood, 72, 190–7, 200–2
    girl power, 42
    girls' education, 4, 7, 29, 32, 35–36, 38, 41
    identity, 31
    legal, 16
    masochism, 182
    media, 6–7, 211
    melancholia, 182
    neoliberal, 33
    political, 107
    rescue, 29, 38–39
    same-sex love, 81
    settler, 129
    sexuality, 192
    social and environmental issues, 100
    spectacular, 40
    Western, 35, 37, 41
    young women, 4
Dobson, Amy, 192, 196
Dorao, Marisol, 144
Douglas, Mary, 177, 183
Downham, Jenny, 48
Downie, Pamela, 130, 139
Driscoll, Catherine, 35, 60, 67
Durham, M. Gigi, 169
Dworkin, Shari, 66

E

education, 10, 25, 38, 99, 114, 129, 137, 145–7, 151, 197, 224, 233
    activism, 7
    ban on female education, 100
    coeducational institutions, 83
    discourses, 7, 36, 38
    domestic education, 149
    educational association, 232
    educational institutions, 154
    educational research, 208, 219
    educational television series, 45
    Eurocentric models of, 139
    in Southern Africa, 3
    neoliberal, 15, 191
    of girls, 3–4, 26, 29–42, 81, 87, 89, 106
    of Inuvialuit girls, 139
    PhD in, 24
    physical education curriculum, 104
    policy, 4, 67
    pre-service teacher education, 26
    primary, 33
    private, 15
    privilege of, 3
    settler educational systems, 131, 133
    sex education, 57, 67, 71
    single-sex educational institutions, 81
    theses in, 23
    Western-style, 34

Eigenbrod, Renate, 129
Ellis, Havelock, 80
Elsewhere, 51–52
empowerment, 164, 184, 186, 218
    and desire, 63–66
    and girl power, 63
    and objectification, 63
    and sexuality, 63–66, 69
    female, 101, 191
    individualistic visions of, 32
    language of, 67
    meaning of, 41
    of girls, 7, 26, 32–33, 64, 68–69, 154–5, 209, 211, 215
    of Muslim girls, 5, 107
    political, 91
    postfeminism, 63
    through education, 3, 139, 209
    Western models of, 41
Eppink, Jason, 199
Escobar, María del Prado, 152
Estournel, Nicolas, 166
ethics,
    and desire, 8
    ethical narrative, 165–7
    of consent, 168, 170
    of girls' victimization, 166, 168, 170
    of *Lolita*, 6, 158–9, 167, 170–1
    reader's ethical stance, 163, 168

F

fairy tales, 6, 8, 174–6, 179–81, 183–6
Fanon, Franz, 3
Farmer, Leslie, 214
Fatty Legs, 127–8, 131, 133–5, 137
feminism, 38–39, 63, 220
    advancements of, 150
    and education, 87
    and girls, 62
    depoliticization of, 63
    fear of, 103
    feminist act, 63, 66, 178
    feminist consciousness, 3
    feminist criticism, 159–60
    feminist framework, 21, 31, 62, 154
    feminist readers, 159, 166
    feminist re-figuration of the schoolgirl, 9
    feminist resistance, 31
    feminist scholars, 15, 30, 158–9, 162, 224
    feminist solidarity, 202
    feminist values, 145
    feminist writing, 150, 167, 178–9, 186, 224, 230
    feminist zone, 104
    intersectional feminism, 101
    issues, 102
    Muslim feminism, 39, 97, 103
    post-feminism, 4, 17, 62–6, 191–2, 194, 201
    proto-feminist narrative, 166
    second wave feminism, 62
First Nations, 128, 131, 136–7
Fish, Stanley, 14, 17
Fortún, Elena, 5–6, 9, 143–55
Fraga, María Jesús, 151
Freud, Sigmund, 81, 178–80, 182–4, 225
    Freudian (psycho)analysis, 178

G

Gannon, Susanne, 15
Gill, Alexandra, 160
Gill, Rosalind, 31–32, 64
Gilmore, Leigh, 29, 31
Girl Effect, 30, 32, 33
Girls and Sex, 60–61, 65
GLAAD (Gay and Lesbian Alliance Against Defamation), 90
Gogi, 5, 94–96, 101, 106–7
Going Gogi, 95, 101–2
Goldman-Segall, Ricki, 208
Gottschall, Jonathan, 45
Grant, Catherine, 224–5
Green, John, 48
Grogan, Christine, 166
Grumet, Madeline, 15

H

Hains, Rebecca, 207
Hall, Radclyffe, 89
Harper's Bazaar, 82
Harris, Anita, 72, 225
Haug, Frigga, 15
Hellman, Lillian, 89
heroism, 5, 95–96
    fictional heroes, 7
    heroine, 151–2
    Muslim superheroine, 10, 95–101, 103
    western superhero trope, 5, 99–100
heteroglossia, 14, 17
Hobbs, Renee, 208
Hocquenghem, Guy, 171
homosexuality, 5, 68, 78–83, 85–86, 88–90

I

identity, 186
    affirmation, 119
    and homosexuality, 85–86
    and virginity, 68
    bicultural, 114
    discourses, 31
    formation, 145, 150, 152, 190, 208
    gendered, 224
    girl, 225
    hybridity, 99
    Indigenous, 128
    of youth, 62
    performative and iterative, 17
    relational, 197
    sexual, 66, 224
incest, 10, 158, 160–1, 163, 167
independence,
    desire for, 151, 154
    empowered through literature, 155
    female, 103
    financial, 78, 89
    of college life, 79
    sense of, 87
    through education, 81

Inness, Sherrie, 80
Inuvialuit, 10, 130–3, 135–9

J

Jordan-Fenton, Christy, 8, 127, 140
July, Miranda, 176–7, 186

K

Kauffman, Linda, 159–60, 164
Kearney, Mary Celeste, 208–9, 212
Khoja-Moolji, Shenila, 35
Koffman, Ofra, 31–32
Kohler, Sheila, 6–7, 223, 225–6, 229, 231, 235–6
Kristeva, Julia, 177, 179

L

Ladies Home Journal, 81
Laforet, Carmen, 144, 151–5
Lal, Ruby, 104
Lamb, Christina, 35
Lamb, Sharon, 64
Lapsley, Mary, 89
Lerum, Kari, 66
lesbian, 5, 7, 10, 80–81, 85, 87, 89–90
Lewis, David, 95–96
LGBTQ+
    movement, 90
    people of color, 224
    youth, 90
literacy,
    and confidence, 133
    and cultural autonomy, 133, 135
    and social imagination, 197
    desire for, 133
    media, 211–2
    pre-service teacher educator, 18
    through residential school, 5
literature, 165
    academic, 35, 84
    characterization of lesbians, 89
    children's, 129, 144, 147, 155
    English, 20, 26
    Nadal literature prize, 152
    of immigrants, 113

on bullying, 112
girl-centered, 230
girlhood, 212
on girls' education 31–32, 35, 41
pornographic, 184
psychological, 168
romance novel, 152
Spanish, 6, 9, 153, 155
study of, 17, 25, 197
young adult (YA), 4, 7, 9, 35, 47, 112–3, 123
Lolita, 6, 8, 158–60, 162, 164–71
Long, Paul, 208
Lo's Diary, 158, 160, 163

M

Mahali, Alude, 231
Maistry, Suriamurthee, 233, 235
Marshall, Elizabeth, 29, 31, 33
Martin, Keavy, 129
Martín Gaite, Carmen, 144–5, 151–4
McCormick, Patricia, 35
McCracken, Timothy, 160, 167
McRobbie, Angela, 15, 17, 191–3, 197
media, 45, 131, 191, 195, 209, 210, 212, 228, 234
    about girlhood, 60
    analysis, 219
    and memory, 4
    campaign, 208
    coverage of bullycide, 57
    coverage of teen suicide, 56
    counter-narratives, 209
    criticism, 219–20
    culture, 15, 208, 210–1, 214–6, 218, 220
    digital, 8, 192, 219
    education research, 219
    girl, 214–5
    hegemonic discourses, 6, 207, 211, 220
    landscapes, 62
    literacy, 211–2
    mainstream, 214, 216, 219
    mass, 62
    misrepresentations of girls, 11, 208, 211
    news, 16, 95
    popular, 16, 64, 209, 215, 218
    production, 208–10, 213–4, 216, 218–20
    relationships, 211
    scripts, 210, 220
    sexualization of girlhood, 66
    social, 4, 56, 61, 64, 72, 193, 196
    stereotyping, 216, 219
    studies, 210, 212
    texts, 6, 8, 11, 16, 61, 207–9, 211–2, 215–6, 218–20
    UK, 36
Me and You and Everyone We Know, 176
Mean Girls, 60
meaning making, 208, 229
memory, 4, 20, 175–7, 185–6, 229
    memory box, 177–8
    memory work, 16
misery, 139, 152, 164
Mitchell, Claudia, 15, 18, 210, 219
modern woman, 145–6, 149–50, 154
Moeller, Kathryn, 33
Mohr, Nicholasa, 5, 8, 111–8, 120–4
Moix, Ana María, 152
Molins, Patricia, 154
Morrissey, Kim, 158, 160–5, 170
Mulvey, Laura, 178–9, 182–3
My Name is Seepeetza, 129

N

Nabokov, Vladimir, 6, 8, 10, 158–60, 163, 165–6, 169, 171
narrative, 39, 41, 62, 105, 119–20, 134, 178–9
    approach, 14, 159, 185, 228, 233
    by dead girls, 47, 58
    character's narrative drive, 181–2
    counter-, 209, 211
    cultural, 46, 57–58, 60, 64–65, 177–8
    desire, 181
    ethical, 165

fictional, 115
first-person, 116–7, 120, 175, 184
girls-at-risk, 61, 63, 70–71
Gogi, 95
graphic, 5, 94–95, 100–1
individualistic, 33
Inuit, 129
Latina, 111
neoliberal, 40
nested (*mise-en-abyme*), 176
of accountability, 70–71
of casual sexual encounters, 69–70
of consent, 71, 171
of girlhood, 41, 46, 58, 60–62, 65, 225
of girls' sexuality, 60–61, 63–66
girls sexualized by men, 167, 171
of international development policy, 30
of Muslim girlhood, 107
of rape, 71
of Spanish literature, 6
of virginity, 67–68
of young adult literature, 47
patronizing, 34
personal, 98, 127, 129, 139, 186
postfeminist, 66
proto-feminist, 166
reading, 229–30
rescue, 94
residential school, 5, 127, 129, 137, 139
theatrical, 229
third-person, 175
US dominant, 114
victim/savior, 100
vignettes, 16
Nayar, Pramod K., 95, 101
Nazar, Nigar, 5, 94–95, 101–3, 106
Nesdale, Dale, 117
Noel, Alyson, 52
Not My Girl, 127–8, 134, 136, 138

O

Olalquiaga, Celeste, 177
Oliver, Lauren, 51, 53–54, 56
Orenstein, Peggy, 4, 60–61, 63–69, 71–72
Orri, Massimiliano, 47, 56

P

Paglia, Camile, 160
panoramic, 96, 104, 106
Parable of the Virgins, 89
Patnoe, Elizabeth, 160
Pease, Allison, 168
Pera, Pia, 158, 160, 162–3
Perrault, Charles, 180, 182
Peterson, Zoe, 64
Pillay, Daisy, 227
Pilinovsky, Helen, 185
Pithouse-Morgan, Kathleen, 229
Poems for Men Who Dream of Lolita, 158, 160
popular culture, 14–15, 17–18, 35, 46, 57, 63, 90, 184, 219
postcolonial,
    framework, 31
    girlhood, 36
    states, 34
    writers, 31
power,
    girl power, 32–33, 60, 63–64, 67, 144
    imbalance, 113
    of the burka, 97
    of stories, 135
    of white masculinity, 94–95, 99, 103
    patriarchal, 104
    powerful organizations, 4
Prager, Emily, 158, 160–2, 164, 169
Projansky, Sarah, 34
public, 8, 38, 40, 81, 193, 195, 199
    access, 202
    attitudes, 85
    boundaries, 201
    consciousness, 208

digital, 6, 190–2, 195, 200
feelings of commonality, 201
formation of, 195, 197–8
girlhood-based, 199, 202
inclusive, 201
knowledges of girlhood, 197
participant, 197
role, 39
romantic relationship, 83–84
social imaginary, 197, 199
-speaking, 40, 66, 117
sphere, 191

Q
Quayle, Susan, 166
queer
    genderqueer, 209
    histories in South Africa, 223–4
    scholarship, 224
    youth, 68, 90
Quinby, Lee, 31

R
Radiance, 52
rebel, 2, 9, 24, 144, 149–52, 154–5, 177, 183, 231
rescue, 29, 31–32, 34, 36, 38, 94, 105, 135, 178, 183
resilience, 5, 128–9, 137, 152
resistance, 20, 96
    feminist, 31
    girls', 36–38, 41
    in reading, 20
    of First Nations people, 131, 136
    of Indigenous girls, 127–30, 133, 136
    sexuality as, 63, 67
    through autobiography, 41
    to colonial oppressions, 5, 128–30, 136, 139–40
    to ethics of consent, 170
    to girlhood stereotypes, 212, 219
    to governmental and religious institutions, 30
    to heteronormative expectations, 5
    to indoctrination, 151
    to patronizing assumptions girlhood, 36
    to powerful discourses, 30
    to sexual coercion, 159
    to spectacularization, 39–40
    to Western depictions, 32, 35, 38
revisionary texts, 6, 10, 158, 169
rewriting, 29, 160–1, 178–80
Richards, Amy, 63
Roger Fishbite, 158, 160–1, 163–4
romantic friendship, 78–79, 81–82, 88
Rosenblatt, Louise, 14, 17, 191, 197–9, 202
Rothenberg, Jess, 50, 53–54

S
Sales, Nancy Jo, 4, 61, 63–69, 71–72
Sartre, Jean-Paul, 3
Schleining, Lon, 176
school,
    administrators, 81, 84
    Australian boarding schools, 130
    Canadian Residential School, 5, 7–8, 10, 127–9, 131–40
    Catholic schools, 127–8, 132, 150
    children, 104–5
    co-educational school, 22
    culture, 79
    dangers, 83
    elementary schools, 8, 209
    environment, 90
    girls' boarding schools, 11, 80, 89, 223
    girls' schools, 37–38, 105, 227
    Hebrew school, 118
    high school, 45, 181
    holidays, 2
    law school, 193
    mission school, 2, 128
    officials, 79, 81, 84, 88
    opportunity, 1
    physician, 89
    policies, 81
    private girls' school, 21–22
    private schools, 9

residential school inmate, 129
residential school survivor, 130
schoolboy, 13
schoolgirl, 4, 9, 13–16, 18–19, 25–26, 223, 226, 229
schoolgirl crushes, 79–80, 88
schoolgirlhood, 21
schooling, 31–32
schoolmates, 67
secondary school, 21
Senior School, 21
South African boarding school, 7–8, 224
teacher, 96, 98
theological school, 104
uniform, 22, 25–26, 37, 39
U.S. schools, 112
Sebold, Alice, 49, 56
seduction, 80–81, 159–60, 162, 170–2
Seidel, John, 212
Sensoy, Özlem, 33
Sewell, William, 216
sexual,
  abuse, 168
  agency, 4, 6, 158, 162, 167–71
  aggressors, 82, 162
  assault, 49, 64, 66, 70–71, 161
  attention, 178
  attraction, 85
  attractiveness, 192
  child, 168
  consent, 8, 10, 161, 170
  constraints, 57
  curiosity, 169
  desirability, 67
  desire, 6, 10, 78–82, 85, 158, 167–70, 177, 181
  double standards, 192
  exploitation, 166
  exploration, 49
  feelings, 63, 82
  freedom, 64
  hypersexualized, 61, 71, 99
  identity, 224, 231
  images, 63
  immorality, 80
  intimacy, 57
  inversion, 79–80, 88
  liberation, 174
  maturing, 177
  object, 7, 61, 63–66, 167
  partners, 10, 66, 68–70
  pleasure, 168
  postfeminist sexual contract, 191
  practices, 61, 63, 65–66, 68–70, 79–80, 82–83, 130, 166
  presentation, 63
  psycho-sexual development, 179
  relationships, 55, 82–83, 86, 89, 161
  research, 185
  rival, 194
  sexualization of girls, 63, 66, 167–8
  slavery of children, 160
  subject, 4–5, 7, 60, 63–66, 69
  subjectivity, 63–64, 69, 71, 170–1
  threat of romantic friendships, 82
  undertones of female friendships, 5, 78, 88
  victimization, 46–47, 50, 56–57
sexuality, 21, 46–47, 49, 57, 64, 80, 82, 169, 184, 191, 215
  as resistance, 63
  as risk, 63
  postfeminist discourses of, 192
  young women's sexuality, 57–58, 63, 78–79, 82
Shin-chi's Canoe, 129
Shi-shi-etko, 129
Slipperjack, Ruby, 129
Smith, Dorothy, 15
Smith, Linda Tuhiwai, 139–40
Sprague, Joey, 61
Stage, Sarah, 82
Steinhardt, David Irving, 82
stereotype, 117
  media stereotyping, 216, 219
  of a Middle Eastern town, 104
  of femininity, 219, 224
  of gender, 209–10, 216, 220
  of girlhood, 212, 218

of LGBTQ youth, 90
of Muslim girls, 10
of Muslim men, 97
of the burqa, 97
oppressive, 214–6
stereotypical characters, 231
stereotypical classroom, 234
Sterling, Shirley, 129
Stewart, Susan, 181
Stockton, Kathryn Bond, 168
Stuart, Jean, 219
subject,
 agentic, 10, 169
 autonomous, 177
 and object, 63, 65
 body as, 67
 desiring, 61, 63
 female, 5, 111, 177
 inferior, 36
 in girlhood discourses, 195
 non-conformist, 155
 position, 56–57
 sexual, 4–5, 7, 60, 63–66, 69
 test, 214
 unified, 31
 universal human, 30
subjectivity, 10, 31, 61–62, 64, 179
 creative, 145
 reflexive, 185
 sexual, 4, 63–64, 69, 71, 170–1
 theories of, 169
submission, 148–52,
 nonsubmissive, 155
suicide, 4, 7, 9, 45–47, 51, 54, 56, 86–90, 145, 182, 185
superheroism, *See* heroism.
Superman, 100
Sutherland, Alexandra, 228–30, 236
Switzer, Heather, 33

T

Talmey, Bernard, 83
Tanning, Dorothea, 177–8, 186
Ten Sex Talks to Girls, 82
The Catastrophic History of You and Me, 50

The Children's Hour, 89
The Dead Girls Detective Agency, 50
The Fault in our Stars, 48
The Lovely Bones, 49, 56
The Well of Loneliness, 89
The Wretched of the Earth, 3
These Are My Words, 129
Thirteen Reasons Why, 45–46, 50
Tolman, Deborah, 63–64, 167
transnational, 10
 African transnationalist, 3
 corporations, 32
 ethnic communities, 2
 girl, 1
 girlhoods, 8, 11
 girlhood studies, 8, 10–11
 issues affecting Muslim girls, 107
 Transnational Girlhoods, 7
 transnationalism, 1–2, 8–11
 transnationalist, 9–10
Truth and Reconciliation Commission, 127–9, 131

U

Ugly Betty [television show], 35, 39

V

Vaingurt, Julia, 160
von Krafft-Ebing, Richard, 79–80
vulnerable,
 emotionally, 217
 from bullying, 118, 121
 girl, 15, 29, 31, 36–37
 teens, 45–46
 to media, 208

W

Walkerdine, Valerie, 14–16, 18–19, 25–26
Wall, Tim, 208
Warner, Michael, 191, 195, 200–1
Waxman, Lori, 224–5
Weber, Sandra, 15, 18
weird girls, 9, 152–3, 155

Wesley-Esquimaux, Cynthia, 131, 137, 139–40
When I Was Eight, 127–8, 133–4, 136
Williams, Patricia, 15–16
Winnicott, D.W., 179, 186
Wolf, Naomi, 160
Wolfe, Melissa, 26
Wonder Woman, 100
Wood, Michael, 171
World Health Organization, 46

Y

Yousafzai, Malala, 4, 7, 9, 14, 29–32, 34–41, 96, 100

Z

Zevin, Gabrielle, 51, 54